Lady Colin Campbell

Lady C

THE LIONESS UNLEASHED

The woman who first broke the news of Princess Diana's unhappy marriage and star of *I'M A CELEBRITY... Get Me Out Of Here!*, *Lady C and the Castle* and *A Cup of Tea With Lady C.*

By
Robert Garv Dodds

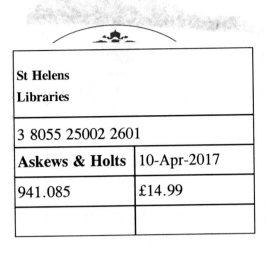
www.dynastypress.co.uk

First published in this version by Dynasty Press Ltd.

ISBN: 978-09935780-6-9

Cover artwork design by **Rupert Dixon**

Typeset by **Biddles**, Blackborough End, Norfolk.

Printed and bound in the United Kingdom.

Lady C was the *real* Queen of the Jungle *I'm a Celebrity… Get Me Out of Here!* reality TV show, as many of the British media reported. Lady Colin Campbell made for compelling viewing, whether you loved her or hated her, and was so unpredictable. *"What is she going to say next?"* She had everybody sitting on the edge of their seats, night after night!

This book is about the woman who broke the news before anyone else of Princess Diana's unhappy marriage, who is the star of two British TV reality shows and who has performed at the world-renowned Edinburgh Fringe Festival.

When you get to know the *real* Lady C in reading this book, judge for yourself if you love her or, if you didn't like her before, have you changed your mind?

Some of the book's new revelations, claims and quotes:

- An attempted murder.
- Who Lady C nearly married.
- An almost Royal affair.
- Major James Hewitt and the author's twist of fate.
- Hear from Lord Colin Campbell and the present Duke of Argyll.
- Reality TV shows, over-manipulation and editing?
- Quotes from fellow Jungle contestants Kieron Dyer and Chris Eubank.
- Lady C's acerbic comments on Tony Blair, Brexit and US politics today.
- Her caustic remarks that are reserved for the French.

About The Author

ROBERT GARY DODDS was born in England and married into one of Jamaica's established colonial families in the 70s. He is highly adept at assessing and reading people, and counts a lot of established families in Jamaica as old friends this last 40 years. Remember Jamaica's motto: '*Out of Many – One People.*'

Gary has a quick wit and sense of humor and is known for being a born diplomat, honesty, and telling it as it is. His reach through friends and connections covers most continents and those who know him say that he has a high level of integrity, and that he's someone who's great at keeping in touch with people.

He has done a lot of work with charities wherever he's lived, such as with terminally ill children in the former Vietnamese refugee camp in Hong Kong. He was a Governor of The Hong Kong Sea School for Boys, and helped out at a home for disabled children in Dubai. He sits on Rwanda and Burundi's Akilah Women's Institute Global Advisory Council.

With Mary, his wife of 38 years, they have homes in the United States and England. Their son Alexander and their daughter Rebecca and her family live a ten minute walk away from their North Carolina home. Gary travels extensively and works as a management consultant and advisor with a number of international companies, in the US, the West Indies, South America, Asia, Europe, the Middle East, Africa and India.

Contents

Foreword

by
H.H. Princess Olga Andreevna Romanoff of Russia

I HAVE KNOWN GEORGIE, Lady Colin Campbell, since the mid-70s. She knew my cousin Henry and we moved in many of the same circles, crossing paths at many of the same parties and events. We met again at a Ball in 2000, of which I happen to be Patron, and we've become close friends ever since.

She has an exotic background and has certainly had a colorful life. What I like about this book is that it has looked at Georgie with fresh, unbiased eyes, has been well researched, and has unearthed vital new facts and anecdotes on her.

Georgie doesn't claim to be an angel, and there are certainly differing opinions of her. The author has delved into all aspects of her life and seems to have left no stone unturned to bring us the real woman behind the name.

One thing I can tell you, Georgie is an incredibly loyal, dear friend to all her chums. She has a huge sense of humor and truly cares about people, and is a brilliant mother who absolutely loves her two sons, and her dogs and cats.

I like the author's natural and unfussy style of writing, delivered with a good balance of humor, hard facts, and new revelations that even took me by surprise. Georgie is an extraordinary woman, a woman very much of our time and who lives life to the full without apology. I love her for that.

Olga Romanoff

This Book is Dedicated to My Family

TO MY LITTLE GRANDSONS Kai and Charlie Shimkets in America, and my little granddaughters, Isabel and Chloe Tomlinson in England.

The book is especially dedicated to our granddaughters' late Mummy, our eldest daughter Nicola, whom we lost to cancer unexpectedly in November 2013 in Houston, Texas, aged just 34. We miss her dearly.

The book is also dedicated to my darling wife Mary whose patience and support over the last year as I have researched, interviewed and written this book - without making hardly any income as she reminds me - made it possible.

I also dedicate it to my son, Alexander Dodds, and my daughter Rebecca Shimkets and her husband Peter who all live in the same neighborhood as we do in North Carolina – and in England to my elder sister Pamela Smith (I always remind her that she is *older* than me!), and her husband George, who has been a constant in my life since pre-teenage years.

It would be remiss not to mention a dedication to our only living parent, Mary's Mummy, known to the whole family as Grandma Harvey. She is a blessing in all of our lives and the family's matriarch to whom we all look up with love and admiration, who retired to England from Jamaica some years ago.

These make up my immediate family who I live for and who inspire me, just as I am also inspired by our wider family members and my friends globally.

Robert Gary Dodds

Acknowledgements

IT WOULD HAVE BEEN IMPOSSIBLE to complete my research and write this book if it wasn't for the likes of:

The Hon. Oliver Clarke, O.J., Chairman of Jamaica's oldest national newspaper *The Gleaner*, for giving me unparalleled access to the newspaper's historical archives; and *The Gleaner's* Librarian, Ms. Sheree Rhoden, who assisted me greatly.

Nicola Crosswell-Mair, who introduced me to many people and sources of research when I was in Jamaica. I discovered that if she didn't know someone, then they probably were not worth knowing. Being a past Miss Air Jamaica helped!

A handful of friends kindly read the early incomplete working draft manuscript of this book to comment on its flow or parts that didn't make sense. I must thank Lillian Foreman, Joanne Lerner and Pamela and George Smith for doing this. I especially thank George who acted as a proofreader of my final draft, earning my undying thanks.

All of Lady C's family, friends and acquaintances who have in speaking or communicating with me allowed me to quote them and share their stories, anecdotes, material or photographs – thank you, each of you, I owe you a great debt.

Various detractors and Press reports going back over 40 years which I have read, many absolutely vilifying Lady C at the time, become the other side of the story already widely in the public domain that enabled me to gain a balanced view of who this woman is.

Lastly, I must thank the Lady herself, Lady C, who agreed to allow me to write this biography on her. She gave me unprecedented access and not only cooperated with me at every step of the way, but also gave her time willingly whenever I asked. Throughout this book, I make no revelations or claims of my own, nor judge anyone I write about. I am writing Lady Colin Campbell's *real* story, from what the Press or others have written about her, and as I've heard it directly from her and others who have spoken to me.

Introduction

"LADY COLIN CAMPBELL, you can't say that!" – and yet she did!

If you want to read the *real* in depth story of a woman of our time, who's as controversial a celebrity as they come right now, then read on.

If you want to read a book that talks about glamorous socialites, sex, drugs, alcohol and has claims of child sexual abuse - and a not known before attempted murder claim – then this is *definitely* the book for you!

We even have a pair of young, twenty-something eligible Russian bachelors!

Lady Colin Campbell is an international and New York Times multiple award winning, best-selling author, a socialite, a British TV star, a stage personality and a survivor. She is known to her friends and family as Georgie. To the British public who watched the 2015 TV reality show *I'm a Celebrity… Get Me Out of Here!* she'll now always be known as Lady C. She's also referred to as *Lady C and the Castle* from her second and own British reality TV show, and has performed *A Cup of Tea With Lady C* live on stage at The Edinburgh Fringe Festival in Scotland.

Her chosen first names are Georgia, Arianna; and her maiden name was Ziadie.

I will usually refer to Lady Colin Campbell throughout this book by the less formal and popular British public term Lady C, or as seems appropriate when her friends are talking about her, Georgie.

Lady C was born on August 17th 1949, in the parish of St Andrews, Kingston, Jamaica, biologically female with a fused labia and deformed clitoris. She was a girl in mind, body, and spirit who had, to go to a conservative, all-boys Catholic school. Sadly she was wrongly raised as a boy until, aged 21, she was free to have the corrective surgery she needed to complete her womanhood without her parents stopping her, and later you'll discover why they raised her as a boy.

Lady C was mercilessly bullied at school and made fun of for being so feminine, a trauma that has stayed with her for her whole life, and we are going to hear for the *first time* from some of her old school classmates in Jamaica and the tales they have to tell. She went on to study at the prestigious Fashion Institute of Technology in New York and became a successful female model – at a time which aligned with the hedonistic lifestyle of the 70s and 80s. She led a young, smart set social whirl life in New York and London, whilst popping in and out of bed with a string of high profile male lovers!

Lady C came from a wealthy Jamaican family that had good connections. She walked away from the American billionaire who was wooing her to marry Lord Colin Ivar Campbell in 1974. He was the youngest son of the 11th Duke of Argyll, and she had a flash of innate instinct that he was her destiny. As it turns out, he was, but not in the way she could ever have imagined I'm sure.

We'll touch on what started as a fairytale and became a disastrous marriage, being hospitalized by her husband breaking her jaw as she has said. This drove her eventually to walk away from her marriage with a man who at the time was frequently on drugs and alcohol, as claimed by Lady C and witnessed by others. A new revelation from an independent witness has emerged that Lord Colin Campbell was in a private clinic not long before Lady C met him, for drugs and alcohol rehabilitation, which if true, somewhat belies his claim that he never had a problem with drugs or alcohol.

We'll hear from Lord Colin Campbell's public statement in December 2015, who says that such birth circumstance as his wife's, as reported at the time of their divorce, he now realizes were wrong. The resulting newspaper smears from this media exposure at the time of their divorce have stayed with Lady C for over 40 years, up to this day.

We're going to take a look from a different perspective at the Campbell family into whom she married, and look back at the Argyll history of sensational divorces, and the historical record of betrayal and massacres. You are going to read an astonishing story from a victim of a claimed murder attempt by someone in Lord Colin's immediate family. We'll also hear claims of Argyll male sexual abuse.

The reader can decide for him or herself who they believe in the marriage disintegration of Lord Colin Campbell and Lady C when you've read what's been researched and written about it, and what both sides have had to say.

Is Lady C entitled to use the title Lady, and continue to use her husband's name? Was she aristocratic before the marriage or not? I'll answer these frequently asked questions in the media, and you will hear what Debrett's, the arbiters of British peerage and titles, have to say.

Before her first big reality TV show in late 2015, her fame and celebrity were built on not just her earlier life circumstances and moving in society circles on both sides of the Atlantic Ocean, but primarily from her disastrous marriage, and the stream of often controversial but highly successful books which she wrote over the last twenty four years. In 1992, she was *the very first person* to break the news to the world that Diana, Princess of Wales, felt trapped in an unhappy marriage and wanted to seek a divorce – and I am going to explore those books and summarize some of the claims that came out of them – which, by the way, made three of them New York Times best sellers.

I am going to take you into the private world of Lady C, and talk to her family and friends about her and who she really is away from the public gaze. She's lived in and owned some amazing homes, from apartments in London's Mayfair and Belgravia, to a Chateau in France and now a Castle and a London town house in England. Let's have a look at those and hear about some of them in more detail, including pictures of the restoration work that was going on in Castle Goring when I was doing my research.

Ladies, you may have heard about her collection of fabulous tiaras and matching jewelry when she was in *I'm A Celebrity... Get Me Out of Here!* Well, you are going to get to see them, and some of her stunning couture ball gowns and clothes too.

Lady C has given me unprecedented access to herself, to her family and to her friends with the writing of this biography because, as she said herself, and which I think is quite insightful – well I would, wouldn't I:

"Few could understand Jamaican cultural and smart set norms which underpin my personality and character, other than someone born into the same families or someone like the author, who himself married into an old, elite Jamaican family. He married into the Harvey family (think Sherry, Darling), members of the established Jamaican sugar plantocracy whose history goes back hundreds of years."

She has talked about the author, because of his age, connections and marriage, being one of the few people she'd help to write a biography on her, because of his understanding of the world she grew up in. She has said that only someone who understands those social norms and the Catholic faith, and who has lived and worked in the Middle East and knows those cultural norms also, can know and write about her. She's from Lebanese Christian, European as well as Jewish stock, remember.

"The author understands these things and that's why I agreed to cooperate with his biography of me."

I interviewed Lady C over the last year for countless hours, both in person at her homes in London and at Castle Goring, and over the phone from my home in the United States. She was always candid and open, straightforward and plain speaking. She called a spade a spade, and was forever extremely polite and thoughtful as to answers to my questions, sensitive not to cause offense to others, and the first to admit her shortcomings. She showed great respect for people, was constantly laughing about situations and herself, and she never attempted to dodge or refused to answer even the most personal of questions.

How did I meet Georgie? Well, my wife Mary had been at school in Jamaica with her younger sister, Margaret (known as Puss to her family and pals). So Mary knew the family and had met Georgie, as she'd seen her often when Lady C came to pick up Puss from the school that they both went to, Servite Convent, where Mary boarded. She next saw Georgie nine years ago, and I'd never met her until then.

We welcomed Lady Colin Campbell into our home situated just outside of central London for dinner. She came with an old mutual Jamaican friend, Nicola Crosswell-Mair, who I'd known from the heady days of the early 70s when Nicola had lived in Hampstead in London. We also had some other old-Jamaican family friends of ours at the time for dinner, Richard & Becky Bayley and Harold & Lyn Dunn.

Hearing only rumors from others of Lady Colin Campbell's early life raised as a boy, I thought what the heck, it was the naughty's, and we'd lived through the hedonistic 70s, so who cared. But deep down, I did feel a little uncomfortable and jokingly said so later as I got to know Lady C when interviewing her for this book.

Well, the champagne and rum flowed during our dinner party (there's a lovely saying that *"time flies when you're having rum"*) and the Jamaican patois did too, and six hours later, as we said goodbye to Georgie and our other guests, I was left utterly flabbergasted at this woman's story. How she had risen, almost phoenix-like from the ashes, time and time again; from the trials of her life, childhood, marriage, the media furor around her divorce and some of her books, as if each sought to burn her out of existence; but she'd survived and prospered.

Fate saw Major James Hewitt in my family's life briefly at the time that his affair with Princess Diana hit the newspapers, post the revelation from Lady C's book on Diana - but more anon. Fate also saw me approaching a UK publisher to write an up-to-date biography of Lady C, and there came a stage early on, before I started my research and interviews for this book, when I seriously asked myself the question, had I taken on too big a task? At that very moment it reminded me of a funny Jamaican countryside, colloquial saying, which perfectly described how I felt: *"If goat knew the size of 'im batty* (batty is Jamaican slang for butt), *he'd not swallow mango seed."* Meaning, that if I had realized the enormity of the task I was taking on, I may not have signed the contract with the publisher.

After the dinner party mentioned above, I set about reading all the books Georgie had written up until then, and felt after doing so that I had a better understanding of who she was. I've since read and re-read each book that she's ever written as part of my research for this biography, in order to *feel* and discover the true identity of the woman Lady Colin Campbell.

Her autobiography *A Life Worth Living* was written nearly 20 years ago now, and her life has grown exponentially since. She's written five more books, often highly controversial ones, and we're going to hear a lot about those last twenty years too. I've also read *mountains* of old press clippings from the seventies and eighties, good and unpleasant newspaper articles written on her. I conducted interviews with her family and friends in Jamaica, America, Mexico, the UK and elsewhere. I believe I have come to know her very well, as well as others perceive her.

No biography on Lady C would be complete without talking of *I'm A Celebrity... Get Me out of Here!* and the sensation she caused on British TV at the end of 2015. So we will look at that, and her claims of bullying and unfavorable TV show editing! The UK's Daily Mirror newspaper said during the reality TV show, "*The super-posh celeb is fast becoming the darling of the Jungle, despite branding viewers oiks.*" We'll look at why that *wasn't* a slur on the British working class as suggested by some in the Press at the time!

Someone commented during that reality TV show that she was like Marmite, a British spread with a salty, beefy taste whose advertising tagline is "Love it or hate it". Meaning that you either love her, or you hate her, there is little in-between! Based on TV viewer ratings it's a true statement, and either way as I discovered, she's okay with that.

"*Lady C, you can't say that!*" was a constant refrain from the producers, as she belted out one cutting remark or expletive after another on live TV to fellow contestants in the Jungle, day after day.

So, who is the person behind the name Lady C? Is she a nasty person as sometimes portrayed in newspaper articles, or a decent fun person who's suffered from an over-edited portrayal in a reality TV show, and someone who's often been given a bad rap in the Press over the years. Let's find out! Does she have two personalities? Maybe she does!

We'll look at how 'the man in the street' seems to be absolutely in tune with her, as I've witnessed, with her being mobbed by people in supermarkets, wanting a 'selfie' photograph with her – and not one negative word said against her, quite the opposite. Not quite the bitch some people talk about, she was genuinely warm, thoughtful, witty and very engaging, especially with the younger generation.

If at times she metaphorically (or literally!) puts one finger up to her detractors and gives them a mouth full of expletives when attacked or bullied, maybe it's because she has nothing to hide, and has learned not to take it and to knock detractors out quick. She succeeded in life against all odds and came out on top, and trust me she doesn't suffer fools gladly. Which one of us can't empathize a little with that?

If Lady C's personality and character were forged in the fires of her life-events spread over these last six-plus decades, in the end, we see a steely, no-nonsense character, but one with a soft heart and the kind nature I've discovered. Those that know her know that Lady Colin Campbell can be feisty and plucky, but is also invariably funny and profoundly witty. She's as sharp as a razor blade, and her tongue can be too. Often cutting in her remarks, but straight talking, her statements are frequently accompanied by colorful language, sometimes a little too vulgar for some. She's also seen as brilliant, highly intellectual, and a caring and thoughtful woman and mother. She has a huge heart, great compassion for the underdog, and is someone her friends say is uncompromisingly loyal.

In writing this biography on Lady C, I am fortunate that I was not close enough to be influenced by her or anyone else in coming to my conclusions and writing her story as I see it. Yet I knew her, and had insight into who she is and was given unprecedented access by her, to herself and her family and friends.

So who is Lady C, as the British public knows Lady Colin Campbell today? My hope is that you will get to know the real woman behind the public image as you read this book, and what's influenced today's portrait of who she is from her cultural heritage of Lebanese and Jamaican descent – and from her life's trials too. I want you to get a sense of how her character and that feisty personality we saw on the reality show *I'm a Celebrity... Get Me Out of Here!* were formed and shaped over years of baptism by fire. As with any of us, her collective life experiences have shaped the personality and character we know today. If we wonder why she sometimes comes out fighting, tough and un-lady like – I think it's because she's a survivor with nothing to hide, no one to impress and nothing to lose!

There's a saying that life is not about the hand of cards God dealt you, but how you play that hand. Well, I think you are about to discover (whether you like her or not), that she has played and continues to play that hand as best she can. Her 'Gusband' Peter Coleman described Lady C as two women, Georgie Ziadie the party girl, and Lady Colin Campbell, the formal and correct woman.

One woman, with two sides to her personality, forged in the fires of an extraordinary lifetime of experiences – this is Lady C.

Chapter 1
Exotic heritage and colonial society

FOR HIS UK TV SERIES *The Tudors* Michael Hirst had a wonderfully apt opening line to each episode: *"You think you know a story, but you only know its end. To get to the heart of a story, you have to go back to the beginning."*

You cannot begin to understand the psyche of the cultured, feisty and accomplished woman who Lady C is today if you do not understand the customs and culture of her paternal Lebanese heritage, her religion and family, within all of which she was raised. In fact her paternal ancestry stretches back to the Phoenician in origin, and on her maternal side her family hails from Anglo-Irish aristocrats and from Sephardic Jewish descent as she shared with me. Lady C has the most wonderfully exotic genes and heritage.

Nor can you understand her if you are not aware of the influence of the Jamaica of the 50s – 70s, the morals, freedoms, politics and crime. They will all have influenced and shaped the personality and character of the woman we know today.

So let's go back to the beginnings of Lady C's story and spend a moment discovering their significance – and I think you'll see how they have influenced the women she is today.

Lebanon, Palestine and Syria are all parts of the Middle East previously known in the West as the Levant. In the 1800s and much earlier most people from the area around Mount Lebanon in the greater region known as Syria were called Lebanese, everyone else were simply known as Syrian. The average Jamaican will often refer to all Jamaicans of Arab descent as being Syrian, no matter from where their heritage.

Lady C's paternal ancestors, the Ziadies, came from Lebanon and were Phoenician in origin and Christian Maronites of the Catholic Church since the sixth century, becoming main stream Catholic from the eighteenth century. They originally hail from the town of Kesselwan, with ancestors moving to the Spice Route town of Choueifat at the end of the eighteenth century from where they eventually migrated to Jamaica. They had moved to Choueifat primarily because it had in its time become a major centre of commerce, and because it was where the centre of the Greek and Russian Orthodox Christian Churches in the country were based. It was around 1890 that Lady C's paternal Grandfather, George Ferris Ziadie, and his four brothers migrated to Jamaica.

Immigrants from China and India had begun arriving in Jamaica in the mid-1800s as indentured laborers. However, the Lebanese came of their own free will, like the Jews who were immigrants a hundred years earlier. The Lebanese or Syrian Christians were fleeing mainly from religious persecution of their Islamic Ottoman Empire overlords; whereas most Jews who immigrated to Jamaica did so to escape the horrid Catholic Inquisition in Spain and Portugal in the early 18th century. Similar to what Christians faced under the Ottoman Empire a hundred plus years later, Jews could convert to Christianity, emigrate or be put to death! Sound familiar? - Look what's happening in parts of Syria, Iraq and other places today. The survivors are those that manage to flee first and have formed, in 2016, one of the biggest mass migrations into Europe in history, itself causing huge divides there. The UK's Brexit political battle-ground was partly drawn up on these fears.

Immigrants like the Ziadies, and former Jamaican Prime Minister Edward Seaga's grandmother, and the Hannas… they had all come from a region in the then greater Syria called Choueifat, sometimes spelt Schweifat or Choueifat. It was originally just a farming and trading community in the hills overlooking Beirut. The Issas (Palestinians from Jerusalem originally) and the Hannas were two of the earliest 'Syrian' families to settle in Jamaica, and were well known for giving those that followed them their start. Most got a small shop and discounted material to sell on to the public at competitive prices. This is how the Ziadies got their break, through the Hannas.

Lady C's paternal grandfather started as many others did in Jamaica, knocking door to door, selling fabric from the back of a cart; they then got a shop with the Hanna Empire's financial help and support. This help they never forgot. Lady C is proud of their humble Jamaican beginnings, when the family had lost everything in Lebanon and started all over again in Jamaica from scratch – it wouldn't be the last time either. A hurricane in the early 1900s wiped out their shop and growing empire, and they had to start all over again.

Early on the Ziadies decided to sell to the masses. They bought less expensive but good quality materials which they could sell at much lower prices than their competitors' high-end stock, and this appealed to the Jamaican working woman in the villages – they went for what we'd call today the supermarket principal, lower prices at a higher volume. From these humble off the back of a cart beginnings which Lady C is very proud of, the family having had power and wealth in Lebanon and having lost it all to escape religious persecution, the Ziadies worked hard and successfully built their small empire up over a 100 years and became, like others, quite wealthy and raised themselves into Jamaican upper class circles.

By the 1930s and 40s the Ziadies in Jamaica had done very well. They had a lovely home in Kingston with 5 acres of pristine and cherished gardens, the Ziadie family of cousins owned a chain of racehorses between them as well, and hardly a race took place without one Ziadie family horse or another taking part. Some of the founding immigrants' sons married into established British colonial families and Lady C's father did too, which unintentionally broke down some barriers for them in the then British colonial world of Jamaica.

Lady C's mother was a Smedmore and whose father, Lady C's adored maternal Grandfather was Lucius Smedmore. He was one of nine brothers and sisters, the 8th to be born to William Dey Smedmore and his wife, Amanda, née, Brown ancestry sites show. He was born in the rather palatial 6-bedroom family home of 49 Beeston Street, Port Royal (Kingston) Jamaica on November 18th 1899. His sister Maud Smedmore married in the family home and there's a charming photo of the very grand looking couple in the book, sat in the garden of the house with the servant's quarters in the background. Their wedding as I found in The Daily Gleaner national newspaper archives was considered 'the' social event of the season.

The Smedmores seem to be related to a number of old European Jamaican families, and William Dey Smedmore (Lucius' father) married in Port Royal, in 1882, and was a 'Writer', being a civil employee working for The Royal Navy at His Majesty's Dockyard, Port Royal.

There is a lovely photo of Lady C's adored grandfather in the book which like many others, she kindly supplied.

Lucius' father died in 1914 of a cerebral hemorrhage, when Lucius would have been around fifteen years old. He had married Carrie May Burke Lady C advised, known as Maysie to everyone. She was the daughter of Aubrey Burke and his wife, Amy de Pass, a very old Jewish family whom I speak about earlier. Aubrey is believed to be descended from the Earl's of Mayo, and old Anglo-Irish family.

Lucius (Cousin, Dorothy Kew's research showed) became a freemason and worked for Henderson & Company, eventually becoming Company Secretary for two of their sugar plantations, Orange Valley and Georges Valley in Trelawney. Lady C as corroborated by others, said that he was considered a pillar of the community and of his Church, as was his brother, Rodney.

Rodney, Dorothy's research shows, was an always perfectly attired gentleman and had a reputation for speaking English as Lady C's mother Gloria did (Rodney's niece), with a very English, Oxford accent.

Lucius and Maysie had two daughters, Marjorie, and Gloria, Lady C's Mother; sadly Lucius' marriage ended in divorce in 1956 when Lady C was just seven. Lucius moved to his daughter Marjorie and her husband's home to live with his own quarters and study.

On her grandmother's maternal side, Lady C's great-grandmother was a member of two of the oldest and most eminent Sephardic Jewish families in the west, the De Passes mentioned above, and the Lindos. The Lindo family is an old Sephardic Jewish family originating in Medieval Spain. Many Jews fled Spain to avoid the Catholic Inquisition when the Spanish King won back Spain and drove the Islamic Moors out. The pattern of emigration of the family follows the ups and downs of Sephardic Jews along the path of history. Many Sephardic families next went to Portugal until the Inquisition came there too around 1530 when many left for Italy, Holland, England and elsewhere. Two members of different branches of the Lindo family ended up in Jamaica. One was first recorded in Jamaica by 1765, nearly a hundred years before the first Lebanese migration to Jamaica occurred.

Lady C's maternal Jewish ancestors found freedom of religion in Jamaica and helped form what is today the oldest colony of Jewish people in the western world. In the Jamaica of the 1800s there were as many as eight synagogues and roughly 2,500 Jews. But tides of Jewish migration dwindled over the centuries and their numbers are around just 200 today, and only one synagogue remains. It is seeking to keep the community alive, partly through religious tourism. Anti-Jewish sentiment is an alien concept in Jamaica by the way.

Lady C may epitomize Jamaica's national motto '*Out of Many, One People*' with her heritage of both Christian and Jewish decent and with ancestors hailing from the Middle East and Europe, to form a rich century or more of Jamaicans that Lady C herself grew out of and with all of whose influences she was raised.

Understanding Lebanese Society and Culture

We can more easily appreciate Lady C's European heritage from her maternal family, and I can share Lebanese heritage with you from my own personal experiences living on and off in the Middle East from 1980 to 2014, as well as interviews of those Lebanese families in Jamaica who I have spoken to. I believe that my summaries hold as true today as they did in the 1940s and onward in Jamaica.

The primary differences between people in Lebanon have been and are those between Muslim and Christian sects. Little has changed in over 150 years from what I can see. Ultimately their differences caused huge social tensions and the long, drawn out civil wars of recent times were born out of such divergence of beliefs. Sad really, as both religions believe in the one God. The government today officially recognizes multiple sects of Christianity, Islam, and Judaism, and I suspect as many as 60 years ago.

Imagine that people like the Ziadies, Issas and Hannas gave up their home, lands, businesses and wealth (and often times influential positions in their community) and left to start new lives overseas in strange lands, because they were persecuted for being Christian – but they held their faith. How does that impact on the instinct to survive and drive your every focus, and how does that reflect on their children and grandchildren like Lady C and how they were raised, and how they think? Those are things that will be innate to Lady C's character.

From the mid-1800s emigration from greater Syria, look 150 plus years later at the refugee crisis in Europe today. It is much fueled by religious persecution in the Middle East, often times between different sects of the same religion, sometimes because of different tribal allegiances. Will we ever accept that out of many, we really are just one people, the human race, and wouldn't it be a sad world if we all had the same beliefs and traditions?

The Lebanese name and honor

This is another crucial building block in really understanding Lady C, as it is part of the cultural heritage in which she was raised at home that a person's name and honor are a cherished possession. As in most Middle-Eastern societies today, and even more proudly so back in the 40s, 50s and 60s, when Lady C was in her teens and still being brought up as a boy, her concern was not to embarrass her parents by standing up to them publicly. This meant pleading only within the private family circle. Lebanon and its early immigrant descendants, like most of the Muslim world today was a male dominated society, so to publicly go against your father's word in a Lebanese household was a complete no, no. It was unacceptable and simply did not happen. What you said from inside the family's private world was another story.

It is crucial for Lebanese to maintain their dignity, honor, and reputation. And, funny that I should make this next comment the reader who has seen Lady C's performance in the Jungle may feel, but Lady C would never in her normal day-to-day life seek to embarrass anyone in public, unless they attack or bully her first. The Lebanese are proud of their tradition of hospitality. This is a culture where, like in most Middle East cultures today, it is considered an honor to have a guest in your home, even a complete stranger. Everyone I have spoken to has indicated in one way or another that Lady C is innately a *most* gracious and hospitable hostess and welcomes everyone, friend or stranger, with the same honor and genuine warmth.

The Lebanese are also a very 'touchy-feely' people and I've seen that in Lady C. However, if they think that their honor has been attacked or challenged, they will raise their voice and unleash *sweeping* hand gestures in a vehement attempt to restore their honor, as we've seen Lady C do in the reality TV show. I've witnessed many such a Lebanese drama unfold over the years. Combine a violation on her honor with perceived bullying, and all inherited social norms fly out the window and all hell is going to break loose from Lady C. You are going to get a piece of her mind and colorful language to accompany it – and we've certainly seen that!

Where did non-British colonial families sit in Jamaican Society?

I spoke with lots of people during my research on this point, both old Lebanese families and British colonial ones. I did so because something said by someone from one of those old British colonial families at the very beginning of my research made me want to look into it further.

It was clear that the old British establishment back in the 1940s, 50s and 60s saw virtually all other ethnic groups, no matter how wealthy, as 'not being quite one of us.' Having myself lived in Hong Kong for many years, primarily when it was still a British colony, I can tell you that the same attitude was still partially prevalent there even in the 1980s. I am sure it was the same in India and other outposts of Empire in their day as well; they were different times 60 plus years ago. There was in Jamaica in those days when Lady C was born and raised, a sort of social glass ceiling. While all mixed socially in a wider sense, and in business, the very British colonial 'reserves', the gentleman's clubs for example, did not have many non-British heritage members until they started to ease up and change in the 60s onwards when Lady C was growing up. Often the exclusive formal parties would subtly see the 'not quite one of us' members of society not quite included on the prestigious gold-edged invitations that were sent out.

Charles Hanna, scion of the Hanna family today, has noticed that one Lebanese family substantially broke through this barrier, and it was the Ziadies. Some of the Brothers of the Founding Father, and Lady C's father's siblings had married into British colonial Jamaican families. They intermixed socially more than the rest of that circle of Lebanese heritage families, even sometimes being invited to establishment events, as Lady C remembers. The Hannas, who were one of the two most prominent Lebanese families, were still under that colonial glass ceiling if they're honest with themselves – but it all soon melted into one come the 70s and 80s.

In my discussions with Lady C's cousin Enrique Ziadie he remembered wealth, not ethnic group, as the key differentiator, and he recalled a funny story of going to school in Jamaica in a Cadillac: *"I was teased at school for arriving in that car, as remember, a car in those days was almost the price of an average person's house."*

Enrique's mother, Helen, was a very good friend of Lady C's mother Gloria and her only sister, Marjorie. Likewise Enrique and Georgie were extraordinarily close as cousins, the bond of friendship passed on by their mothers' friendship to them.

Most who I spoke to in Jamaica said that when they grew up in the 50s and 60s there was hardly any color or ethnic discrimination at all – discrimination, if any, was economic, and the haves and have-nots was the divide, as it probably was globally, and maybe still is anywhere in the world today, if truth is known.

Violent crime and safety – the role of politics and economics

Politics had its part to play in the crucial growing up years of Lady C in the 50s and 60s and it influenced her young adult mind in the 70s and whenever she was in Jamaica.

Now if this way of life in Jamaica in the 60s and 70s didn't have an unconscious and subtle effect on Lady C and her thinking, I am not sure what would, so we need to talk about it. Violent crime and a lack of safety become engrained into your hidden psyche.

Violent gangs connected with the JLP (Jamaica Labour Party) and the PNP (People's National Party) began to attack each other with guns and extreme violence. They were and remain the two main opposing political parties in Jamaica. Prime Minister Bustamante and then his cousin, Prime Minister Norman Manley, oversaw a period where gang violence and a high death rate were accepted as the norm, as they were believed rightly or wrongly to have tacitly funded weapons to their followers. They were, if it's true, perpetuating the violence but neither acknowledged such a role. Under Michael Manley (Norman's son) and the Seaga era of the 70s and 80s, as I witnessed firsthand on a number of occasions, it grew 'far' worse and more prolific and dangerous. Both have been accused of tacitly supporting their followers' gun violence too.

We need to understand the racial and economic issues in Jamaica at this time as well, and the economic promises made to the people in the 70s by Michael Manley and the PNP that as history shows could not be delivered to the level the people expected. Combine that with the high crime and murder rate that came with them, and they *must* have impacted on Lady C's personality as it was forming through those informative years, from a child to a young woman.

During these years, her maternal grandfather, Lucius Smedmore, was murdered, and she had the horror of seeing his body immediately afterward where he was slain. The impact on her, and the shock and devastation at her loss, cannot be underestimated, as she adored him. Lucius was a true gentleman of fine social sensibilities, as Lady C recalled, and her grandparents held a high profile position in society.

An aunt was killed, shot in the head while sitting in her car at the traffic lights on her way home. A cousin was buried alive, albeit that he survived – and there was the constant threat of break-in, violent crime and murder.

These were now the heady days of the 70s with the Caribbean and Western world experiencing marijuana, reggae and sexual freedom. As for crime, every home I knew in Jamaica by the 70s had wrought iron bars on the outside of all windows, and oftentimes on the inside of all windows and doors too! Surely in such an environment you become tougher and quick to defend yourself innately? This *'norm'* of a Jamaica environment to grow up in must affect you.

Crime in Jamaica when I was last there in early 2016 appeared to be less, and I felt safer than I have done for many, many years, but Jamaica still has one of the highest murder per capita rates in the world. However I do not see the same racial tensions that existed in the 70s, as Jamaica is slowly slipping back to the pre-Manley days of more harmony. Manley came to power blaming European families for holding all the wealth and keeping the African race down. It's taken 40 years to start to turn the clock back on Manley's socialist economic experiment of stripping the rich to give to the poor, which was an abject failure, and took the country to the brink of bankruptcy. The IMF is still helping out today.

Hopefully the new JLP party, which came back into power in 2016, can continue the *Out of Many, One People* ideal of the country's motto. Jamaica needs all, all of its people, regardless of color, race or religion, to build strength for a successful nation. Those in poverty must be the priority, to raise them up, because as they say in Jamaica, a hungry man is an angry man.

Margaret Thatcher famously said: *"The problem with socialism is that you eventually run out of other people's money."* So did Manley's socialist experiment, and Jamaica paid a heavy price for it.

Chapter 2

School days to marriage

FOR ANYONE BORN BEFORE 1977, the chances that they have read Lady C's autobiography *A Life Worth Living*, written 20 years ago as I alluded to earlier, are pretty slim – so I feel the need to address readers with her earlier life story and give a good summary of it, to enable you to know her background.

School days

Lady C was always known as Georgie, and at school was by many simply called 'Ziadie'. It was very common in boarding schools in those days to be known by your family name. Georgie attended an all boys' Catholic school in Kingston, Jamaica as a day pupil, St. George's College,

Those that knew Georgie throughout her teenage years, as neighbors and friends remember her, and many described her as someone who'd built up a high level of self-confidence for her age and was clearly a girl in behavior not a boy. She was quite a partygoer too, usually in the company of her brother Michael, who chaperoned her to most places.

Some thought that her boldness in taking on sneers and snide remarks full on, made her stand out as someone you'd not willingly pick a fight with. This was in an era where being gay as a boy was not only illegal but virtually unacceptable. A gay friend of their circle set himself alight and killed himself, rather than face a life of humiliation.

It's all the more astonishing that being born as she was, a girl trapped in a body not yet complete as the woman she would be, that she did not hide from society, but boldly strode into it at every opportunity and acted just as she was and who she was. One friend described how when Georgie entered a room or party everybody started talking about her and whispering, both admiringly and, often as not, mockingly. However, being the center of attention, even if it were due to muffled remarks being made about her, built her level of self-awareness and drove her on to be just who she became, someone with no pretense.

If she was known amongst her friends as someone who was very courageous, who'd stride into the midst of every event, party or gathering with her head held high, she was also known for her wit and humor even as a teenager. And she was known for her extravagant and feminine hand and arm gestures and outward self-confidence. It was noticed in her late teens how she was developing a quick retort and sharpness of tongue when spoken to off hand, which developed, as she got older into an art form. I suspect she developed her own mechanism early on as a way of protecting herself from frequent aggression and attacks over her sexuality. Most who did not know her, her friends recalled, guys especially, stayed out of her way. The guys at her school wouldn't get too friendly or wouldn't want to be seen to know her either - but most accepted her - and she did brilliantly at school academically as everyone recalled, including her teachers.

She may have been different to everybody else, but one thing she would not be, and that's silenced, or cowered into embarrassment. She stood her ground early on and she wrote her own script for living her life.

There's a lovely story of how Georgie 'hated' one neighborhood girl at first as they both had a serious crush on the same guy, as did another neighborhood girl. Georgie of course could not declare publicly her interest in boys as she was supposed to be one! Her friends thought it so evident that she was a girl that no one who knew her thought differently. She was simply Georgie.

This other young girl thought Georgie hated her like poison because she was going out with the object of Georgie's eye. She had never met Georgie at that point but had had feedback from other friends and ignored it. Fascinated as she was with Georgie all the same, as she had never met someone like her before, they finally met at a party. Georgie *"sashayed into the party with a flourish,"* head poised and held high. She asked the hostess where Susie was, and her friend thought she sought another Susie who was present and said, *"Over there,"* pointing to another girl. Georgie in a loud *dismissive* and terribly English accented voice, said, *"Please don't insult me, that's not Susie."* The girl who shared a crush with her over the same boy heard all of this was Suzanne Chin, and she thought Georgie terribly funny and sensed she was going to like her. Eventually they found themselves talking to each other at the party and became friends thereafter, which evolved into a very real friendship which has remained to this day.

Georgie grew up in a household where her mother certainly spoke very proper English, and what's sometimes seen by some today as an affected aristocratic accent, truly is, her friends recall, how Georgie always spoke from childhood – it's simply how she was raised and who she is, with a slight island lilt to her accent.

Aged 13, Lady C summonsed the courage to consult a gynecologist in private about her condition, seeking to present her parents with a solution once she could gather all the facts that showed them she needed to be made whole as a woman. The Doctor proved very understanding and gave her reassurance and confidence, allowed her as a minor in the circumstances to be seen, and invited her back a week later to come with her parents. In between time he would do in-depth study to present the best case to them of why corrective surgery to make her the girl and woman she was born to be was the right thing to do. However, a maid reported her leaving the house the second time and staff were sent to bring her back.

Now the matter of her desire to do something about her condition was out in the open with her parents, but it all went the wrong way, as her father insisted on ignoring the specialist he did not know, and placing her in the care of a German Doctor and his psychiatric Doctor wife. Lady C was subjected to horrific forced hormone treatment from one Doctor, and psychological pressure to accept that she was maladjusted from the other or why would she want to swap gender. She felt that it was clear that neither had any knowledge of her condition, being born biologically a female, and neither made any attempt to understand. They were going to make her male come what may! Just short of her 14th birthday puberty she showed all the feminine signs of a higher voice, smooth hairless skin and budding nipples.

However she was forcibly hospitalized and shot full of male's hormones for an entire month, with daily psychological treatment in an attempt to restructure her personality to that of a male. So began on her birthday, with cold calculation, three weeks of terrifying treatment, both hormonal and physiologically. Her treatment she said was carried out with sadistic deliberation to destroy the person she was. Her voice started deepening, some hair started growing and she was drugged heavily all the time.

She finally decided to play along and earn trust in order to get out, and succeeded being allowed to go home for three weeks as they thought she was accepting psychologically the necessary change.

She flushed all the hormone medication down the toilet as soon as she got out. She told her mother what was happening and that she wasn't going back, and said so calmly to her father, and he decided not to force her back - the horrid treatment and brain washing stopped. She felt that it took months to overcome the combined treatments and then was faced with being in limbo for years to come – but the almost criminal behavior of the medical duo was over and school continued.

Teenage friends remember how all their girlfriends knew Georgie as a really lovely, caring person. One friend recalled how, as a teenager, she was so inquisitive that she asked Georgie very personal questions about her sexuality. As no one did that, she felt that it broke a barrier for Georgie and brought them both close together as she learned to rely on another's confidentiality and opened up about her condition.

She was known to have a hilarious sense of humor, and was the talk of the town in her teenage set as you can imagine, with her poise, self-confidence and an air of mystery about her. Her 'crowd' would often go to the Junkanoo Lounge at the old Sheraton Hotel in Kingston. They were underage but ordered alcohol and nobody really cared in those days in Jamaica, they looked grown up and must have been around age 16. A bunch of six to eight of her crowd went there with Georgie's brother Mickey one evening when he was in town. Georgie was in her element and *'outrageous'*, she was telling one joke after another and even her brother Mickey, who was reserved and quieter, was laughing out loud. Mickey her brother said, *"We are not amused,"* in reply to some antic of Georgie's. Georgie without missing a beat apparently, replied that, *"Queen Victoria would have been amused to hear you say that,"* and their whole party fell about laughing. Georgie's humor, her ability to tease and quick wit were developing even then into a quick, sharp and instant response to situations.

In her circle she was very popular as a teenager, she loved to dance, and often danced with girlfriends as any two girls would at that age. She was growing a reputation too as someone who came to life on the dance floor, making as one friend described her *'a spectacle of abandoned joy'*, and she didn't care what people thought of what or who she was. She was more feminine than any of her girlfriends, and her clothes as a teenage 'boy' were more and more outrageous for those times. She was forced to dress as a boy, but did so with abandoned female flair, with wide, wide bell-bottom trousers and floral shirts, and hair which draped slightly over her face. She looked fantastic, as many described her to me.

Just before Georgie left on her own to start a new life studying in New York, aged just 17 she created a sensation amongst friends and neighbors which had everybody abuzz with comment. She drove by in an open top car on the main road in her district dressed entirely as a woman, with makeup, lipstick and a wig. She said to one friend afterwards that there had been some to-do or other with her mother, who did not believe her when she had said to her that, *"One day I'll be a woman."* This was her first public breaking out and showing what she was to become: a fully-fledged woman – she knew then in her own mind that she was going to have corrective surgery and she started the long uphill battle to get there, which was to take her four plus years.

Georgie only ever wanted her mother's love and blessing, and her mother, it seems, was always belittling her and thinking of herself. Her mother was thought of by some as a wicked woman toward her children, and more often than not could be found drunk, at any time of day or night. Her alcoholism was to prove necessary the sending away of her youngest daughter for her safety, and eventually it caused an unreachable chasm between her mother and Lady C. Her friend Suzanne Chin remembered that she and her friends nicknamed Lady C's mother

"Mah Nerves", because she was always complaining about "my nerves" with comments like, *"My nerves can't take it."*

Lady C had had to fight so many battles already as she contemplated moving to New York, but she survived, mostly all on her own. She was turning into a young adult who could stand on her own two feet. During her early teenage years, as Lady C became more and more naturally feminine and flamboyant, which I read as a reaction to hold her ground on her own against constant whispering wherever she went, it was recognized that she was often the brunt of many of her own mother's jokes. Her mother talked, one friend recalled, about *"Having to live with it."* That must have been so hurtful.

What did Lady C's former classmates at St. George's College have to say about the bullying which she claimed she went through at school? Lady C was at St. George's College, the all-boys private school in Jamaica, right through to high school graduation in the class of '67. We have never before heard stories from first hand witnesses of the supposed bullying of Lady C at school, as she claimed during the *I'm a Celebrity… Get Me Out of Here!* reality TV show.

I wanted to ascertain whether Lady C was bullied at school or not; and if so, what form of bullying she went through. With a friend's help I managed to track down a number of her former classmates who spoke at length to me about those dark times in Lady C's life and their recollections of her. Their memories and stories create another layer of understanding of how Lady C's character was formed. '

It seemed clear from those I spoke to, who were in the same class as her or a class below, that Lady C had a very difficult time during her school years. Georgie, or Ziadie as she was known, stood out, as she was so feminine and she expressed herself so differently from all the other boys. A number of people recalled that the way she wore her hair and the way she wore her school uniform was the big talk of people at school.

Georgie was a slim young person, always neatly put together, with a shine to her thick hair and an unusually pretty face for a 'boy', who acted very effeminate. Her hair, always a little longer than most boys', hung a little across her face. Years later, hearing about what 'she' went through all made sense to those I spoke to; that in reality she was not a boy but a girl all along. When old classmates heard years later that she had had surgery to correct the birth deformities they'd heard about in school, they all knew to a man today that it was the right thing to have done, and they told me so.

That Georgie was bullied all the time at school is irrefutable from my numerous interviews. She was, year in, year out, teased and ridiculed, with disparaging remarks being made right through her school days. It was relentless it seems. Those that didn't take part nevertheless didn't want to be 'seen' to be closely associated with her and draw attention to themselves from the class bullies. It must have been a very lonely part of her life; being seen alone and sensing her loneliness was felt by sympathetic classmates who kept quiet. But now, in opening up to me, they felt great remorse for doing nothing, and indicated great admiration for the woman who she is today.

Lady C went through a horrific experience when a bunch of the class tough guys forcibly held her down on the floor. With her trying to stop them, yelling, screaming and crying, they almost succeeded pulling off her long pants to *'see what was down there,'* because of all the rumors that went through school about her being born with deformed female genitals. If it were not for the timely arrival of a teacher breaking up the kerfuffle, it would have been all the more horrific. As some witnesses look back now with the hindsight of adulthood they wish they had done something to intervene. But, when the class bullies are picking on someone and you are not one of the class tough guys, most people just shut up and don't draw attention to themselves. One doesn't just experience that at school. Often times we witness it as adults in a work environment, don't we?

Some boys' tongues were so sharp. They almost hated her, and standing out in an all boys' school made her a target for attack. Throughout her school days, Georgie was severely treated – it must have been so difficult in a school of all young men and I wonder now, how on earth did she cope with it? She would by her mid-to-late teens have found her feminine hormones kicking in and be beginning to fancy boys, which would have made it all the more conflicting and impossible. Many people would have had a mental breakdown, but the girl who was to become Lady C was made of sterner stuff.

The consensus among those I spoke to was that she truly was given an unfair and indeed hard time, a very, very hard time at school. Boys, and Jamaican boys especially I think, found it very hard to accept one of their number being so different. Most of the class did not take part in such bullying, but it happened, and the majority did nothing to stop it, as so often is the case. When her classmates rushed to play football or rugby, Georgie didn't want to take part. She would have been happier going off to do more feminine things. Literally everyone remembered one other outstanding thing about her school days, which was that she excelled in anything academic; she was always up there at the top of the class in any subject.

Bullying at school, not by physically hitting or anything you understand they would never have gotten away with that at a Catholic school, but by intimidating Georgie with horrid remarks about her sexual identity or effeminate ways, or poking, jabbing or shoving. Kids can be very cruel, and many heard frequently about how the Sixth Form had *'Had a go at her'* again. It must have been terrible. No wonder then that when it came to higher education she wanted to undertake studies overseas, where her persona, history, tormentors and past life could all be left behind and she could recreate herself afresh!

Cookie Kinkead, the famous Jamaican photographer, knew Georgie from around age twelve. She would often see her when she was home from school and knew how challenging her mother could be. Lady C's mother was well known for always being found on the back verandah of the house with a drink in one hand and a cigarette in a long, ivory cigarette holder in the other. As the front of the house was kept locked for safety and security, the only way out was through the garden and the back of the house. But there sat Mummy Ziadie, smoking, and no one could escape unnoticed! *"She was known for her deep, quiet voice and sadly, a conversation that was mainly peppered with snide remarks about everything and everyone,"* Cookie said.

Well-known alumni of St. George's school in Jamaica include Bob Marley's son Ziggy and Kristopher Cooper an actor in the 1993 movie *Cool Runnings* went there too – as did Professor Emeritus Anthony Chen, a member of the Nobel Prize Team in 2007.

Her teachers seemed very concerned about Georgie coping in an all boys' school when clearly something was very different about her, but they treasured her because she was so intelligent and successful in every academic subject, and they encouraged her in her studies and, some boys felt, tried to shield her. Maybe if she were not born as she was, and had not gone through what she did in her school days, she would not have turned to academics as a way of escape and to be able to stand out in her own way, and she wouldn't be who she is today either.

She was, looking back and as all recalled, clearly a genuinely nice, caring person and so thoughtful of others despite everything happening to her, and she was known to come from a well-respected family. Most families at this level in society knew each other or knew of each other, so there were awkward bonds to deal with when one of their 'sons' was so out of the box compared to all the others.

Years later, after school days were long behind her, Georgie had come back to Jamaica from the States having had corrective surgery and was now fully realized as a woman. One old classmate remembers running into her for the first time since school at a party in Kingston. *"It was, amazing, she looked stunning, had a fabulous figure, her hair and looks, wow and every man in sight tried to make it with her,"* he said. I heard the same comments from many who were eligible bachelors in those days, who did not know her from school but moved in the upper echelons of Jamaica society as young men. Everybody can change, and when she came back to Jamaica after her surgery as a fully-fledged woman, many school classmates remember thinking, '*Good for you,*' and seemed glad for her that she had found her rightful place in life.

It's sorrowful looking back and now knowing her full story, that her parents didn't do the corrective surgery she as a female needed when she was young. Almost everybody I spoke to from her early years said that her parents should have done it and spared her from such a horrid childhood of bullying. That included her aunt, who tried to influence her parents to do something when she was three years of age. It was, in my opinion, a grave injustice to her that her parents did nothing.

New York days and a hedonistic time of discovery

When she first went to New York at 17 years of age, Georgie attended the prestigious Fashion Institute of Technology (FIT), the design school of the State University of New York. However, she was still registered as a boy.

While by now her parents were going through the motions of trying to help plan corrective surgery, she began to realize that until she was aged 21 and an adult in the eyes of the law and could do what she liked, her desperately wanted surgery to make her womanhood whole was unlikely to happen. Her parents seemed to constantly delay and prevaricate, avoiding taking accountability for the change she needed. To me it is almost as if doing so would have forced them to admit that they had done wrong by her over her whole life – as indeed I believe they had!

Approaching each day when you look and behave, naturally, every ounce a woman, but being known as a boy, was an acute embarrassment and as she's said, "*Just getting through each day made life unbearable from the start.*"

People knew that she was feminine and worked out that she was not a gay boy. However, they could not work out what she was, and it's that which seemed to perturb people. Once at the FIT a teacher said in front of the whole class: "*Could you look less like a girl please?*" And she replied with her now growing wit with an instant retort: "*If you can make an equal effort to behave less like a swine.*" The remark brought that house down, with all in fits of laughter, to the teacher's great embarrassment and, I suspect, anger.

She was growing her ability to fight back and how to use her words and quips to stop bullies in their tracks, no matter who they were. After other equally degrading and similar incidents, she decided to leave the school. Even so, she made the Dean's list for the first semester that she was at FIT, loved creatively draping garments and sketching designs, but did not feel intellectually challenged and had had enough of the degrading attitude of others. Academically she was always one of the brightest at FIT, with echoes of St. George's School coming to mind and following a pattern that matches her extremely intelligent reputation today.

Now, with her mother up in New York from Jamaica, she started looking at which hospital had the best expertise to deal with her medical condition and the necessary corrective surgery. She knew that she wanted to go to the Johns Hopkins hospital, the best in its field, as she had researched it completely. However, her father had been recommended to somewhere else, and she played along while seeking ways to get to Johns Hopkins when the decision was entirely in her hands. Here pops out that innate, Lebanese culture of trying not to offend the father of the household, and yet she told me that she was determined she would go to Johns Hopkins and nowhere else.

Her cousin Enrique remembers that she would have been 18 when he was back in Jamaica from boarding school in England, and Georgie was back from New York for a while. It was on the way back from the airport with his mother after he had landed from England that he learnt for the first time of the whole story of Georgie's birth circumstances. *"No one in our families ever spoke about it, so I honestly did not know,"* he said. *"We just knew Georgie as she was,"* he said. *"Georgie, was just Georgie."*

Back in New York after her vacation at home in Jamaica, Lady C decided to try her hand at writing, as she now needed to do something if she wasn't to live off the family funds forever. She determined to write an article for a magazine on male models, having just seen a program on them on TV. She interviewed some male models at the Paul Wagner Agency, and when she finished the interviews Zolie, who ran the agency, asked her if she had ever thought about modeling herself. The firm managed both male and female models and Zolie said that Lady C had a unique look, and wasn't trying to be somebody else, that she could be the next Twiggy, with her distinct looks and slim body. Lady C said yes, and embarked on a modeling career for one of New York's top agencies, still not surgically changed to a complete female but living as a female. And no one knew different, nor did anyone ask – all merely saw her as a stunning young woman and model.

"It all seemed very glamorous," Lady C said, and for the first few months she found her part time modeling both exacting and exciting, and it helped fund her living expenses. However the gilt was soon off the lily so to speak, as after a while she realized that every modeling day was a long, dreadful slog. She has enormous respect for models she told me, knowing firsthand what hard work modeling is. But it was 1968, and the sexual revolution was at its peak! *"When photographer after photographer unzipped his trousers and assumed you wanted it,"* as she said, she became disenchanted by the modeling industry.

It was now 1968, she was 19 years of age and still a couple of years away from an age for surgery when no one could stop her, as her parents *still* kept delaying. She knew that until she was 21 there was nothing she could do. She was now back, once again, studying at FIT in New York, even though she felt as though she had been browbeaten into returning. She said, *"I knew deep down though that FIT was a passport to a vastly improved life, so I had to make it work. Half a life in New York was better than none in Jamaica."* These were the Big Apple glory days; the city was vibrant and clean, and full of prosperous and high-powered socialites who gave the most fantastic parties.

Lady C contacted friends and found a new apartment through Prince Serge Obolensky, the former husband of Tsar Alexander II's morganatic daughter, who was instrumental in many of New York's main social events of the day. She was in high society's social scene and raring to go! She soon met Bob Taplinger, renowned for throwing great showbiz parties, and at such parties Lady C met stars like Cary Grant, Joan Fontaine, Rosalind Russell and Gloria Vanderbilt. *"I met Ted Kennedy at the Diamond Ball in 1969 who made a play for me, but I managed to escape when yet another lovely woman sidetracked him."* Remember, she was 20 and had not yet had her surgery.

At this time the nightclub scene in New York was electrifying. Clubs like Numero Uno, whose opening night she went to on September 25th 1968 (it was closed down a year later for not having the right liquor license), and its rival Le Club – New York's most chic nightclub for a year or two where she met Aristotle Onassis, who treated her with great decorum and was vastly entertaining she said. Numero Uno was owned by Igor Cassini and his elder brother, Oleg, who was the fashion designer and official couturier for Jacqueline Kennedy when she was First Lady. Igor is also given credit for coining the phrase 'Jet Set' to describe the free-living, free roaming international rich. He was proud of the fact that he had picked Mrs. Kennedy as 'debutante of the year' in 1948, in the days when she was plain Miss Jacqueline Bouvier.

Attending the premiere of the film *Midnight Cowboy*, Georgie met Tucker Fredrickson – he was at that time a quarterback for the New York Giants and a hugely popular national jock. Lady C says that he was, *'devastatingly handsome'*, but they were not fated to go beyond one night of passionate embraces and didn't, as she couldn't yet go all the way with a relationship despite wanting to, and could hardly wait to have the much desired corrective surgery to be a whole woman.

Through Tucker she met one of his best friends, Bill Swain, a dead ringer she said for Clark Kent, Superman's day job persona! Bill was a linebacker for the New York Giants and another hugely popular national sports jock, who operated the nightclub Swains in the off-season. She has said that she fell in love with

Bill. She had not had her surgery yet, so played the shy girl wanting to wait to have sex, and toyed with the idea of telling him about her condition, as she truly adored him. However, as it seemed not to be a relationship that was going to turn into the marrying kind, she kept her counsel and it didn't go any further.

The Vietnam War was now raging and the anti-war movement began, mostly on college campuses where students could express their opposition to the war. The majority of the American population still supported the government's policy in Vietnam, but the student movement was making its voice heard. By December 1969 the government had instituted the first U.S. draft into the military, causing many young men to flee overseas to avoid conscription. Tensions ran higher than ever, spurred on by mass demonstrations, and President Johnson and the war became increasingly unpopular across the nation. Lady C tried to avoid the protest marches that many of her friends from FIT were on, as she did not want to draw attention to herself and be deported.

In February 1970, she graduated from FIT. She attended the Viennese Opera Ball at the Waldorf Astoria to celebrate, and her father let her stay on in New York, as she talked him into letting her get work experience. Later she later went back to Jamaica for six months and was often out with many of her Ziadie cousins. All of the women in her family told her that they were 100% behind her in her planned surgery, which was now close to becoming a reality. The surgery to correct her birth defects was within grasp, and she knew that she could never live life as a man, and all of her friends knew that she wasn't one and could never live such a lie.

It was during this gap period before going back to New York for her surgery that, like many people in her fortunate economic position, she too felt that no compassionate person could fail to be moved by the plight of the poor. Townships bordered all of the smart enclaves of Kingston, Jamaica's capital. One of her early charity actions that she was to instigate herself (having been raised in a family of women who all did charity work and who involved the children in helping), was doing volunteer work in the Department of Pediatrics at the University Hospital of the West Indies (UWI). Interestingly the Scottish husband of a Jamaican aunt of my wife, Professor Eric Cruikshank, created and set up the medical school of the UWI in Jamaica. Here too, my wife's middle brother, David Harvey, attended the faculty of medicine and graduated a Doctor, so beginning his career in Jamaica, England, and now Australia in semi-retirement.

By August, Lady C had her gynecologist in New York lined up, her research having shown that he had a reputation as the finest surgeon in the exact corrective surgery that she needed. He specialized in vaginal reconstruction, and had extensive experience in malformed female genitals. Her cousin, Enrique said to me that, *"Georgie went off to New York for surgery to make her the whole woman that we all knew she was."*

It was the early 70s and the Age of Aquarius, and people were coming out all the time as gay or lesbian, and no one cared. You either liked somebody or you didn't, it did not matter what their sexual preference or condition; that no one by now thought of Georgie as anything but a girl is clear from all those whom I have spoken to. As Enrique said, *"You just didn't think about it; Georgie was Georgie, and we all loved her for who she was."*

New York and the long awaited surgery.

She returned to New York in September 1970 and was admitted with her grandmother's kind funding to the Johns Hopkins hospital. As she said, *"No one ever faced the knife more eagerly as me!"*

She had the life-changing surgery that she had dreamed of her whole conscious life, to become the whole woman for which she had been born to live. Her three closest friends in FIT, Carolyn Kelton, Jill Sprinczellis and Jennifer McFarlane, all knew the truth before her surgery, and each offered support without pity, which got her through this terrible yet exacting time. That she could never be made to live the life of a boy again was her main thought as she woke up from surgery, with a profound disbelief that she had lived through it all and it was now all in the past. The *new* Georgie awoke!

Georgia Arianna emerged like a fresh butterfly from its cocoon, and she was an already stunningly beautiful young women. She spread her wings with entirely new self-confidence – and could now, as she said, respond to the attractive men always coming on to her who, in the sexual revolution of the 70s, wanted full penetrative sex. *"Now I could accommodate them, and I wanted them too!"* she said.

The surgeon told her that it did not take much work sorting out her vagina, but that he was worried that she was, in his words, clearly anorexic. He would not discharge her without someone to care for her, and her friend Frances Bacall and her mother, who flew up from Jamaica, nursed her to full health in the weeks and months ahead.

If you think that the American transgender icon, Kellie Maloney, or Bruce Jenner the all-American athlete and movie star, Caitlyn Jenner as she is now, is an amazing person for choosing to make a transgender change as an adult - which was indeed a brave thing to do and has opened up the whole topic for people to talk about - just imagine being born biologically female and being raised as a boy with no choice in the matter, then being sent to an all-boys' school when you are pumping out female hormones – now that's character forming – and then turning out to be a successful international author, businesswoman and celebrity of TV and the stage. Now that's amazing!

After the first few weeks convalescing Georgie and her mother went up to Canada to stay with relatives for another few weeks of recuperation. By November 1970 she was ready to face the second step, having the paperwork changed that ensured she was recognized as female. Registering with the Jamaican authorities was necessary and she went back to Jamaica to commence this bureaucratic marathon.

The media had somehow been alerted to her story, but the then Editor of the Jamaican national newspaper *The Gleaner* said that her mother had done so much for charity that the family deserved privacy over this and did not publish or report on her surgery. The family's influence came to her rescue with the media on this occasion.

Her original birth certificate listing her as male could not be changed; it was a matter of public record that her sex was wrongly declared and recorded by the doctor who delivered her, not knowing what to do and knowing her father's desire for a son. Finally, with the kind help of the Registrar of Births, they issued a second birth certificate, which made no mention of the sex recorded at birth. It simply listed her new female names, Georgia Arianna Ziadie, her date of birth and sex: female.

It must have been that first certificate that was discovered later by the Argylls, which they used to claim wrongly that Lord Colin Campbell had married a man!

She stayed a little longer, recuperating at home in Jamaica, and decided to give up her New York apartment. She dabbled as a freelance designer and model to earn enough money to buy the occasional air ticket return to New York and get a buzz being in the city, seeing and staying with friends and enjoying the nightlife. When her cousin Enrique arrived in Jamaica from England around the same time that Georgie had come back after her surgery, his mother told him on the way back from the airport (this seemed to be a theme with his mother) that, *"Georgie is coming back from New York a woman."* She also shared with him for the first time what she had told Georgie's mother when Georgie was three that Georgie should have had corrective surgery done at that age. *"We were not brought up to talk about these things but my mother was cross with her friend for failing to do something back in 1952 when she begged her to,"* he said.

We now know that Helen (Lady C's cousin Enrique's mother) and Marjorie (Lady C's mother's sister), both asked Lady C's mother Gloria, when Lady C was three, to do something about her birth circumstances and give her the surgery which she needed to make her fully female. I know from hearing it from Enrique that his mother was very upset with Gloria for not doing the needed corrective surgery for Lady C when a toddler. It just lends credence to the reality of her story and what came out later as evidenced by medical reports during the time of her divorce and defamation lawsuits, that she was born biologically female. Newspapers wrongly reported that she'd been born a man or was a trans-sexual.

Jamaica was a beautiful place, but she was in danger of being bored as husband material was thin on the ground for all in her circles, not just Lady C. When she returned from New York her family and her close Jamaican friends spread the word that Georgie was a beautiful, in demand model in New York socialite circles. Friends like Cookie Kinkead, a well-known society photographer, and Pam Seaga who set the pace, Suzanne Chin, and Maxine Walters. The result seemed to be that everyone else followed suit and she was quickly welcomed with open arms wherever she went in Jamaica.

It was Pam Seaga who played a vital part in introducing her to the first Jamaican man she felt could be husband material, and he was a wealthy landowner in the country, with a house in town. However, she felt she could do better, find a better love match. As it turns out, the woman this man married suffered after the first five years, having to put up with a string of mistresses which he kept in Town. Not for her.

Now that she was a woman in every sense of the word, she was just waiting for the right man to come along, and it didn't have to be for love or marriage either, just someone she fancied!

Let's look at other lovers; well, at least those we know about!

Pam Seaga was the matchmaker again in introducing Georgie to a young man who, like both of them, was someone from a leading Lebanese family in Jamaica; aged 37 Maurice Shoucair was the head of his family clan. All her girlfriends encouraged her and said that a good-looking Lebanese man was the best and gentlest introduction to love making. He was separated and going through a divorce.

He won her father over as he telephoned him first, not Lady C, and asked permission to court his daughter in the old fashioned way, which was important in Lebanese culture and to her father. Her attractive beau was the first man to deflower her womanhood, and she said it was a mixed blessing, as the first time was painful, but with it she could discern the pleasure that lay beneath.

However, her father was concerned that a three times divorced man whose elder brother inherited the bulk of his family's wealth was not capable of keeping his daughter in the style he expected. Her father was worried that her beau was still married despite being separated, and that Lady C would be cited in a divorce case with the whole damn thing of her birth circumstances exploding in her face if she continued with the relationship. Lady C agreed to step back from the relationship for a while, and sadly it was only a few months later that her first lover died of sudden heart attack.

She next dated a charming American, Eugene Brown, someone who she felt just might be ideal husband material. The only problem was that she wasn't completely sure that she fancied him sexually.

Next came a German shipping magnate she had met in New York, who came to Jamaica and spoke to her father about his interest in marriage to Lady C. He was a gentleman indeed and very well off, which made her father happy, but she simply did not fancy him, period.

By now it was 1971, and stepping out to a hotel nightclub with cousins and friends, she saw an Adonis across the room and felt an instant *lustful* attraction. One of her friends knew the chap the Adonis was sitting with and took her across to meet them. The next thing she knew, Bill Madden, the object of her lust, asked her to dance and as quickly said, *"I want you badly"*; and as quick, she replied, *"So do I."*

That was it; they were off to his hotel room and made mad passionate love. She said that she never before or since has been so instantly attracted to someone as she was to Bill. She saw him as marriage material and was totally in love *and* in lust. However, she realized sooner rather than later that he was a bit too prissy for her modern approach to life, so she never became Mrs. Madden.

She was back in New York staying at a friend's apartment while he was away for the summer. With a cousin she went to a dinner party and met Russell Price again. Russell had studied for the Catholic Priesthood, but abandoned it for an old girlfriend of Lady C's, who he had now left. They landed up going to bed and had a three-month passionate affair, but it ran its course and she did not see him as husband material either. She left shortly afterward to spend Christmas at home in Jamaica with family and friends.

Her second touch of charity work occurred when she reflected on how lucky they were as a family to have a happy Christmas and gifts. She knew that for so many it was a time of want, and parents who could not afford gifts for their children like those that they would have. She came up with an idea, and roped in family and friends who owned shops, stores and factories to donate presents to her, which she and her friends could then distribute among the poor children who lived in communities nearby. She worked tirelessly, knocking on doors and extending her reach to people she had never met before. Before long, she had had several hundred gifts donated.

She asked a family friend, the Attorney General Victor Grant, for his thoughts on the best way to distribute the gifts. Come the appointed day she says, *"He whisked us off in a car with a huge van behind us carrying all the presents,"* and they were driven from one unknown village to another. She was so angry when she realized that he was having her gifts handed out *only* to children in *his* parliamentary constituency and *only* to *his* supporters.

She was stunned, but learnt a lesson. Her next charitable drive was to seek to raise money for the University of West Indies (UWI) hospital department of obstetrics & gynecology, which needed a machine to monitor the heartbeat of fetuses. She asked the well-known French pianist Andrée Juliette Brun (the Russian Princess Oukhtomskaya in her private life) to give a Gala Concert recital at the Jamaican State Theatre in aid of the cause. Andrée dedicated her time and flew down from New York with her boyfriend, and Lady C talked BOAC, as British Airways was then known, into sponsoring their air tickets and the Skyline hotel into putting them up complimentary.

The Gala was a sell-out, with anyone who loved music wanting to be there, and anyone wanting a chance to meet a Russian Princess scrambling for tickets. The program sold advertising space, mainly supported by Ziadie family and friends businesses. The event raised a small fortune for the hospital. Even the Governor-General of Jamaica turned up.

I've since discovered that Lady C went on constantly, throughout her life, to organize charity balls; she would sit on ball committees and when it became too demanding on her time she would buy whole tables and ensure that she filled them with friends who she knew would buy prizes and donate sizable amounts of money to the charities the events represented. She remains a favorite invitee to many charity balls still, for that very reason.

Up and onwards on the male front!

There was a dalliance with a Ron from Wales, who seems to have hung around for quite some time, but whose family name has escaped time. She says he was good looking, a rugby player type, but it seems someone who was proactively anti the upper class, and so eventually the friendship waned and fell to one side.

But the path towards marriage was now in sight, and she was at the Jamaican Jockey Club racetrack, owned by the father of a friend as that journey began to unfold. Kari Lai and Lady C had become great friends and through her, Lady C had met the then Duke of Marlborough's sister, Lady Sarah Spencer-Churchill (the family associated of course with Winston Churchill and Lady Diana Spencer, later Diana, Princess of Wales). Sarah lived huge chunks of the year in Jamaica in her elegant home named *Content* in Montego Bay. Two weeks after breaking up with Ron she was invited by Lady Sarah to spend a long weekend there. Other houseguests were Kari, her brother, and Ian Hamilton. Ian had flown in with Sarah's brother, and she had become drawn to Ian. Back in Kingston at her brother Mickey's pied-à-terre, Ian and Lady C hopped into bed and consummated their mutual attraction!

Ian owned a stud farm in England, and his elder brother at the time owned the sugar estate Caymanas Park, next to the Caymanas racecourse in Jamaica. He was not wealthy, but well off. Of course as they both loved and kept racehorses this boded well for her father's approval, should she ever feel he was the one. Ian had to return to England shortly and he asked Lady C to visit him there.

In the meantime as a frequent guest and now friend of Lady Sarah, she was at a long weekend house party of hers some time later when the movie *Papillon* was being filmed at Montego Bay with Steve McQueen and Dustin Hoffman, with the Art Director, Tony Masters. Ali McGraw was with Steve, and Dustin had his wife with him. Lady C got to know them a little over this long weekend. There are some amusing stories about Lady C's advice to Steve McQueen.

There were regular guests coming and staying at Lady Sarah's, her sister Lady Caroline Spencer-Churchill, lady-in-waiting to Princess Alexandra, visited. Soon afterward, her son Michael flew out and stayed with his good friend Mark Shand who came with him. Mark was the brother of Camilla Parker-Bowles née Shand, the future Duchess of Cornwall, and later Mark became an intrepid explorer and founder of Elephant Family, a wildlife foundation. Both men were ruggedly good looking but not quite her type, but Lady C had great fun in their company during their Jamaica visit. She felt Mark kept flirting with her, but whenever she showed interest he pulled back again. Shortly he returned to London.

Back in London herself some time later, she ran into Mark at Annabel's in Berkeley Square, the exclusive and elegant members only nightclub for the well-known and the well-heeled. If you've been to Annabel's you know that it's always crowded, and the small Buddha bar area is stunning, as is the wine-cellar private dining room. Mark made a beeline to her through the crowd, and he asked Lady C to dance, and at evening's end he asked if he could drop her home rather than her friend do so. She agreed, wondering whether this was going to develop or not, after the somewhat non-starter of Jamaica.

Mark's conduct in the flat where she was staying in those days in Bina Gardens still brings a smile to her face 44 years later. He became so infatuated with Lady C she says, that he bought the flat below her within a few weeks. One evening when he was visiting she had gone to the kitchen to get drinks and when she returned she said: *"Mark stood naked from the waist down with a proud erection!"*

She was shocked, and who knows how different the future would have been had she said yes and jumped into bed with him – maybe married and then sister-in-law of the Prince of Wales? However, taken aback at his behavior, she asked him to get dressed. He always remained very friendly and courteous to her she says, but unsurprisingly never tried to make advances again. It was not meant to be.

　While in England she visited Ian Hamilton at his horse stud farm in Newbury. However, she found that two weeks there was enough to kill off any relationship. She was too excited by the social whirl of London to become a country girl and wasn't raised one. She woke up one morning and could not face another barren day with Ian happily pottering in the garden or around the stud.

After returning to London and staying with friends temporarily, she moved into another flat in Bina Gardens and shared with two other girls. Many of her Jamaican friends were in London at this time and were well placed, so she received impeccable introductions. She met many English girls through the equine bloodstock agency owned by the Cecils, and was invited to countless dinners and parties. To pay people back for their hospitality she would throw drinks parties for twenty plus friends at a time at her small flat every couple of weeks, in order to say thank you.

Now came a proposal of marriage!

By now Lady C was in a furiously intense relationship with the Honorable Serge Beddington-Behrens, the son of Russian Princess Irina Obolensky and Sir Edward Beddington-Behrens. Sir Edward was a famous banker who bailed out King George V when Daisy, Countess of Warwick, blackmailed the Royal Family over her love affair with the King's father, Edward VII. She had a short-lived affair with Serge, with him proposing marriage after their third date. Lady C was then becoming increasingly keen on him, but talk of marriage so soon threw her off balance. It quickly became apparent to her that whilst he was a tiger in bed as she described him, he wanted to live life as a hippy. He tried but could not wean her off dressing up and her love of the social calendar, and she could not wean him off wanting to dress down and wishing to opt out of the real world. Nor was she listening to his request that she become a vegetarian – after all, lobster, caviar and champagne are a staple diet, surely! After some months they parted, somewhat acrimoniously she said.

She was only 24 so marriage could wait, and moral support came in the guise of her little sister Margaret who was by now at school in England, and Mary Anne Innes Ker, as well as Mary Anne Rutherfurd (Mary Anne's grandmother Lucy Mercer was President Roosevelt's great love and mistress, and was with him when he died Lady C said). She decided to take a break from men and started writing a book on philosophy. She worked at it every day with ideas pouring out.

In the evenings, she went out with friends to dinner and parties, or to Tramps, the London discotheque part owned by Jackie Collins at the time. The dancing there was better than at Annabel's, and while she knew fewer of the members she bumped into the likes of Bianca Jagger and Ryan O'Neal.

David Koch

Lady C attended an American Thanksgiving luncheon in London hosted by Dulany Howland, who was a dear friend. One of his guests was fellow American David Koch, who was visiting England. She had no idea at the time when they met that he was one of the richest men in the world, an American businessman, philanthropist and political activist. In 1970 David had joined the family business Koch Industries, a conglomerate that was the second largest privately held company in the United States. Forbes estimated his net worth in 2015 as US$44.3 billion.

David asked her out to dinner, and, as she described it, it was a truly lovely swansong period in her life. She now sees, looking back, that this was the end of a carefree period in life until decades more would pass – but she wasn't yet to know this.

David went back to New York. She intended to stay in England until she found an agent and publisher for her book. The three-day week was going to come into effect in England, and did from January 1974. She knew that this foretold extensive periods of power cuts and no electricity or heating in winter months, so in early December 1973 she took off to New York as well, to stay with her friend Lady Sarah Spencer-Churchill at her East Seventy-Second Street townhouse.

Once in New York she started to see David regularly, and got to know him better. By now she knew that he and his brother were filthy rich, but she simply knew him as a charming, considerate, gentleman. Their friendship soon became passionate, after just a few weeks she claims, and she describes him as an extremely considerate lover. It was a time when both were single and yet she did not feel the same passion for him as she did Serge. She began to wonder if she expected too much from a future husband and whether sexual fireworks were necessary, as here she was in bed with one of the most eligible bachelors in the world and their relationship was growing and she really, really liked him.

She only pulled herself away from David and New York to attend Christmas at home with family in Jamaica, and in January David followed her to Jamaica for a long weekend. He clearly was taking this relationship as seriously as she was. She asked her brother Mickey to chaperone her, and David asked his best friend Roger Samet, to join him. She also invited her childhood friend and now celebrated artist Judy Ann McMillan to make up a house party. Her brother was, unusually for him, being quite obnoxious towards everybody and at supper in front of everyone she rounded on him, asking him if he was trying to ruin the weekend for her and David. David only endeared himself to her all the more when he said, *"Brothers! I know all about them. I have three."*

Back in New York after Christmas David got his best friend Roger to ask Lady C to stay in New York, as he wanted to pursue the relationship with her. She told Roger that if David loved her so much he could ask her himself, and not send an emissary. Roger said, *"Do you realize how rich David is?"* as they ate lunch at the restaurant Maxwell's Plum, which to her was not the point. Clearly David wanted her in his life, but she felt then, as now, that money has limited value, and that if David really wanted her, he'd keep chasing her. As both were busy with a thousand and one other things in the weeks ahead, she agreed to have dinner in a few weeks' time with David and talk things through.

Lady C has not disclosed before that David was the American billionaire who she mentioned without naming in her autobiography of nearly 20 years ago. She says that he nearly swept her off her feet and was the one who she thought she would land up marrying - until after some six or more charming months of romance, Colin Campbell came onto the scene. Looking back, I wonder if she now sees that more akin to an ominous dark cloud appearing over a bright sunny summer? She was at this time busy arranging to stay with a friend in New York, Jeanne Campbell, the second wife of Norman Mailer the famous novelist, author and two times Pulitzer Prize winner. Jeanne was also the daughter of the 11th Duke of Argyll (and Colin's sister). Little did Lady C know that her glory days and carefree life was about to come to an end.

Enter Lord Colin Campbell, stage right, or should I say, stage fright!

Jeanne Campbell's stepbrother, Lord Colin Campbell, the younger son of the 11th Duke of Argyll by his second wife Louise Clews, came to New York to visit his sister and stay with her, supposedly for vacation. He was aged 27 when Lady C met him, and she thought him a romantic textbook figure. He was, *"Tall, dark, handsome and a mix of adventurousness and non-conformity,"* she said, and he certainly looks handsome and dashing in photos of the time. The only problem was, he was as thin as a stick, and she preferred her men husky and athletic, the Adonis types. She felt that he had the strongest personality of anybody she had met before, and Jeanne had pre-warned her that he loved pretty girls - but not to jump into bed with him that easy or he'd lose respect for her. Impulsive as she was becoming when she fell in lust, she still behaved ladylike and would have been thankful for the advice.

After Jeanne's other guests had left a drinks party that she'd hosted three days after Colin arrived and at which Georgie was present, the three of them went out to have a burger together: Jeanne, Colin and herself. They came back to the apartment and Jeanne went to bed, and Lady C and Colin stayed up talking. *"We chatted for hours, his jet lag keeping him wide awake having just come in from London,"* she says, captivated by him, it seems. She felt that they had so much in common, and, when he leaned over to kiss her, Lady C let him. He started getting hot and heavy but she said, *"Not now,"* to his intimating he wanted to go to bed.

Right then and there, on meeting for the first time, he asked her to marry him.

Lady C says he said, *"You're the most beautiful girl I've ever seen,"* and went on to say that he felt he had known her all his life and that his sister Jeanne said that she was from a good family and had a great character. He continued that she was everything he wanted in a wife.

She was stunned and could not help but draw parallels with Serge and his asking her to marry him after just three days! She had always wondered if she would ever find the ideal man and suspected that here was an opportunity to put things right, having turned Serge down, being distracted and now unsure if David was the one, and here was a chance to get married as she always dreamed of doing.

There was David in the wings though, the billionaire who was very properly and traditionally courting her and wanting her to stay in New York – she began to toy with the idea that she had David in the wings if it didn't work out with Colin that week.

Whatever else she may be thinking, she knew that she was smitten with Colin and did not want to wreck another relationship with too much prevarication. She stalled for time, gently suggesting that they hardly knew each other. He proposed that they ask Jeanne what she thought, and she agreed. She wasn't expecting him to walk straight into Jeanne's room then and there and wake her, but he did!

When asked, Jeanne said that she thought it was a marvelous idea. Lady C gently counseled waiting, and Jeanne said, *"Look, whether any marriage works is the luck of the draw, I've known people who got married a week after meeting who are still happily married years later, and individuals who knew each other beforehand for years, only to divorce within months."*

It all began to move a bit too fast for Lady C when Colin called his brother Ian in Scotland. She desperately tried to think the whole thing through whilst he was on the call. To cut a long story short, after Colin and Jeanne had spoken to Ian, who seemed thrilled about it, she and Colin went off into the living room to talk some more. To her own surprise and caught up in the romance of the whole thing, she impulsively accepted his proposal of marriage, and said, *"Yes!"*

Colin then wanted to tell her two important details about himself. Firstly, that he had a chronic stomach problem, which made her feel closer to him as her father also suffered from such a problem. Secondly, he said he didn't want children: *"You can't marry me if you want children,"* he said. She remained silent, but sensed he knew all about her past already. Only after they were married did he let on that he knew Jamaica well, and had learned all about her and her family before they met. His stepsister Jeanne had a house in Hopewell, just outside of Kingston in Jamaica. Georgie says that in turn she told him about her upbringing which he took in his stride, but more about that later.

Jeanne arranged for them to be married in the 'Gretna Green' of America, Elkton, Maryland as it could be done with 48 hours residency, whereas New York required another 11 days residency before granting a marriage license.

Meanwhile, Jeanne said, *"How truly sweet Colin was, and how his mother was beastly to him."* When Colin's mother's marriage to the 11th Duke (Colin's father) no longer worked, and before her divorce, the then Duchess took a lover, Prince Dmitri of Russia. He was one of the last Tsar of Russia's nephews, and when he refused to marry her if she left the Duke, she took out all her spite on Colin. Lady C felt sympathy for Colin and decided to throw caution to the winds and run off with him and enjoy the romance of it all.

She then stopped, and thought about how on earth she was going to tell David, who seemed to be working towards asking her to marry him, and tell him that she'd decided to marry somebody else?

All of this happened Lady C said, during those two or three weeks when David was away on business and before they had met up for dinner as planned. *"Colin and my romance of just a few days was to change my life forever,"* she said.

She was busy dealing with the paperwork of getting a marriage license sorted out for Colin and herself when she suddenly realized that it was that evening that she was supposed to go to dinner with David. She agonized over how she was going to tell him, felt elated at her decision to marry Colin, but was saddened to let David down, as he was such a gentleman. She went to the dinner and dropped the bombshell on David right out front - that she had met someone else and was getting married. His best friend Roger was there at her request to make it easier for them all – and in a very gentlemanly way David said that he understood, made no attempt to change her mind and wished her well. *"He was a truly lovely man,"* as she said.

Planning a wedding.

Getting her news out in the open after he had shared his wish not to have children, she had asked Colin again if he knew about her birth circumstances and being raised wrongly as a boy? She claims that she told him clearly that: *"I'm not sure if you're aware that I was brought up a boy, are you?"* as she never wanted that coming up later and standing between them. He seemed a little stumped that she was raising it again, and said, *"It's not run of the mill, is it?"* and went on to say that he didn't care for bullshit like that. She added that she could not have children either, and he stated that he had already said he didn't want kids and added: *"I can't stand the little buggers."*

With that hurdle out the way, Colin, Jeanne and Georgie went down to his trustees for him to draw out a sum that enabled him to buy her an engagement ring and to pay for their elopement to Elkton.

Whilst they had to wait 48 hours for State residency to be granted permission to be married, she kept thinking how romantic it all was, how real. However, she was a bit surprised when she realized that it took second place to Colin's searching his baggage to find drugs to get over his jet lag. Warning bells should have rung, but it did not occur to her then that he had a serious drug problem.

The evening before the wedding, a friend had come across to where they were, and they had, as she describes it, a riotous dinner. Afterwards they all turned in early, but she and Colin had still not made love, as they had never been alone long enough to, not for one minute since the whole whirlwind started, Lady C said.

The wedding took place on Saturday, March 23rd, 1974, on a chilly but sunny morning, and this was it, she was getting married. She felt surer than ever that she was doing the right thing and off they set.

She hadn't been expecting members of the Press and photographers to be present, as they were supposedly eloping, and she wondered how on earth they knew. It turned out that the Campbells measured their worth in terms of publicity and had ensured that the media knew all about the wedding. She only realized later why they thought her the perfect match and why there was such a rush to land her before she escaped.

The Campbells she believed, knew that if the marriage worked she would prove a great asset hanging on Colin's arm; he'd have a real beauty and a big chunk of her father's money, surely. If the marriage failed he could as easily follow the example of his father and great-great-uncle and sell her birth story to the Press and divorce her. Looking back with hindsight, they may have envisaged making a killing in cash if the marriage failed so may have seen it as a win–win situation, who knows?

At the time she felt happy that she was marrying a great looking guy, one from a suitable background, albeit that he clearly had no money in terms she was used to in her family. But she felt that they were both young, and they could forge their own future and success. Besides, Colin wanted to make a new life in Fiji, and that seemed to her to be a romantic, as well as a sound economic idea, with the lower cost of living there.

Colin asked her to sign a document waiving her rights to his trust fund should anything go wrong with the marriage. She claims he said, *"It produces a minuscule income, and I can only just live off it myself."* She didn't care. She was in love and paid no attention. Other than this meager amount it appeared that he was penniless, but she agreed willingly and signed the document – yet looking back it should have set off another warning bell.

Chapter 3
Marriage to Lord Colin Campbell
and what went wrong

WHAT'S LORD COLIN CAMPBELL'S current side of the story? In a year-end 2015 interview with The Sun on Sunday newspaper, his first comments publicly in many years about his divorce and Lady C during the reality TV show *I'm a Celebrity... Get Me Out of Here!*, there was one revelation where he admitted they were wrong, otherwise he repeated the same views he had 40 years ago.

Of his divorce he said: *"I was stunned. I just could not believe what I was hearing. After she told me, I could not even bring myself to look at my wife, let alone touch her."*

The revelation: his brother the Duke of Argyll telephoned Lord Colin and asked him: *""Do you realize you have married a man?"* He was wrong about that, I now realize,"* Lord Colin said in his *Sun* interview in 2015. But he also said that it was a massive shock at the time.

He talked about their whirlwind romance and Lady C's beauty, her attractiveness and flirtatiousness. He talked of how their sex was normal and how they had lots of it on their honeymoon, and had had a fantastic time. He also talked about his being a randy young man and said that, *"her body was that of a normal woman."* He admitted that he was pretty drunk at the time of the revelations hitting the newspapers. He also said that he'd, *"Hit the bottle as I struggled to cope with the scandal,"* and described himself at the time as being young, impulsive, stupid and silly. He talked of Lady C being *"trouble with a capital T"*, and of her being lovely and charming but deep down a monster. And he urged contestants in the Jungle to avoid her at all costs.

In her autobiography Lady C claimed that Colin was an alcoholic and a sometimes violent drug addict, which he denies. But he admitted that they simply were not compatible. He found her voice and her aristocratic accent, which he clearly thought false, irritating, and he acknowledged that they had constant vicious rows. He said, *"I have not spoken to her since the day we divorced in 1975."* He told reporters that he had not watched *I'm A Celebrity*, which was not available anyway to viewers in the US (as I knew, as I couldn't obtain it, other than snippets via YouTube) and he added, *"She's bad news, and I hope I never have to lay eyes on her again."*

Sex and the Marriage

Steady on old boy! Interesting that Colin mentioned that on their honeymoon they had regular sex and lots of it. Lady C has been quoted as saying that they did not make love on the first night after their registry office wedding, as he had said to her that he was too tired from jet lag. She had hoped that when he awoke the next day he'd leap on top of her, and she encouraged him as she so wanted to consummate the marriage, but he didn't she said. The great romance was certainly not following any script known to lovers, as he suggested they go for a walk through the city instead. Alarm bells ought to have been clanging in the background by now I'd have thought, meshed with everything else that had happened to-date. But she was too in love to see it, and patiently waited.

A surprise revelation

On honeymoon, when it came to bedtime Colin kept prevaricating, and Lady C claims he suddenly commented that, *"I'm uptight because I might not be able to satisfy you."* Dropping the first bombshell he added, *"I've never had a relationship with a girl in my life,"* but added that he'd, *"had sex with women before, but all prostitutes."* His father had sent him to a bordello when he was sixteen apparently. Such a rite of passage was not unusual in upper-class circles, to prepare male offspring for their duty to marry and deliver heirs. Given the previous days palaver over uppers and downers she wondered if she had married the male version of a Drama Queen.

A bombshell revelation

They went back to New York the following day and to the apartment of a friend who had loaned it to them. Here the second bombshell hit. Lady C said that Colin told her: *"I wasn't totally honest with you yesterday; I have a hang up about physical contact."* He named a male relation she says, who, *"used to force himself upon me as a little boy."* Wait until you hear who Lady C says Colin claimed it was in an upcoming chapter. Oh My God!

Lady C felt staggered but sympathetic towards Colin. Now they both had shared traumatic sexual pasts she believed they were building an unshakable bond as a couple. She was annoyed that he hadn't told her about this hang up before the wedding, when she had told him about her circumstances of birth and how she was raised, something he's always denied knowing about. But now he had shared it, and she was glad he had opened up to her. It was also during these few days in New York, before going down to Jamaica for the first wedding reception, that she says she became aware of his excessive pot smoking (marijuana); and despite it being part of the 70s and accepting that no one saw great danger in it, it seemed to her an *excessive* use of the drug. A tinkling of the alarm bells?

Mind you, here we are in 2016 and multiple States in America have already or are considering making marijuana legal for medicinal purposes. Jamaica made that legal in 2015 – so times change.

Wikipedia and Lord Colin Campbell

What's interesting is that when I looked up Lord Colin Campbell on Wikipedia it said the only page available was on the Lord Colin Campbell from the 1800s who was Lady C's husband's Great-Great Uncle, who also divorced his wife spectacularly in the media, something unheard of in Victorian Britain. The only option for Lord Colin's correct full names, Lord Colin Ivar Campbell brought up Lady Colin Campbell. It only referred to Lord Colin Campbell as the ex-husband of Lady Colin Campbell. Ouch! No matter how hard I tried in Google, Wikipedia and other sources, I could find no record on the current Lord Colin anywhere other than newspaper interview reports. When you look at Lady Colin Campbell's Wikipedia page, it says, rather embarrassingly for the Campbells, that the Campbell family are best known for their relationship with her. Not that she's best known for her relationship with them. Ouch, and double ouch!

What else didn't sound right to me in Lord Colin's 2015 Press statement?

The money:

Lady C said that he wanted a prenuptial signed so that she couldn't touch *"his miserly trust fund"* as she described it. He did not build into that prenuptial that he sought to swap a title for money, or say that he wanted a dowry, as surely this was the time and place to ask for it she said – not wait until after they were married and then start demanding that she ask her father for an annual allowance, *"as that's the deal. Get your Father to settle an annual income on you."* She told him that her father was not like that and nothing would be forthcoming, nor would she ask. Lord Colin had a $12,000 a year trust fund income - that's around $61,000 a year in 2016, or just over £42,000 a year.

Some have claimed that she had assumed that she was not just marrying a title, which she wanted, but great wealth by marrying into a Ducal family, and was shocked to find that they were all relatively penniless. Lady C has always said that the title wasn't important to her, although it's been useful since as she's always admitted, and that she knew fully that Colin was relatively penniless before she said yes, and married for love.

When they were still in New York and just 48 hours after their wedding, Colin tried to persuade Lady C to sell her jewelry to raise funds to furnish the apartment they had in mind. She had them undervalued deliberately to make it look pointless trying to sell the mainly family pieces which she had inherited or been given as gifts. She had no intention of selling them. She felt that she was their custodian not their owner, and had no right to sell them.

Was the future looking brighter?

A few days after the wedding and back in New York city, he initiated the first kiss for a change and made love to her she said, albeit it that, "*he laid back with his eyes closed*" and left it all to her. His lack of experience and insensitivity was showing, and even though he was no good in bed, she felt at least that the marriage had finally been consummated, which gave her hope for the future.

Jamaica and the first wedding reception.

On the morning after they arrived in Jamaica for the first wedding reception Colin raised the idea again, that she should ask her father for an annual income, and she says she told him that, "*Daddy will never agree to something like that,*" and that, "*I'd sooner starve than put myself in a position of asking.*"

Lady C says that upon arrival in Jamaica Colin's wardrobe consisted of one of this, and one of that - one pair of shoes, one pair of swimming trunks, one pair of slacks, and everything worn and dilapidated. She didn't want to be embarrassed and carry him around town to meet friends dressed so poorly, so she had one of her father's retail shops send an extensive amount of clothes and shoes to the house for him to try on. She helped to create a new wardrobe for him, which *she* paid for. At this point she says Colin said, "*I hope you don't think I married you for your father's money?*" She was quick to tell him again that there was no magic pot of money coming her way.

Her cousin Enrique remembers meeting Colin for the first time when they came down from New York for these wedding celebrations at her family home in Jamaica. He said, "*Georgie brought him to meet us, and they seemed well suited, and he seemed very nice.*" He talked of when suddenly months later it all turned very vile, and that Georgie's family said nothing more than that they found it all very disappointing.

One morning in Jamaica during this honeymoon period Colin was found making a series of calls to his elder brother, Ian, the 12th Duke of Argyll. These calls to Scotland he made on Lady C's parents' house phone. As long-distance calls were terribly expensive in those days, especially from Jamaica to Europe, it seemed very odd, because Lady C recalls that he hadn't asked her parents' permission. Remember too, that these were the pre-mobile phone days, there was only the family landline – and no one could text, fax, Face-time or Skype. They did not exist! If you had 'a house phone' in Jamaica in the mid-Seventies you were already somebody.

Later that same day, Lady C's father took a call from the *Daily Telegraph* in London saying, *"We have been informed that your daughter changed sex, is that true?"* Clearly the calls from Colin to his brother in the morning and this one were too coincidental to be unconnected, and her father and she herself were shocked. Lady C felt a wave of panic come over her.

Ten minutes later a relative who worked at *The Gleaner*, the national newspaper of Jamaica, rang saying that the British tabloid *The Sunday People* had contacted them, asking for someone on their behalf at *The Gleaner* to check Lady C out locally and see what they could find out about her birth – following a tip-off earlier that day, from a *"well-placed source"*, that she'd been born a man. The request was passed to the Social Editor at the time, who was a Ziadie family friend, and she said no to *The Sunday People*, and warned Lady C's father to expect another call shortly, as she was going to see the then Editor about it. She rang back to say that the Editor wasn't going to publish or help anyone publish such a scandalous story. There could be no way that Colin's calls that morning with his step-brother were not connected she thought.

In the meantime Colin had said to Lady C that, *"the publicity doesn't matter to me, you can sell your story for a small fortune, and the controversy will help you get your book published"* – her philosophy book. She thought at the time that he was just trying to be consoling and maybe hadn't been personally involved after all, but clearly, when we read everything else above and to come, this seems like a concerted plan with his elder brother to get a "small fortune" for Colin from the newspapers. How do you read it? And they had only just got married. But Daddy and Lady C were not playing ball, coughing up an annual allowance or selling her jewelry?

Georgie's family had discreetly suggested to many attending the Jamaican wedding reception that the 'happy couple' would value cash donations to help set up home, a common thing for many couples today and frequent in Lebanese and Arabic households through the ages, as indeed in many Jewish and Greek families too. Their wedding reception guests generously gifted enough to them that they were able to furnish their New York apartment, primarily with lots of lovely antiques.

Nothing further seems to have come of the Press inquiries from London, with the local Jamaican Press not co-operating, nor of the earlier threats by the Campbells, and at this stage all went quiet - for now.

Further wedding receptions in Britain

Receptions were planned for their friends and families in London and Scotland, and in New York when they returned to establish the marital home. Ian, the 12th Duke of Argyll, planned wedding receptions for them at his London house and at the family seat Inveraray Castle. She met lots of charming and warm people, and she said that all without exception were very welcoming. They fared less well in the wedding present department than they had in Jamaica all the same, and the Duke and his brother seemed to chat a lot about the fantastic press coverage the wedding had brought and how Colin was now famous.

Invited to Inveraray Castle for the wedding reception was a dear American friend of Lady C's, Mary Michele Rutherfurd. Mary Michele is the great granddaughter of former American Vice-President, Levi Morton (1889–1893). It was all very romantic and a fairytale weekend house party, and it must have been even more romantic to an American to wake to the bagpipes playing in the morning. Colin was home with his brother Ian, the Duke. What most people may not know and as Mary Michele said to me as a firsthand witness present during the festivities, *"was that I knew that they were both enrolled in Alcoholics Anonymous, and all of them seemed to have emotional problems and yet none of them were in therapy."* It must have been emotionally draining as a guest to say the least, as one would be on tenterhooks the whole time.

Not long after they had all arrived at the family seat of Inveraray Castle in Scotland, Colin received a letter from the attorney who had handled his late mother's estate. The bottom line was that the kitty was empty. Other than the $12,000 annuity each brother received from their $225,000 stake in their maternal grandfather's trust. Lady C claims that Colin freaked out. He told her the estate owed him around $20,000, which is over $100,000 today, or £69,000. What had caused this was dear brother Ian she says. Apparently when he had become the 12th Duke of Argyll his mother had guaranteed a loan for him to buy a house in London, in Park Walk. But he'd never, ever, made any repayments as he had no real job or any real income. Upon his mother's death the bank demanded immediate payment of the outstanding loan, and the executors of her estate were obliged to satisfy the debt from in-hand funds, leaving nothing for Colin as Lady C explained it.

It was at this time that Colin was beside himself, as he also received a bill for an outstanding debt from some years earlier from The Priory, a private clinic in Roehampton, London, famous for drying people out from drug and alcohol addiction. They had now called the outstanding debt in and threatened to take legal action for any further delay in payment. He was panicked as the expected money to pay the bill wasn't forthcoming and if The Priory sued it would get out that he not only had financial problems, but true or false, they'd say he had a drink and drug problem too. The Priory, where a witness claimed Colin had been treated for his drink and drug problems before he met Georgie, were threatening to sue him for over £2,000 which was a debt way overdue, Lady C claimed; that's around £10,000 or $15,000 in today's money.

We'll read shortly of an independent witness to Colin being in The Priory just one or two years before the wedding and way before he met Lady C, which somewhat belies the perception that he never had a drink or drug problem before and only took to the bottle to cope with the astonishing divorce embarrassment and claims that he'd married a man.

Colin demanded his brother settle The Priory debt as he had caused the default on his mother's loan (by failing to ever make monthly payments on that loan) and that this had deprived him of his inheritance Lady C said, and that Ian refused to do so. The Duke also declined to sell his house in London to pay the debt owed to the trustees of his mother's estate to free up Colin's inheritance and as Colin had asked, as Lady C relates it. Colin rounded straight on Lady C again, pushing her to have her father settle his debts – and suggested money left over from the funds gifted to them at the wedding party in Jamaica and not fully used to furnish their New York apartment be handed over to him to help pay some of his outstanding debt.

But Colin had been heavily dipping into this wedding fund overage and behaving as the *big-up* Lord, buying things here and there Lady C says, trying hair treatments for his thinning head of hair, and buying rounds of drinks *on the house* wherever he went. These extravagances and others such as chauffeured limousines were all paid for with wedding gifted money Lady C said, so there was virtually nothing left to buy out some of his debt. There simply wasn't enough left to pay The Priory bill and she knew him well enough by now, and said to herself, *"that he'd wait like his father for what would be to me the least expected moment and clear out our joint bank accounts."* His father the 11th Duke during *his* honeymoon grabbed his first wife's inherited family diamond tiara and sold it to pay off his gambling debts, without asking his wife Lady C says she was told.

Colin's famous comment to her during another drinking marathon was, she claims, *"My father didn't work a day in his life. His wives supported him. That's what wives are for. That's what you are for, you stupid bitch."* – Nice guy!

She had known she was *"stepping down"* to a lesser lifestyle than she was used to, but she was in love, and it did not matter she said – but had she known him to have a habitual alcohol and drug problem as she claims and others attest, she was clear to me that she would not have married him and would have followed David Koch's wooing.

As neither Colin nor Lady C have ever said or claimed that a request for a dowry upon marriage in exchange for the title was made, it seems a reasonable assumption that it was never discussed before the marriage by anyone. However, it seems nevertheless to have been Colin's expectation, based on everything we've read. Money for Colin was not on Lady C's or her father's radar or thinking. As she said, *"My father thought him a penniless drunk with a drug problem and wasn't going to give him a penny."* You cannot feed such habits, it doesn't solve anything and you land up with the same problems you started with, but broke.

Georgie tried to lead as normal a life as possible during all this drama and stress. She would go out on the town in New York now that they were back in the Big Apple, spend an afternoon with friends or go to dinner parties with people like Mark Friend, Huntington Hartford, or with dear friends Barbara Taylor-Bradford or Lady Sarah Spencer-Churchill.

Not long afterward as Lady C recounts, Colin's brother Ian, the 12th Duke, came to New York and the brothers talked amicably. They visited their mother's estate attorney together and seemed happy and reconciled. She felt pleased, and Colin suddenly said to her that they'd found a way to pay off their joint debts without sacrifice to themselves (we're about to read how). Apparently Colin then turned to her when she said how pleased she was that the brothers had reconciled and said ominously: *"You've made a big mistake taking me on Georgie, and you'll pay for it."*

She felt a very dark cloud settle over everything, and looking back Lady C says it seems that this was most likely when the brothers hatched the idea of blatantly selling the story to the newspapers that Colin had no idea when he married that Lady C was raised as a man - triggering divorce. It was certainly a plan to make a killing from selling the story, pay off all their debts and file for divorce Lady C believes. What bright guys! – but 'gentlemen', I think not – not if it were true.

Just six weeks after marrying and back in London again, Lady C didn't have to wait too long before regular drunken and drug-fueled physical attacks started she said. One turned into a rage which broke her jaw, as she has claimed. Colin, she said, promised her that it would never happen again and begged her to stay. They continued on and off, and when she finally said she was going and would shortly file for divorce a whole 14 months after marriage and constantly trying to make it work, he begged her to stay just one more week, as he wanted a week to come to terms with her finally leaving. She felt him genuine and whilst she had made up her mind to leave him permanently this time, she saw staying that week as a compassionate thing to do. Then, on her last day of that week, as she prepared to leave, suddenly, collective headline news across all the newspapers said: - **Lord**

Colin Campbell sues for divorce – has thrown his wife out – he didn't know when he married that his wife was born a man!

Her horrid life suddenly became a vicious nightmare, but looking back, at least it was the beginning of the end and the start of a new life. As it turns out, as painful as that journey has been, it led to Lady C forging by her own hand, by her determination, sheer willpower and hard work, a new and exciting life. However, that was all decades in the future.

The £100,000 Lady C believes Colin and the Duke were paid by the *Sunday People* newspaper for the initial exclusive of their sensational story, would be around £314,000 or $455,000 in today's money. That would have paid off all of the stepbrother Duke and Colin's debts as Lady C understood them, and made a nice little profit for both Ian and Colin, wouldn't it?

Oh, my, God, what a dirty rotten scheme if so.

Embarrassment to the Argyll family?

Colin had said in the *Sun on Sunday* interview quoted earlier that: "*Things were not so liberal back then, and the scandal was deeply embarrassing for my family.*" Hang on a moment. In my research I have not been able to find any public knowledge or scandal *until* Colin and his brother the Duke sold the scandalous story to the newspapers, as Lady C had claimed. Therefore, surely it is *they* who created the scandal and embarrassment. It was not there before, nor did the public know of it until then.

The brothers created the shock and furor it seems. They sold the story for the newspapers to make scandalous headlines, Lady C claimed.

Colin has said himself that this story that he had married a man is what his brother Ian the 12th Duke told him, who he said claimed to have evidence. He implies that if it were not true, as he said in his 2015 interview he knew it wasn't, then it was not his fault but his late stepbrother's – dead men tell no tales.

We've heard Lady C say that she told him herself about her birth circumstances and mistakenly being raised as a boy before they married, and that he knew she was from a relatively wealthy Jamaican family. So he should have known and had no shock, and it appears that during the honeymoon itself he was plotting with his stepbrother to sell the story to English newspapers when she would not ask her father for an annual allowance, or later ask her father to settle his Priory debt. It seems that English newspapers were making just such inquiries of Jamaican newspapers during their honeymoon, so he certainly seems to have known from that time. So why not 'sell the story' then if he was so repulsed? Some have said that they believe that he had not given up hope of getting a dowry or annual allowance at this stage, as Lady C has claimed he was continuously after one or the other, and/or because they did not yet have the original birth certificate that she was first registered as a boy, which only came out a year later.

Let's also look at the fact, as Lady C says, that she knew his step-sister Jeanne and that Jeanne knew her story before Lady C met Colin through her. It would be quite a stretch of the imagination to believe that his step-sister didn't tell Lord Colin first about Lady C's birth circumstances, before they married, and she was there at the time with them both. Their mutual girlfriends all knew, and it seems logical that Jeanne would have told Colin how Lady C was born and raised, and that the family was well-to-do – were these by chance the reasons why Colin rushed into the marriage as he did not want to let the golden goose that ought to lay plenty of golden eggs get away, as Lady C perceived?

He might get a dowry and annuity with a happy marriage, failing which he could sell the story to newspapers through divorce and have money either way?

Lady C believes, in fairness to Colin, that he was just naively following in the wake of his father's example, at his brother's bidding – a four times married and three times divorced Duke who appears to have made money out of each wife. She said that, "*They seemed to have connived together from beginning to end to elicit money out of me or my family, one way or another.*" I'm not saying they did; I'm just looking at what others and Lady C have said and leave you, again, to make your own assumption.

Some I interviewed felt, rightly or wrongly, that the motive to marriage all along was money and a valuable by-product of ending it too. In selling the lie that she was born a man both brothers made money from it, it seems. From asking Lady C to sell off her jewelry and asking her repeatedly to seek a dowry or an annual allowance from her father as she claims on all counts – to beating her numerous times in drunken, drug-fueled rages because she wouldn't ask her father for money are, if true, shows that the marriage was all about the money from beginning to end. Who do you, believe?

Did Lord Colin have a drink and drug problem, which he denies:

Critical to the story is that Lady C claims in her autobiography that Colin was from day one always drunk or on drugs or both (and he had said himself that when they first met, "*I was pretty inebriated,*" which was just one incident of course – and in his 2015 *Sun* interview he says that he "*hit the bottle*" from the embarrassment of the newspaper articles on his "*marrying a man*"). However, he seemed unable to control his moods and rages according to her, resulting on numerous occasions with his ranting that she must get her father to give him money, as he had nothing to speak of.

Witnesses have said he always seemed drunk in Jamaica, and witnesses felt that he had a problem, and we had Lady C's father's comment that he felt Colin was a penniless drunken bum. People certainly didn't seem to have a high opinion of him.

A fresh and new independent witness says he did have a problem.

Baron Marc Burca, who was previously the Editor of a major London City magazine and who didn't know Lady C at the time, says that his brother Richard had been in hospital at the same time as Lord Colin Campbell in the early 70s when, as he said, *"They were both drying out in The Priory …. both were in for drug addiction problems, and Brian Jones of the Rolling Stones was there at the same time."*

The Priory is the famous private hospital in London that specializes in drying out people with drug and alcohol addiction. So here we have an independent witness to Colin's problems with drugs which was around a year or two before he met and married Lady C – which backs up her story – and yet Colin claims he didn't have a drink or drug problem.

Georgie said that her unwillingness to ask her father led three times to Colin beating her over that inglorious 14 months of marriage. The worst was when he broke her jaw and she had to be hospitalized she has claimed. Close friends who saw her right afterward at the hospital testified, and as she says her doctor did too, that it was not an accident or a case of having fallen down the stairs, as she first said upon arriving in hospital, wanting to keep it all under wraps. Colin she has claimed had indeed broken her jaw in yet another drunken drug induced rage.

She had left him on a couple of occasions temporarily before, to bring him to his senses, and then when he begged her to come back each time he promised to sober up, and she went back to him each time she said because in the end she still loved him and wanted everything to work out.

Her cousin Enrique stayed with Lady C in her West Eaton Place flat in Belgravia some time later, when she was going out with the actor Larry Lamb. She recounted to him her story of how Colin had beaten her and broken her jaw. Enrique knew Jeanne, Colin's sister, and Jeanne *knew* what happened he said, and he could not believe Jeanne had kept quiet, brother or no brother. Now 40 years later Colin makes statements as if nothing happened, which has surprised Enrique.

Cousin Enrique stayed with Georgie for a whole year throughout the divorce period. They'd meet for an hour each evening no matter what else was going on in their lives, with Enrique at the time opening a retail shop in Lowndes Square in London and Georgie typically going off to a Ball or Annabel's – *"She just carried on,"* he said to me. She was very traumatized by the revelations in the newspapers;

and she developed anorexia from the tremendous stress and strain that she was under. She couldn't eat properly – and yet at the same time, *"She lifted her head up, and carried on with steely determination"* – just as she had faced all the whispering when entering a party as a teenager in Jamaica.

When Colin said in his 2015 interview that it was an embarrassment to his family and the divorce newspaper headings drove him to take up the bottle, it seems from everybody else's lens that he merely carried on where he left off before Lady C's beating, and went 'back' to the bottle!

Such a scandalous story involving a British Ducal family was massive headline news back in the 70s. If it wasn't about money, then why did Colin and the Duke 'sell the story' to the newspapers as Lady C has claimed, and which they have never denied? Colin could have quietly filed for divorce. It would have all come out in the trial and become public news anyway - the same scandal and embarrassment for Lady C, but no money for the brothers - and how gentlemen surely would have behaved. The only logical conclusion many will make is that the story was sold deliberately to make money out of it, and that this was a motive for divorce.

Was she an aristocrat before she married? This is a frequently asked question.

Lady C did a lot of research into her family background with a documentary team that traveled with her in Lebanon some years ago. They looked into the Ottoman Empire occupied period, when leading Orthodox Christian families were sometimes granted courtesy titles of nobility as Counts of Russia. Her father she believed was descended from Lebanese awarded such a title, granted to try and influence internal politics and people from within Lebanon, to pave the way for a Russian invasion and take-over of Lebanon.

She said that they tracked a lot of circumstantial evidence and from what elders in the community remembered and stories told, her father's ancestor was indeed granted the title of nobility, that of Count. They had pro-actively dropped the title when Russia's influence slid away and the Turkish became dominant again she said, as to be seen to be linked to Russia would have been a death sentence under the Turks. The family slipped into lesser influence and wealth quite quickly and kept their heads down. Eventually, persecuted for being Christian by the Ottomans, they finally fled Lebanon as we've heard earlier, and landed up penniless in Jamaica - but they were alive.

Here, though, came a dead end in Lebanon for Lady C and the documentary team. The hunt for black and white evidence saw news that all Letters Patent from the Russian Court assigning Titles of Nobility in Lebanon were assumed destroyed during the Lebanese civil war of modern times. The town hall in her ancestral home where such records were believed to have been held were destroyed in that war. The documentary team that traveled with her to Lebanon to find physical evidence of stories passed down through her father's family came to an end. They were left with a lot of circumstantial evidence, but nothing hard in black and white.

One friend, Suzanne Chin stated that Lady C's mother Gloria was very pretentious and obsessed at one stage with saying that the Smedmores, her side of the family, were descended from French aristocracy and Charlemagne. But no one ever heard how that was and she would have produced evidence if she could – so it may have been a fantasy in her mind, as she suffered from constant drunkenness by this time. However, aristocracy takes another form, as we'll read shortly, and her mother did come from old European stock of, which they could be proud.

Was she a social climber? as some old Press reports insinuated

Lady C, it's been reported by some journalists, was a social climber who married upward for the title. However, she came from a wealthier family than Lord Colin Campbell it seems, and he was the younger son of a Peer with no property to inherit and a small annuity. Coming as she did from within Jamaica's version of 'aristocracy' (we'll review that claim shortly), and whose new husband expected a sizeable dowry from Lady C's father (but had not asked for one before the marriage), she wasn't exactly marrying upward and social climbing was she; as time would sadly prove, wasn't it more a case of falling down a slippery slope?

Did she marry for a title?

Having turned down the advances of an American billionaire to marry Lord Colin Campbell with a title and no money, one might be drawn to the conclusion that she married down. To marry for love a relatively penniless Lord or to stay in the game and hope to get married to a billionaire was the choice. She chose, tragically as it was, to marry for love, and knowing that she would not have the wealth she was accustomed to, but that they would have to work for it on their own. And yes, there would be the title, which was some small consolation.

What of Lady C's claims of coming from Jamaican aristocracy?

It's been said that she was not an aristocrat in her own right as she's claimed, and why is it that, when divorced for over forty years, she is still using her husband's title?

We ought to look at what that means, as in English terms she had no title before marriage, that's for sure. However, Debrett's advice confirms to me that she is entitled to retain her title after divorce, that of Lady; but more on that shortly. Just as importantly, anyone raised in privileged circumstances in Jamaica in the 1950s and 60s will know what that privilege brought, and acknowledge how fortunate they were.

I think the Oxford Dictionary's definition puts this matter to bed: *Aristocracy - noun - The highest classes in certain societies especially those holding hereditary titles or offices. Synonyms – include nobility and peerage, but they 'also' include Gentry, Upper class, Ruling elite, high society, Establishment, and Haut monde.*

So when she talks about coming from Jamaican 'aristocracy' – the term 'aristocracy' is okay to describe the wealthy gentry and upper classes of Jamaica. It is not due to a title by peerage as we think of it in Europe, but the term 'aristocracy', meaning as the Oxford Dictionary describes, from a top level of privilege and wealth in their country, and that the Ziadies eventually had in Jamaica.

Lady C, and all those raised in Jamaican that were by wealth and privilege at the upper echelons of society, can rightly be referred to as 'Jamaican aristocracy'. They were either major trading families who had built up sizeable wealth and empires, or, at the top of the tree, the major landed families in Jamaica who owned vast swathes of land and sugar plantations developed over centuries, such as the Beckfords, Kerr-Jarretts, the Harveys, Parnells, Clarkes, Campbells, McConnells, Sharps, etc., etc. all known as coming from the 'plantocracy'.

Privilege still meant in the 1940s and 50s, and to some degree in the 60s, that such a typical home of those from 'Jamaican aristocracy' came with anything from 6-12 servants depending on the size of the property. It was quite common for people to have a country estate and at least 6-12 house servants (plus estate workers) and a townhouse, with at least 4-6 servants there. Between numerous maids, cooks, nannies, gardeners, a driver, a butler for many, and even, in my wife's family case, a man who only cleaned her father's shotguns and cars, and collected the post. Their townhouse had 10 servants including three nannies at one time, as they had 5 small children – a good Catholic family!

The Jamaican aristocracy lived a life of privilege that most European aristocrats, such as titled British Peers, could no longer afford by the 1950s and 60s. Titled British families lived that way in the last century, but few had more than a handful of servants by the 1960s – two world wars had swept those days away in Britain. Many were already renting out their homes and castles for day-trip visitors, weddings and sporting events, to help pay for their estate's upkeep. Countless other grand houses were abandoned and left to ruin, and numerous estates and family piles were eventually split up and sold off. The British *Country Life* magazine was full of such sales. Georgie also has those links to her ancestors who were the Earls of Mayo as she has shared with us.

When Lady C married Lord Colin Campbell he was relatively penniless, he had asked her to sell her jewelry and push her father to give her an annual income and he had no servants. Even his elder brother the Duke had only a handful of staff by then. The difference is then that she came from a family within 'Jamaican aristocracy', of relative wealth with no title, and he had little to no wealth but a title of peerage – that may well be considered as Lady C had married down – and was not marrying up into the aristocracy. Her mother would have wanted her to have the title nevertheless, and indeed encouraged the marriage.

Lady C would be the first to say, as she did to me, that of course she valued having a title, but she would not have married a man who was not rich other than she was truly in love, and the title was not what drove her to accept his proposal. While she would have happily given up her title after her divorce, she said that her husband was putting it about at the time that 'they' were going to force her to give up the title, and *this* she says made her decide to keep it, as she was entitled to by law, and let him feel ashamed of his actions in how he divorced her every time someone called *her* Lady Colin Campbell.

She'd also be the first to say that in British and European society that title has done her no harm either!

Chapter 4

The divorce

GEORGIE SAID THAT SHE did not know at the time of Colin's constant calls to his brother, just before the newspaper stories hit the headlines in Britain, that they were planning a stunning betrayal of her to save the family's face – by selling a lie to the newspapers for money.

She realized after the fact and wished she'd realized beforehand, that if it came out first unchallenged that Colin, in one of his drunken, drug-fueled rages had broken her jaw as she would claim, and frequently beat her, it would clearly sully the Argyll family name in the divorce courts. Now because she left 'after' these scandalous newspaper headlines, which also crushed her spirit by the way, it looked to the public as if she was 'thrown' out rather than left, and fueled the belief that 'their' story must be true.

The story told on behalf of the 12th Duke of Argyll, that my *poor brother had no idea that he had married a man, who had transgender surgery to become a woman"* – this stunning claim and as it turned out lie, as Lord Colin understood in his 2015 interview, was front-page news. It was explosive and utterly destroyed Georgie's image in society. It left her reeling in shock, a shock that took a long time and therapy to come through. To have not only such private matters dragged across every newspaper for everyone to read, but that they were also told as lies was devastating!

She said that in defending herself against such lies cost her a small fortune in legal fees and nearly destroyed her financially despite her father supporting her case with funds early on. She stood up not just to the Argylls but to the wealthy tabloid newspapers as well. Her lawyer felt that she would win her case, but that the revenues from the *Sun*'s increased circulation would be far more money than their legal fees, which is why they brought the case Lady C claimed her lawyer said, as counsel believed that they could not win *but financially they could not lose.*

The Argylls needed to be a step ahead of the tabloids telling Lady C's story I suppose, so they sold their story to the media first as Lady C claims, before she filed for divorce and the can of worms was opened. This story brought the 'family' not just a face-saving solution, to what otherwise would have been a media furor over the Ducal family history of selling divorce stories to the media (more on that anon), and Lord Colin being a drug and alcohol crazed wife-beater, as Lady C would have claimed. They sold a sensational lie as she said, and it had to be a good money earner didn't it!?

Life after divorce.

The first year back in England was fraught with lawsuits which she enacted against the *Sunday People* and others who had repeated the lie of her being born a man, which eventually were all settled to her satisfaction, and the *Sunday People* apologized for what they had printed, Lady C said.

By October of that following year Colin arrived in London to collect paintings of his, which included ones she knew she says that he'd taken out of his step-sister Jeanne's house in Jamaica without her knowledge. But before Colin had arrived Lady C gave them back to Jeanne to ensure that she got them, which caused a row between them.

James Adeane was coming to take Lady C for dinner when Colin arrived at her flat and made a scene, asking James, *"Why do you want a bitch like her?"* When he was leaving Colin' asked Lady C if he could borrow the money for a cab home, and with contempt, she recalls, she said, *"No, you will have to walk home I'm afraid, I do not have a pound to lend you. Goodbye Colin, and good luck."* She is pleased never to have seen him since.

Returning to a normal life was far from easy, particularly since whenever she entered the room at any event or party, reminiscent of her teenage years in Jamaica, even strangers whispered to others as soon as she turned away. Knowing that most continued to view her with all the misconceptions peddled by the newspapers, and trying to retain her dignity must have been an appalling weight to carry on her shoulders.

A year had passed since the divorce but she still felt fragile, and was always reminded of the past with the ongoing libel lawsuits she had taken out, and they were all but draining her of her personal wealth. Lady C said to me, as she's often said to the Press over the years, *"I was caught in a dance macabre,"* and only divorce from Lord Colin Campbell could stop the vile music.

Lord Colin, of course, may feel the same. Even for a dance macabre, it takes two, at least: but the Argyll marital dance has a historical variation - with steps for two partners, four co-respondents and a judge.

Did you know that nasty divorces seem to run in the Argyll family?

We ought to consider the divorce history of the Argylls up to this time. Some may conclude that taking a dance partner who's a Campbell is a macabre risk!

Lord Colin's father (also an Ian, like his elder brother), Lord Ian Douglas Campbell, 11th Duke of Argyll, had divorced his first three wives, and the third wife the popular socialite and heiress to a millionaire father, Margaret (neé Whigham), Duchess of Argyll, was divorced spectacularly. Colin's father married four times in all, and it seems like the family didn't cope too well with being married, or did great financial planning, whichever way you read it.

It was on March 22nd, 1951, a few months before I was born, that Margaret Whigham became the third wife of Lord Ian Douglas Campbell, 11th Duke of Argyll, and Colin's father. She was considered a great beauty, and was the most celebrated debutante of her time. Her first marriage to the American Charles Sweeny, saw the famous singer songwriter Cole Porter include her in the lyrics of his hit song 'You're the Top': *'You're the nimble tread of the feet of Fred Astaire, you're Mussolini, you're Mrs. Sweeny, you're Camembert.'* The Duke had married a stunningly beautiful, charismatic and vivacious young woman - and an heiress. Colin's father divorced Margaret in a famous headline-grabbing scandal, which he sold to the newspapers at the time too, Lady C says. It seemed like that worked well for raising money for him, and it seems entirely believable as Lady C claims, that this is what the 12th Duke, Colin's elder stepbrother suggested to Colin when divorcing Lady C.

'Monkey see, monkey do,' as they say!

Colin's father divorced his third wife, Margaret, Duchess of Argyll, by selling outrageous photographs to the newspapers of his wife, Lady C says. Margaret was seen naked in bed with another man whose head could not be seen – it caused a sensation in the 60s and ruined Margaret in much of the smart set. Mind you Margaret was no genteel wallflower as we'll see, but it does not excuse a story for cash approach if that's true. It would all have come out in the media when he filed for divorce anyway, as we've said about Colin's divorce from Lady C, so the only motive to going to the newspapers before filing for divorce must have been to obtain money, if money he received. It suggests that Colin's father the Duke needed money too, or why would he have sold the story to the Press. Such action is not what I would have expected from a gentleman, let alone a Duke, the most senior peerage of the realm. And shame on him if he sold his story to the Press, but then again, he was only following an earlier Lord Colin Campbell, who set an example in the late 1800's of attempted public humiliation of his wife in the media – but more anon.

Margaret is such an interesting person in her own right, and *très méchant,* very naughty, so let me share with you just a little of who she was as she became a close friend and ally of Lady C. She was the sole heir to George Hay Whigham, her father, who was a Scottish millionaire (my research does not throw up how many millions, however, even if his personal fortune in 1951 was only £1 million that's equal in 2016 to £9.8 million or US$14 million roughly) and it's believed that he was worth many, many times that and may have been a billionaire in today's terms. He was chairman of the Celanese Corporation of Britain and North America and Margaret spent her key childhood years in New York. All in the right social circles spoke of her as being quite a beauty, and it's talked of that she had youthful romances with the playboy Prince Aly Khan and various heirs to family estates and fortunes like her own.

It was claimed in the Press at the time that Margaret at just age 15 had had sex with David Niven, the Hollywood star, when on vacation in England. To the fury of her father she became pregnant as a result, and Margaret was rushed into a London nursing home for a secret termination it was claimed. David Niven would later appear as a co-respondent in her divorce case but until his dying day he maintained that he was not the headless man in the photos supposedly sold to the newspapers by the 11th Duke of Argyll.

In 1930 she was presented at Court (presented to the Court of the King and Queen as part of a well born Ladies' 'coming out' into society, and being eligible for marriage thereafter), and was known as the debutante of the year. Shortly afterwards she announced her engagement to Charles Greville, 7th Earl of Warwick. However the wedding was called off after she fell in love with Charles Sweeny, an American amateur golfer from a wealthy Pennsylvania family.

A bit of a gal was our Margaret it seems – but it does not excuse the money grabbing sale of her infidelity to the media by a so-called gentleman and Duke, if he indeed did and make money out of it. Lady C remembers Margaret telling her some years later that, *"Colin once when in a drunken rage threatened to smash my face in, in London at her townhouse at 48 Upper Grosvenor Street the night of the Inveraray fire."*

Within a few years, the 3rd marriage of the 11th Duke and his Duchess, Margaret, was falling apart. The Duke suspected his wife of infidelity; and, while she was in New York, he employed a locksmith to break open her personal cupboard at their Mayfair pied-à-terre, 48 Upper Grosvenor Street in London. The evidence discovered resulted in the infamous 1963 divorce case in which the 11th Duke of Argyll accused his wife of infidelity (which to be fair was clearly true, and she was found guilty in the court of adultery).

Evidence included a set of Polaroid photographs of the Duchess nude in bed, save for her signature three-strand pearl necklace (the Lady had class). She was in the company of a naked man who was not her husband. There were also photos of the Duchess fellating the naked man whose face was not shown either. A government Minister was whispered to be the headless man, and whilst he vehemently denied it he resigned due to the furor, as he felt it had made his job untenable. David Niven, the British born and famous Hollywood Star, was another as we've said who absolutely denied it, and Douglas Fairbanks Junior, the famous American Hollywood movie star, was another named in court. He had had an affair with Margaret, but a very dear English friend of his, Mark Sykes said to me that Douglas had told him personally that he, *"not only flatly denied it at the time, he hotly denied it to me and denied it right up to his death."*

I share more about the late Duchess of Argyll not to distract from Lady C's story, but because it is an integral part of understanding the Argyll penchant for an almost ingrained habit and history of the family divorcing their wives in spectacular public fashion, and that it seems has bearing on Colin and his brother's actions in Lady C's divorce. Aristocrats divorcing over adultery may not be new but it was still uncommon, and what came out in the court was sensational. Claims of an insatiable woman, unusual sexual practices, blackmail, bribery, a diary listing conquests, encounters with unknown men in bathrooms, naked photographic mementos of these occasions and the so-called "headless man" or men, and rumors of the involvement of Royalty and a cabinet minister; a list of 88 possible co-respondents, pornographic postcards, and more. The huge list of co-respondents is a mirror approach it seems to his great-uncle's spectacular divorce in the late 1800s.

Ian's first wife was Janet Aitken, daughter of Lord Beaverbrook the newspaper tycoon; their daughter Jeanne was Colin's step-sister. The Duchess of Argyll told Lady C that Janet was only 18 when they married, and she claimed that on their honeymoon he took her to spectate at a French brothel. As she subsequently claimed, he spent the money she brought to the marriage, pawned her jewelry, and beat her – the latter a claim Lady C makes of Lord Colin Campbell, the son. The 11th Duke divorced Janet in less than ten years and secondly married Louise Hollingsworth Morris Vanneck, née Clews, another wealthy heiress. It's claimed that his first wife Janet Aitken once asked Louise, his second wife, after they divorced, *"Did he rob you?"* She apparently said, *"He took everything but my trust funds."*

By 1959, the 11th Duke and his Duchess Margaret (his 3rd wife) were living entirely separate lives; he had obtained an injunction barring her from Inveraray Castle Lady C recalled (renovated with £100,000 of her money Lady C says Margaret told her directly, that's about $3 million or £2 million in today's money in 2016) and divorce proceedings had begun. Well done Ian, he had at least renovated his castle at his wife's expense it seems from what we're told, before divorcing her and selling his story for more money, as Lady C claims. At least Lady C is renovating and fully restoring her own Castle Goring at her own expense, with money she has or is raising herself through hard work.

It seems that upon his third divorce, the 11th Duke may have got an unexpected punch in the face so to speak. His London club, one of the oldest and most respected gentlemen's clubs, White's, blackballed him. Founded in 1693, White's is the oldest and also widely considered one of the most exclusive gentleman's clubs in London, based in St. James's. Current members include a friend of mine, Prince Charles, Prince William, and the 13th Duke of Argyll, Colin's nephew.

The 11th Duke married for a fourth time in 1963 and died in 1973. His daughter Lady Jeanne Campbell (Colin's stepsister) married Norman Mailer the American novelist, journalist, essayist, playwright, filmmaker, actor and political activist. He wrote 12 novels and married six times! Poor Jeanne seems to have married a man just like her father, who married one woman after discarding another and so on. There's a pattern of Argyll marriages really not doing too well here, isn't there?

Lady C shared one or two short stories of her dear friend Margaret, Duchess of Argyll, with me. One lovely one being that they were watching the famous UK TV series *Upstairs Downstairs* together in 1976. It was a favorite TV period soap drama series in England at the time, about life above stairs and below stairs in an aristocratic home in Edwardian England – a sort of early version of Downton Abbey. Margaret and Lady C sat in Margaret's library at her home, 48, Upper Grosvenor Street in London, opposite the American Embassy. She leant across as they were eating and said to Lady C, grabbing her arm, "*Sweetie there is something I've meant to tell you for ages!*"

"*What?*" Lady C asked.

"*On the last three occasions I've seen you, you've had a different hair style. Now, take the Queen and me, we've only ever had three hair styles; as a child, young woman, and older Lady – it confuses the public darling to keep changing, you must only have one hairstyle.*"

Lady C said that Margaret cared about her public image very much, and that she dressed in the morning, and if she were going out in the day, formally, she'd change beforehand, and she'd change again for dinner. She kept a personal Ladies Maid right up until she was placed into care. She always wore the same pearls, "*always*" Lady C recalled. I recall a number of friends of my wife's mother in Jamaica who followed the same regime, and if guests were at dinner at home they'd put on their long white gloves which came up to the elbows. This was right up to the 1980s at least. In the grandest Jamaican homes the butler and maids serving dinner were still wearing white gloves during service then.

If you do not wish to read any profane or vulgar words, or are underage, please turn away now and jump to the next chapter.

Lady C remembered another humorous anecdote of Margaret's when Lady C had taken her to see the movie *Goodfellas*, which turned out to be the last movie she ever saw, at the Cinema in St. Martins. The movie was about the Mafia, and had constant bad words with fuck this and fuck that as almost every other word. Margaret turned to Lady C and asked, *"Why do they keep on using such a word and no other vocabulary?"* When someone in front of them turned around and asked Margaret to, *"Shut up – can't you stop fucking talking?"* She turned to Lady C and whispered, *"It's not only a problem on the screen darling, it's in the theater too!"*

Lady C claimed, as told to her by Margaret, that Margaret's father didn't give money to restore Inveraray Castle when asked to by her new husband Ian when they married, but gave the money as a loan, obliging Ian to mortgage other property as collateral – but Ian, Lady C says, fraudulently put up properties he did not own as collateral, and it was taken on trust in those days that they were his by the lending institutions as he was a Duke. So when Margaret's father called in the loans at their divorce, confident that he was right to have followed this strategy in the first place, there was nothing to pay him – so her father lost all of the money, some £250,000 in the 1950s (today worth around £2.5 million). Clever Duke it seems, but again, not something if the story is correct you'd expect a Duke or a gentleman to do.

Some in high society did not want anything to do with Margaret after her divorce, yet she was still one of the great socialite figures of the age. She gained notoriety, but didn't fully lose her position, as many in society stayed loyal to her. Times were changing and society's view of her ex-husband seemed very low, as was that of his club who'd blackballed him, which probably accounted for many not dropping Margaret.

Lady C and Margaret, Duchess of Argyll, had in common their both being divorced by the same family (father and son), and both husbands tried to destroy them for their money it's claimed. Lady C claims that Jeanne, Lord Colin's step-sister, said to her: *"Just as well Colin is not a member of White's, as when Pa sold his story on Margaret – White's cancelled his membership."*

Lady C was stunned when she discovered they had sold her story to the Press. She landed up in therapy when she realized that it was not a mistake, it was a deliberate attempt to destroy her, not just spite her – and she felt that they relished it. Margaret never came to terms with her horrific public divorce; she was in her 60s when Lady C first met her and as therapy wasn't really done in her day she had no help getting through the trauma. Margaret died aged 81, still traumatized by the whole experience.

The 11th Duke's great uncle Lord Colin Campbell divorced, then Ian the 11th Duke divorced his first three wives, and then his son Lord Colin Ivar Campbell divorced Georgie, and Colin's step-sister married a man who married six times – goodness, what a family - they sure liked divorce, didn't they? ?

When the 11th Duke died in 1973 his son, Ian, the older brother of Colin, became the 12th Duke of Argyll, before Lady C met and married Lord Colin in 1974. The 12th Duke's son Torquil is the current and 13th Duke of Argyll. I communicated with the current Duke to understand what the family felt firsthand about the divorce of Lord Colin and Lady C. He said that as children at the time, their father never talked about the divorce, it was never discussed. He said that his uncle did not like his ex-wife continuing to use his title, and said that all he's likely to say on the matter if you speak to him is what he's already said in his interview to *The Sun* newspaper (in late 2015); and he clearly did not wish to put me in touch, which I can understand, and he wished me well with my book. I sought to speak to Lord Colin Campbell himself, but was unable to get through to him in his business in Florida, and knowing from his nephew, I am sure, that I wanted to speak to him, he could easily have called me had he wished to share more of his side of the story.

The current Duke is making a going concern of Inveraray Castle it seems, and it is open to the public most of the year. Paying events such as castle and garden tours, a tearoom, stretches of let fishing and a number of vacation rental cottages are staple revenue makers. The estate also offers shooting for snipe, wildfowling and goose, as well as deerstalking in the estate's 50,000 acres. More revenues come from the holding of an annual Highland Games event and a 'Best of the West' festival. All help pay for the castle's up-keep and earn a living for the family obviously, and good for him. This young man and his Duchess seem to have really turned around the family's fortunes. Lord Torquil came across as a very decent man to me, aged 49. He took the time to communicate with me rather than ignore the conversation, his words were given openly, and he made fair and reasonable comments in the circumstances I thought. He is very much in favour with HM The Queen and appeared with her in a carriage ride, opening one of the days at Royal Ascot races in June 2016.

Hopefully, the divorce cycle of his forbears is broken with the current Duke of Argyll, and I wish him, his family and descendants well, as he appears to represent his ancient name with dignity and honor.

Another earlier and spectacular Argyll divorce. Surely not?

Yes, there is a third, which I have alluded to earlier, which is in fact a second *earlier* precedent for how Argylls previously shamed their wives in public with divorces before Lady C.

An earlier Lord Colin Campbell in the late 1800s sued his wife *after* she sued him first (divorce was almost unheard of during Queen Victoria's days in the British aristocracy). In Queen Victoria's reign this was just not done. After an acrimonious trial, the couple went their separate ways – albeit that a divorce was not granted to either, and they remained married leading separate lives until the late Lord's death, indebted, embittered, and an embarrassment to his family say reports at the time.

This Lord Colin Campbell made public accusations of his wife's infidelity which ruined her in society, in an attempt to deflect a divorce case brought by his wife over her claims of his sexual diseases, which he brought to the marriage without telling her. Her claims, filed first, were that she did not know when she married that her husband had a venereal disease, and that he knowingly married her and infected her in that state – just as 'our' Lord Colin Campbell sought to deflect the likely media field day of his wife's story being heard first, as it might be perceived by some.

This Lord Colin Campbell had been born in 1853, the fifth son of George Douglas Campbell, 8th Duke of Argyll and Lady Elizabeth Georgiana Sutherland-Leveson-Gower. His future wife had been born Gertrude Elizabeth Blood in 1857, the daughter of an old family of County Clare in South West Ireland. She grew up to be a tall, stunningly good looking beauty, acknowledged by her peers at the time. They met during a social visit to Scotland in 1880 that Lord Colin had made. He was the brother-in-law of HRH Princess Louise, Queen Victoria's fourth daughter, who had married the then Duke of Argyll, which turned out a childless marriage as did his own. This is how the family became related to the British Royal Family.

The marriage was twice postponed by Lord Colin because of his ill-health, and when he proposed a pre-nuptial agreement until his doctor felt that he was well enough to consummate the marriage, her father made inquiries as to his condition, whose results suggested that Lord Colin had syphilis. Whilst the Duke did not want him to marry as he considered Colin's future wife below his station, her father did not want her to marry either, due to perceived syphilis in her future husband. However, her mother it was suggested at the time, saw the family's elevation in society and pushed for the marriage to go ahead.

The wedding took place in July 1881. It was later discovered that Lord Colin did indeed have a venereal disease and had infected Gertrude at some time in the first couple of years of marriage. Whilst it is assumed that he had syphilis, there is no conclusive proof as to the nature of the disease that I can evidence, but we can assume by her divorce proceedings that it was so. She filed for divorce in 1884 – although from my research, it seems to have taken two years to come to court.

Later in the same year Lord Colin filed a counter-divorce claim, accusing his wife of multiple extra-marital affairs. Lord Colin accused his wife of adultery, citing four names: George Spencer-Churchill, the son of the Duke of Marlborough, and three others. The only witness to her supposed infidelity with one man, was the Lord's own butler. Hardly an independent witness in those times I would have thought! The judge could not have thought this sound either, as he refused the divorce of both claimants, and I can only assume he refused the Lady's case trying to save the Lord's embarrassment at being found guilty of having a sexual disease. Lady Campbell was ostracized and shut out of polite society, and suffered greatly in those Victorian times.

Once divorced, Gertrude, Lady Colin Campbell, turned her attention to, and subsequently became, an accomplished writer. An interesting coincidence that the current Lady Colin Campbell is a successful writer too, Lady C having made the New York Times Bestsellers list three times, and Margaret, Duchess of Argyll, turned her hand to writing also. It's a strange coincidence that three considered each in their time and youth, great beauties, Gertrude, Margaret, and Lady C - all went through nasty divorces with stories leaked and or sold to newspapers as Lady C has said – all causing huge shock waves in society in their day, and all became writers.

Oscar Wilde said that, *"To lose one parent may be regarded as a misfortune; to lose both looks like carelessness."* We might say that to lose one wife to scandal is unfortunate, but to lose three to such public divorce scandals is careless, if not shameful.

Lady C's additional thoughts on her divorce:

She's often said in the media and to me that she felt *"set-up by my stinking, rotten, drunken brother-in-law."*

In the case of Gertrude, Lady Colin Campbell, in the 1800s the divorce was based on supposed adultery, with Lord Colin's own and certainly not independent witness, his butler being the only evidence he raised. In the case of Margaret, Duchess of Argyll, it focused on the mystery of the headless man. The present Georgia, Lady Colin Campbell, believes that it is no coincidence that her Lord Colin Campbell followed his father and great-great uncle's examples when divorcing her in equally spectacular fashion.

Margaret told me, she said, that, *"Big Ian, the 11th Duke, used Gertrude's divorce as a precedent. It was a complete rerun - down to the number of respondents."*

She has said a number of times that all three scandals sit like a heavy lunch with her. *"Gertrude was destroyed. Margaret never got over the trauma. Never. I've tried to put mine behind me, but it's still hard after all these years."*

Gertrude died just age 53 in 1911 and bequeathed her portrait to the National Portrait Gallery. She died with little wealth and Margaret died almost penniless in a nursing home – both great heiresses whose fortunes transferred to their husbands who divorced them after spending their dowries it appears from what we've been told. Lady C on the other hand seems to have been catapulted into creating her own success to fight back after divorce against how she was treated, and today, thanks to her multiple New York Times bestseller books and other works is doing very nicely thank you. She has a to-die-for house in central London and Castle Goring, an almost completely restored 18th century castle in West Sussex to her name.

So who told the truth about our Lord Colin and Lady C's divorce?

We've now heard about their marriage and fatally flawed life together, and read of the Argyll habit of spectacularly divorcing their wives, at least five, and you'll read shortly about the Argyll history of betrayal and murder going back in history, and we're even going to hear of Colin's sexual abuse claims (as Lady C relays them), and claims of an attempted murder on a family schoolboy by the 12th Duke when he was a young boy himself, directly from the man who said so.

For Lady C and Lord Colin there were completely opposing claims, with Lord Colin saying he had no idea about Lady C's condition of birth or upbringing as a boy before marriage and that this is what drove him to seek divorce and hit the bottle; suggesting he didn't have a drink or drug problem beforehand.

On the other side we have Lady C saying that Lord Colin had a drug and alcohol problem, and we also heard from an independent witness at the time who knew Colin was in the Priory Clinic in London a year or two before he even met Lady C, being treated for drug and or alcohol problems as that independent witness claims, so we know he had a problem before he even met her if that's so.

We've also heard of Colin's sexual hang-ups, which Lady C claims is because, as she said he told her himself during their honeymoon, it was none other his elder step-brother Ian, when Marquess of Lorne (the future 12th Duke of Argyll), who had sexually abused him as a child, forcibly holding him down.

We've also read that when no money was forthcoming, he started to beat her in drunken and drug-fueled rages and, in one of many fits of rage, broke her jaw, requiring hospitalization. Also she says that she had told him about the circumstances of her birth and upbringing, and how his step-sister Jeanne was fully aware, who surely then would have told him.

We've read from Lady C's statements of how from before the marriage he sought to have her sell her jewelry to raise money, saying he only had a $12,000 a year income from a trust. On numerous occasions, he pushed her, as did brother

Ian, by then the 12th Duke, to get her father to give her an annual allowance or give Colin a dowry.

Which side of the divorce story is true?

Based on everything that you have read so far, you decide who you think was telling the truth as to the reason for the divorce - Lord Colin Campbell or Lady C?

Why is it Lady 'Colin' Campbell and why a title of Lady, after divorce?

The short answer to both questions is that she is entitled to use both, but let me explain.

Debrett's, the quintessential arbiter of all things British etiquette, Peerage and titles, confirmed to me when I asked the generic question on correct style in marriage and divorce, that the younger son of a Duke (i.e. Colin) has no peerage title, only the courtesy title of Lord. His wife when he marries becomes a Lady, if she is not born with a title already, and she uses her husband's *'forename'* and *'surname';* so for example it would be Lady Colin Campbell. This is custom and tradition, and Lady C was quite correct when married being styled this way. It would have lacked etiquette and respect for her titled husband to use her own forename. In a traditional or archaic sense, she belonged to him.

Debrett's answer in a divorce is that if divorced the wife of the younger son of a Duke or Marquess would normally then attach her forename to her style of address, whilst retaining her title by marriage and her husband's family name. The Lady would be obliged to call herself, for example, Georgia, Lady Colin Campbell, if her husband remarried, so as to distinguish herself from the Lord's new wife when he married, who'd also be known as Lady Colin Campbell.

They said that if the ex-husband has not remarried, this leaves it open for interpretation as to the divorced wife using her forename or not changing anything. What many such divorced Ladies have done in more modern times, if their ex-husband has not remarried, is to retain the full name that they have used all through their marriage, including their husband's forename.

In Lady C's case she became Lady Colin Campbell upon marriage, and upon divorce would have become, Georgia, Lady Campbell, if Colin Campbell remarried. As Lord Colin Campbell has not remarried, so the *status quo* is open to interpretation as Debrett's have said, and by default it's okay for Lady C to continue to be known as Lady Colin Campbell until such time as her ex-husband may remarry. Until then it's a non-issue, and Lady Colin Campbell it is!

If Lady C were to remarry one day, she'd take her new husband's title unless he had none, in which case she'd become plain Mrs. John Smith for example.

For better or worse, for richer or poorer, in sickness and health… is something Lord Colin Campbell should have thought more about when he rushed to marry Lady C in a matter of a few days, and now not whine about her retaining his name and title I think. What's the old saying, 'buyer beware.' It may partly be the ultimate payback of a woman scorned, admittedly, but she's entitled to use her title and his family name, and I am sure she will continue to do so. The title of Lady doesn't hurt socially either, as Lady C has recognized herself, nor for celebrity.

So now we know that throughout the story of marriage and violence as Lady C has claimed, and through the divorce and after it, none defended Lady C more stalwartly than Colin's stepmother, the late Margaret, Duchess of Argyll, and we'll hear more of this special relationship later.

Chapter 5
A history of murder and betrayal

A sensational attempted murder claim.

A NEW AND SHOCKING CLAIM has been unearthed by the author during his research; that Lord Colin Campbell's late elder brother Ian, the 12th Duke of Argyll, when he was a boy and the then Marquess of Lorne, tried to drown a family pal aged just fourteen. The parents of Mark Sykes, a gentleman I interviewed for this book, were very close friends of the 11th Duke of Argyll (the 12th Duke and Colin's father) and his then wife. Mark was at the time attending Eton, but was on vacation as they often were, the Sykes & Argyll families, at a Cornish seaside house they'd take annually.

Ian and Mark were swimming in the sea together with nobody else around and no-one was in eyeshot at the time. Mark told me that Ian, vigorously and with determination, held him under water. Whenever Mark came up for air, he was held under again by Ian with greater and more forceful determination.

"He had a look of absolute determination on his face and pushed me under every time I struggled to get air, it was no game," he said.

I asked if this was surely not just a schoolboy prank, and maybe it simply just got a bit out of hand, and he emphatically said, *"Absolutely not, this was a determined effort to drown me. I knew it then and know it now."*

He was only saved he felt because his father came along by chance, wondering what the boys were up to, and rescued him – everybody then assumed it was a school boy bit of fun too and didn't believe Mark when he explained what happened. Mark said that much later Ian apologized to him and had said that he'd, *"Always gotten rages every now and again as a child,"* but Mark said that he did not believe him, then or now, and felt betrayed by someone he thought was a family friend.

Mark said to me, *"You can put that in your book, as it is the absolute truth. Ian tried to drown me, deliberately."*

Lord Colin was not present on that holiday Mark said, and in fact Mark's never met Lord Colin Campbell. He only met Lady C some 25 years ago in the early

1990s, way after her marriage and divorce to Colin, *"as we began to move in the same circles in the 90s."* I suppose her divorce from one brother and his attempted drowning as a youth by the other, gave them a shared antipathy towards the Campbells – and they became and remain great friends!

Let me sidetrack briefly, as Mark's ancestor is worthy of it – and for a moment talk about the Sykes-Picot line, as it has a bearing on all the troubles in the Middle East today which in part reflect on Lady C's heritage from Lebanon. Mark Sykes' grandfather was Sir Mark Sykes, 6th Baronet, who's famous from the First World War era for the borderlines that created new states in the Middle East. Drawing with the Frenchman Picot on a map the boundaries of those new nations, known by the name the Sykes-Picot line. Strictly-speaking there was no Sykes-Picot line. It was in fact an agreement made in 1916 between Britain and France with the collusion of Russia, which would divide up the Ottoman Empire between them after it collapsed. Some remnants went to different Arab tribes, and left Palestine under international control due to the holy places, with parts claimed by Jews and parts by Arabs. Oil and access to the Mediterranean in the region may have been a keen motive of the super-powers of the day too, to divide up chunks of the region between their influences.

The agreement fell apart firstly when Italy joined the war and had her claims recognised, and when Russia fell out of the war in 1917 with the collapse of the Tsarist Empire that part was erased. The new communist Russian rulers confided the plan to the Arabs, and so the original plan fell into ruins, and was eventually replaced by the San Remo Conference in 1924.

This Agreement is considered to have shaped the Middle East as we know it today, redefining parts of the old Ottoman Empire and new country borders, and originally created a Palestine meant for Jews and Arabs to protect the holy sites for both.

In 1920 Palestine was ruled as "Mandatory Palestine" and British soldiers were stationed there. It collapsed with the Zionist uprising and the creation of the State of Israel, and a separate Palestinian state did not make it.

The history of Campbell treachery goes back 324 years!

I was mindful to look into this after talking at the end of 2015 to a retired British Royal Naval Polaris Submarine Officer and a very amiable old Scottish friend now living in California with his lovely wife Eileen, Robin Lamont.

I mentioned that I was busy researching a biography I was writing on Lady Colin Campbell. I was momentarily taken aback as he nearly came down the phone at me in an anguished but slightly humorous way, saying, *"Don't mention that treacherous name to a Lamont. Some of us were murdered by the treachery of the*

Campbells in the Massacre at Dunoon (on the Clyde) the first week of June 1646 and I think worse was the massacre of MacDonalds by Campbells at Glencoe in 1692 but there were some Lamont mercenaries helping the Campbells" – these were tough times when clearly loyalty could be bought, and massacres were all too frequent, but Glencoe was particularly shocking and none seem to have forgotten.

Well, that set me off researching this for myself. Over 300 years later it caused distress, even if slightly light-hearted. I recalled such a massacre from school history, but not the detail. Clearly those in Scotland have not forgotten! There's even been a pub in Scotland near Glencoe I discovered with a sign saying: *Campbells not served here!*

The parties responsible for the massacre of some of the MacDonald clan and their vassals were the Earl of Argyll and the regiment of foot of the Clan Campbell, led by Robert Campbell of Glen Lyon – acting for the King's man in London, Lord Dalrymple.

The English King at this time, William of Orange had ascended the throne of James II of England & VII of Scotland (Catholic), when the Protestant English Parliament invited him to marry the English Princess Mary, eldest daughter of King James II. Mary was raised a Protestant. William of Orange's advisors felt that the some of the Highland clans had become out of control and it was "necessary" to deal them a blow. So William's man Lord Dalrymple was tasked with making the Highland Chiefs swear an oath of loyalty to Protestant King William and abandon the exiled Catholic King James.

A deadline for taking of the oath was set for New Year's Day, 1692. Having no real choice, all the Highland Clan Chiefs made their way to Inveraray, the seat of the Argylls and Clan Campbell, and swore their oath, at least to be seen to be loyal if nothing else. However, chieftain McLain of Clan MacDonald either got it famously wrong or sought to sidestep the oath a little longer, his real reason is lost in time. He went to Fort William to take his oath late all the same, (as he claimed he was told to go by Dalrymple, and he felt later that Dalrymple had a personal grudge against him and deliberately misdirected him, making him late - and there is truly no reason to doubt his claim), but upon arrival at Fort William, he was told that the proper place to take his oath was Inveraray. Lord Dalrymple refused his oath when he finally arrived in Inveraray, which then came well past the set deadline. He stated that it was not given in the allotted time – and in Dalrymple's eyes he had to be made an example of.

History suggests that he now personally put in place a plan to massacre MacDonalds with the connivance and support of the Campbells. The place where it eventually went down was in the valley Glencoe, where a small community of McClains and other branches of the clan MacDonald lived. On February 2ⁿᵈ,

1692, in the midst of a harsh Scottish winter, the small group of the MacDonalds and their vassals (McClains), simply referred to as MacDonalds, were visited by a group of Campbells and their Highland tributaries. As with any Highland village of the time, even one's enemies were received with the offer of shelter and food. The Campbells and their Highland tributaries stayed for nearly two weeks it's believed, accepting their hosts' shelter and food. It was by all accounts a particularly harsh winter. These forces were under the command of Robert Campbell of Glen Lyon and Breadalbane of Argyll, who it was believed, had been coerced directly by Lord Dalrymple, and thus the King. Amongst his forces was Duncan who headed the Breadalbane and Argyll branches of the Campbell clans.

All appeared hospitable, but on the early morning of February 13th Campbell's force, without warning, took the sleeping MacDonalds by surprise and a wholesale slaughter took place of men, women and children. The Campbell's orders from King William's man in Scotland, John Dalrymple, "Master of the Stair", were quite clear he believed and he met his master's expectations.

That was in 1692. In 1978 the Clan Campbell Chief, our very own Ian Campbell, the 12th Duke and elder brother of Lord Colin Campbell, (and the man who as a child, Mark Sykes says, tried deliberately to drown him), attempted to explain the massacre when he said, *"We did what we were supposed to do…we were just obeying orders…it was strictly a military operation"* – which seems an inexcusable comment to make, albeit over 324 years later. Today some play the whole thing down, but such comments as these from the late Duke did no good to the name of Campbells 38 years ago, as their forefathers' actions did no good to their name at the time of the massacre. To be fair to the Campbells, massacres were not uncommon or infrequent by one clan or another in this period of history, but this massacre stood out even in its time as horrific. There's still a hatred held by some of the name Campbell in Glencoe in modern times, but for most who make belittling comments, they may well simply be said more as a humorous tourist story. The Clachaig Inn or pub in Glencoe until very recently at least, had a sign on its door that said: *No Hawkers or Campbells.* Another Glencoe pub used to have a sign that read: *No cats, dogs or Campbells.* Maybe it's still there.

In her autobiography *A Life Worth Living* Lady C referred to a funny anecdote when she said that in 1974, when political correctness was certainly an unknown entity, she and Lord Colin were faced with a full and busy restaurant when visiting the Glencoe area and having to wait for a table. So Colin dropped his name and title to the waitress, assuming it would get them a table quicker. The waitress promptly refused to serve them saying: *"I don't soil my hands feeding Campbells."*

For some the massacre still rankles today and antipathy remains.

The Massacre of Monzievaird

Looking into historical records and researching further I found an even earlier massacre in the Scottish Highlands in which the Campbells had a hand. I'm very conscious of the fact that in the 12th - 18th centuries and earlier, clan disputes were commonplace and this resulted in feuding and murder; but here's another massacre, which was notorious and sensational in its day too, like the later Glencoe massacre of 1692.

In 1490 a feud between the Murray and Drummond clans of the Highlands started, it seems from reviewing multiple historical sources, after a Murray lost the stewardship of Strathearn held by him for decades, along with the revenues from the lands that went with it. The Drummonds had evicted the Murrays and when the local Abbey ran short of funds, the Murray-aligned Abbot taxed Drummond lands in Monzievaird and sent his clan friends to raise the funds for him, and they did not do it too gently – which was to result in a bloody response soon afterwards.

The Drummonds launched an attack on the Murrays in a vicious battle. Many were killed and some of the Murray clan escaped and fled towards Ochtertyre. As the Drummonds made their way back to Drummond Castle, tasting success of battle, they came upon Duncan Campbell and his men. The father of Duncan's wife, and his own two sons had been murdered by the Murrays, in an earlier clan altercation. Campbell persuaded Lord Drummond to go after the Murrays, marching with him and their joint armies towards Ochtertyre to deal them a crushing blow.

Historic tales tell of over a hundred Murray survivors hiding in the local church in Ochtertyre at the coming of the Campbells and Drummonds, men, women and children (some accounts differ the numbers from 100 – 200). Remember in these medieval times a church's ground was a Holy Sanctuary, and anyone could claim sanctuary, and Holy Law forbade anyone entering, harming or seeking to remove those granted protection.

Someone from within the church gave the game away by firing an arrow at a member of the threatening troops who'd got too inquisitive of the church, and it killed him. Legend has it that the Campbells and Drummonds then barred the doors and windows, locking the hundred plus people inside, piled dry timber and hay around the outside of the church and set it alight. All the while a single bagpiper played. All but one man was thought to have died in this horrific massacre. A cousin of the man in the attacking force helped him escape, when the Murray managed to climb out of a high window. For helping a Murray escape, he was apparently put into exile forever from his own clan and was lucky to escape with his own life.

Chapter 6
Life after marriage - and in the Jungle

THERE WERE NEW JOBS, new loves, new careers and then there was *I'm a Celebrity... Get Me Out of Here!* the 2015 reality TV show.

Life after marriage

In 1976, with her divorce behind her, Lady C took a summer vacation job at the famous department store Harrods, in London's fashionable Knightsbridge. It gave a small but steady income to pay the daily bills. She worked with pride in the cosmetics department from May until September. Her social life picked up to be as busy as in the past, going to the Opera, friends' dinner parties and nightclubs like Annabel's or Tramps. She said that she felt that she was going everywhere, but that her life was going nowhere; and then it suddenly all changed.

James Buchanan-Jardine

She met James Buchanan-Jardine, the man who was to be the next great love of her life, in Annabel's when her friend Anka introduced her. James was very taken by her. After a lot of doubts about getting involved with someone again so soon and wanting to give herself a bit of breathing space, and Anka confirming that he was separated from and in the process of divorcing his wife, the Earl of Carlisle's daughter, Lady C eventually said, *"Okay, he can meet me next month at the Rainbow Ball."*

This is when Lady C first got to really know James, a member of the Jardine-Matheson family, whose great Hong Kong trading company was founded in 1832 in Canton, China and established in Hong Kong in 1842. A company and some of their executives that with my own fourteen years in Hong Kong I knew well. They helped build Hong Kong from a fishing village to a vibrant trading colony. The firm is now run by the Keswick branch of the family, who are descendants of co-founder William Jardine's older sister Jean Johnstone, through the marriage of her daughter to Thomas Keswick. Today Jardine Matheson are maybe best known for their business arms such as Hong Kong Land, Jardine Strategic, Jardine Insurance and the luxury Mandarin Oriental Hotel Group.

James and Lady C did meet at the Rainbow Ball, and she wondered if she would even like him, but within moments, as their eyes connected, she knew that he was her dream come true. It was December 1976, he was 30 and Lady C was 27, and they were both single and available. She found him very handsome and rugged, masculine and muscular; just as she liked them. She said that they both felt the instant chemistry. She discovered as the evening went on that his father had owned a magnificent home in Jamaica where they all went as children and which they had sold when Jamaican independence approached, so they had a love of Jamaica in common too.

Her cousin Enrique, who by the way she says was her rock, stood beside her in London throughout the divorce and year of newspaper nightmares, was with her and joined them as James took her to Annabel's. She tried being a little cool to the whole thing as she wasn't sure if she wanted to rush into another affair after having not long ago left such an unhappy marriage. Their first proper date after this Ball, where James brought along some old friends of his, the More-Nisbets, was at the then popular Sloane restaurant *Pooh Corner;* and afterwards they again went to Annabel's.

Lady C went to Jamaica to be with the family for Christmas, and James went to Hong Kong, and when they were both back in the UK, James drove down to London to see her from a family country home. Coincidentally, an aunt of my wife lived next to a key Keswick family property in Wiltshire. They finally consummated their attraction to each other and she said that he proved to be a very accomplished lover. She found that he had all the qualities she sought in a man and she talked about how she was born and raised right up front. He understood all about her background and didn't care a damn she said; he loved her just as she was and was secure in his masculinity, and her story did not trouble him one bit. What a relief for Lady C, after all that she had been through.

When I interviewed him, her cousin Enrique said of this time that, *"Georgie's eyes sparkled likes diamonds when she was with him."*

Lady C was absolutely and totally in love and said that she and James would often make love four or five times a night, that he had a huge amount of vigor and that she'd have to spend all day sleeping to recover!

The Jamaican government at this time decided to tighten currency controls, and her father could no longer send out money for her allowance. Within a short period, and like many other families, her family's key assets were nationalized too. Faced with funding three separate libel actions and no funds coming in from her father anymore, she settled out of court. As her QC had said, *"They stand to make more money from newspaper sales than paying you libel compensation and your court costs."* Lady C said the *Daily Express* paid most of her costs, and all newspapers agreed not to reprint the libelous claims again. Maybe not a total victory, but the media was stopped from ever repeating such lies again, so I suspect that a massive weight was lifted from Lady C's shoulders.

James's divorce was nearing, which he handled in a gentlemanly and considerate way to lessen the pain for all, Lady C said, and her libel actions had been brought to a satisfactory end. He started talking marriage – her life truly was turning around. James started making plans to move back to the family firm's chief seat of empire, Hong Kong, and told Lady C that she would love it there. She said that she might well have taken up the offer of marriage, which she thought he was leading up to, and Hong Kong, other than one incident that suddenly changed everything.

One evening he said to her that he had to pop out to see a cousin for supper and arrived back at her place at 11 pm. When they went to bed, she noticed that he'd come back smelling of fresh soap and his hair was freshly combed. If he'd been to an innocent late night dinner with a cousin he'd not have had a shower before he came 'home', and she knew instantly that he was seeing somebody else. She asked herself the question: What if she went to Hong Kong, married and he started to have other affairs? Could she live with it?

James was excellent and everything she could wish for in all other respects Lady C said, but she made the decision not to move to Hong Kong, and she stayed in London when he left amicably a few months later and they drifted apart. She said that whilst she was contemplating what to do before they parted, a friend of his asked if a friend of theirs could stay with him in Hong Kong for just a few days. Irma (Irmgarde Margarethe Boorman) stayed some months and quickly launched a romance with James, Lady C says. Irma and James, after marrying and having two children, began leading separate lives and Georgie and James became an established couple on the social scene. There was talk that they would marry if Irma managed to marry someone else, but that eventuality never transpired, though for years Irma and Georgie attended parties at each other's houses.

Now aged 27 Lady C was okay with the possibility, albeit against the norm of well-born girls in those days, of facing a single life if need be.

A new job!

Some time later Lady C was speaking to a friend who was a diplomat with the American Embassy in London, who said that if Lady C had one thing in bucket loads it was class, and she carried a title too. He suggested that she should write to all the Arab Ambassadors in London, saying that she was available for a suitable post, as most were seeking better PR in Europe in those days and by doing so she might just land a job. The first to reply was the Libyan Ambassador, who was seeking a Social Secretary.

With the Libyan–Egyptian War that summer, in July 1977 President Boumédiène of Algeria and the Palestinian Liberation Leader, Yasser Arafat, brokered peace within a few days of the war breaking out. The Libyans likely saw Lady Colin Campbell as a well-connected addition to helping win some friends in the West. Relations were already strained with the US, who had withdrawn their Ambassador from Libya in 1972 after Gaddafi had nationalized the oil industry, and the London Libyan Embassy functioned as a link for America at the time. It wasn't until two years later that the U.S. Embassy staff were withdrawn from Tripoli after a mob attacked and set fire to the embassy in December 1979 and the U.S. Government designated Libya a "state sponsor of terrorism".

The Ambassador offered her the job, and Lady C took a new flat in West Eaton Terrace in Belgravia. She moved in opposite Andrew Lloyd Webber and his first wife, Sarah Brightman, did up the flat and furnished it with antiques.

Lady C started her job and got on so well that shortly she was playing the role of personal as well as social secretary to the Ambassador. She also learned a lot about the hypocrisy of politics, with newspaper headlines one day saying that the Libyans were not friendly people, and the next day British company Chairmen and government-sponsored arms and munitions people making appointments and doing business with Libya. British government Ministers, people from the foreign office and members of the Royal household were always quietly dropping by – whilst the official line was one of growing distaste for Libya. Britain and America were quietly trading with Libya it seems. Business is business and where there's profit to be made, especially in arms running. It seems we'd sell anything to anybody, sadly. Libya had lots of money and was awarding contracts for this and that, and everybody wanted a slice. Lady C was frequently offered bribes for access to the Ambassador and as often she was offered bribes to keep competitor companies from seeing him – she turned them all down. However, she was quick to work out that the wealth and genuine care of Libyans towards others less fortunate could prove valuable both to their image and to western charities needing philanthropic help. She suggested the idea to her Ambassador that if Libya gave money to charities in Britain it would help their image, and Gaddafi's office said yes. She began slipping news to social gossip columns and the Press that a Libyan Ambassador's Dinner was going to be announced to kick off such philanthropic work, and that it would be sumptuous and the grandest and most lavish diplomatic dinner ever. Suddenly Lady C was inundated with calls.

Organizing this event took up three months of her life. The embassy, having had no precedent for such an event, left Lady C checking the *Who's Who* book for everybody's correct titles, decorations, and order of precedence. 2,000 invitations were dispatched, finally aiming for 1,200 guests maximum. Young socialites were accepting in droves, as were politicians of the time such as Reginald Maudling and Roy Mason (both government Cabinet Ministers) and the likes of Sir James Goldsmith and Lady Annabel Birley (Annabel's nightclub in Berkley Square is named after her). Lady C booked both tiers of the Great Ballroom at the Grosvenor House Hotel on Park Lane for the event. Although they had opted for a cap of 1,200 guests they squeezed in 1,231 in the end, to avoid diplomatic upsets. Peter Snow, the journalist and TV presenter, said to her, *"I didn't know there were so many limousines in the whole of London. This is 'the' diplomatic ball of the decade. How does it feel to have such clout?"*

By December 1997 President Sadat of Egypt reached a peace accord with Israel which pitted Gaddafi against every Western nation - and he could not accept that peace. Libya and the West entered a nasty phase. The Ambassador told Lady C that he regretted that Tripoli had said that it was not in their best interests to be seen to have a British aristocrat in the heart of a key Arab Embassy, and he asked her to resign, whilst asking her to understand and thanking her for her services, and he committed to continuing to support the charities for whom she would ask philanthropic help.

I wish there were lots of juicy Libyan and Western under-the-counter stories and leaks to tell you, but all diplomatic business at the embassy was carried out in Arabic, and all meetings with Western diplomats and companies was conducted in private, with meeting summaries going to Libya via Libyan Arab secretarial translation, so Lady C has no juicy stories to share from her time working there – she simply relished her personal and social secretarial role.

A job with Lloyd's of London underwriters

By February of the next year, 1978, Lady C landed a new job with four Lloyd's underwriters who had advertised for someone to help run their office. As the hours were from 10 am – 4 pm it greatly suited her lifestyle, as she was out most nights of the week and rarely in bed before 2 am. She'd have time to join various charity ball committees too, which she loved doing. She helped her new employers in other ways as well, such as getting their 'Names' on the list for the Royal Enclosure at Ascot, and she lent her title and maybe also her notoriety to impress their clients at lunches.

In 1986 she was doing occasional freelance work for *You* magazine and the *Sunday Express* magazine, in addition to her work at Lloyd's. She was able to use her contacts and connections to pull in people for articles, such as getting the magazine into a gala held for Prince Alfred of Liechtenstein with the President of Austria in attendance; or pull in people like Prince Charles through his old confidante Lady Tyron; or attract the Duchess of Norfolk for features on anything from racing to a charity ball. Her contacts had blossomed with her work at the Libyan Embassy and they were now proving highly valuable, as were the social circle of friends she'd had beforehand.

Her journalistic career took another turn later on when Baron Marc Burca, who'd been a friend for some years and remains a great friend of hers to this day, asked her to become Social Columnist for *Boardroom Magazine*. This was a magazine that could be found in the office of every MD or Chairman of every major British company.

It was to be a purely social column and was a great opportunity, which she took to with enthusiasm. She said that she had never lacked invitations to major social events or friends' parties, Ascot, and the opera etc. but suddenly they inundated her from every PR firm of worth, socialites and charities. She hopes that she wrote a column that was witty and seldom bitchy, and never gossiped. She said that she only accepted invites to attend three types of function: ones organized by her friends, actual or prospective worthy causes, and glamorous events such as The Cartier Queen's Cup for polo at Windsor.

When I spoke to Baron Burca, he explained how his previous Social Editor had been Una-Mary Parker, who was also Social Editor of the *Tatler*. When she retired, he hired Georgie to take over. He said, *"She wrote a great column, with a slightly acerbic tone at times."* He went on to say that occasionally she wrote rather controversial pieces, landing the magazine in hot water and they would have to write an apology. *"But she always wrote amusingly, and knew everybody, which is probably why she never got on with Nigel Dempster."*

Nigel Dempster was a celebrity gossip columnist who had early on taken sides with the Campbells during the time of Georgie's divorce and he'd been a guest at Inveraray Castle during the divorce itself, so seemed well entrenched in their camp. He seems to have never missed an opportunity to take a swipe at her until the day he died; always, always reminding the public in every article he ever wrote about her how she had been raised as a boy - as if it were new news.

Finding love again

Lady C's affairs picked up again as she slowly emerged from the trauma of a violent marriage and the media glare that almost destroyed her self-confidence, and a deep, deep love affair that was not meant to be.

Oliver, Lord Henley, who had succeeded to his father's title, went on to be a Minister in Margaret Thatcher's government and then John Major's. Lady C and Oliver went out often, innocently, and he attended some of her 'At Home' dinners. Six foot tall and very handsome, she liked him. They moved in a set that included Roddy Llewellyn (then Princess Margaret's boyfriend) and Ned Ryan. One evening after dinner Oliver and she ended up in bed together. She said that he was a beautiful, tender lover. He was a barrister and single, and popped a proposal of marriage. She said how very flattered she was, but knew that he wasn't really in love with her and was a romantic, nor was she in love with him. She made light of the matter so as not to offend him, because she wanted their friendship to continue and truly liked his company and friendship. At the same time, she knew that in making such a decision their in-bed intimacy had to end so as not to muddy the waters. *"And we remained friends,"* she said.

Larry Lamb the English actor well known for his parts in the ever-popular TV soap series *EastEnders* and later '*Gavin & Stacey*', was also one of Lady C's lovers. They are pictured during a relationship when she was in her thirties and picking up the threads of her life again. Rough and smooth. Opposites attract some might say. They met at the opening of The Ritz Hotel's casino in London through Edward Duke, the actor best known for his one-man show '*Jeeves*'. Larry arrived with him. Few may know that Larry had starred with Dame Maggie Smith in Canadian repertory, then in the English theater with Joan Plowright, Sir Lawrence Olivier's wife. He was an accomplished stage actor.

Larry was Lady C's type, tall, well-built and ruggedly handsome. They hit it off straight away, but she was off to Jamaica for a vacation. He said he'd take her to the airport and on the evening of her return to London they planned to meet with others for dinner at La Poule au Pot, a fashionable restaurant in London's Belgravia. Her cousin Enrique arranged to collect Larry from his flat and take him to the restaurant and they'd all meet there. Enrique got on with Larry straight away he said to me, and felt he'd be good for Lady C.

It quickly became a full on romance for several months, and she thought him one of the best lovers in bed she had ever had – and as we've heard, she's been pretty enamored with a few good ones already. They got on so well, and he made her laugh. Something I've found with all of her friends, they all talk of valuing her ability to have both in fits of laughter constantly. I have found from my multiple face to face or phone conversations with her that this is absolutely true; she is constantly laughing and teasing, and it's hard to feel down in her company.

Lady C's brother Mickey was as enthusiastic about her match with Larry as cousin Enrique, and all of her girlfriends found him so good-looking. They came from different ends of the social spectrum, which did not stop either of them enjoying everything about the other. Larry had been married twice before, which didn't worry her, and she had told him all about her birth, upbringing and marriage. But it slowly became apparent, she thought, that he wanted to marry again. She didn't see their relationship going *that far* and told him honestly how she felt. She said that he was every inch a gentleman, and remained a friend. She was jubilant for him when he went on to marry his next girlfriend and settle down.

By the following Easter Lady C was again off to Jamaica. She almost tripped over a man's luggage on the flight to Miami from London, and he landed up sitting next to her, a young actor who, upon their both returning to London some weeks later, telephoned her. She was happy; as he was her type to have an affair with, but she knew that it was not going to go further, and his alcohol issues at that time were a warning sign too. She'd learned the hard way to listen to the warning bells in life! They had a very loving affair, and she said that he was very accomplished in bed and that she felt they had a unique bond. His sister had been born with the same medical condition as Lady C. Luckily for his sister, she had been raised a girl. This chap and Lady C fought like cat and dog she said, but nevertheless remained good friends. They remained lovers for two years – but she coyly hasn't named this lover!!

She left Lloyd's in 1981 and went to work for her brother Mickey, who no longer worked as a barrister in Chambers in London, but as a solicitor in the then poor West Indian community of London's Brixton. He wanted his talent to be of use to those that couldn't otherwise afford the best legal representation and to do so amongst his own Jamaican people.

It was 1982 when the love of her past reappeared in her life.

James Buchanan-Jardine returned to live in London after five plus years in Hong Kong. He rang Lady C and invited her to dinner, and she was looking forward to meeting his German wife. But James was on his own when he and Lady C met again after all those years and he explained she said, that his wife was in the South of France with their children, whom he adored. He remained very loyal to his wife and said nothing negative about her. However, reading between the lines, Lady C realized that the marriage had seen better days. James eventually said that they led separate lives now, but he'd never leave her for the children's sake.

Lady C said that she felt that they were both taken aback by how much each still meant to the other. They had a lovely dinner and he said he'd call her the next day and that he had something to tell her. He came through the door of her apartment the next evening, swept her in his arms and told her he still loved her, and she said she still loved him.

For the next eight years they became a couple, very much acknowledging that he would never leave his wife and hurt his children. Lady C accepted the new relationship as it was, and was just happy to have him back in her life. She felt complete. He had a London home very close to hers, and she and James would meet regularly in the mornings to go jogging together. She felt that, had he been free, she would now undoubtedly have married him, but she wanted him to remain married and put his children first, and was happy to live with the arrangement as it was. She had an attentive lover and an excellent companion, and she knew that he needed to continue to be a warm, caring father with his wife - she 'assumed' - accepting their relationship.

However, in an interview for a Sunday newspaper Irma Buchanan-Jardine said of Lady C while *I'm a Celebrity… Get Me Out of Here!* was being screened that, *"She tried to destroy us by driving our family apart. She would not give up despite the heartache she caused for so many years."*

Lady C has denied such claims and we've heard that she had a long affair with James Buchanan-Jardine when he was single, and that he indicated that he wanted to marry her and asked her to move to Hong Kong with him. If James walked back into her life years later, took her to bed and carried on an affair with her for eight years when married, it seems that James would not have continued the relationship if he did not want Lady C in his life. Clearly she was not chasing him, but enjoying being with him – he could have walked away at any time, and chose to stay all those years.

Three years into their new, intensely happy relationship, James gave Lady C a Springer Spaniel puppy. Not something you would do if you were trying to get rid of a woman who you didn't want in your life is it? She was the nine-week-old puppy of James's family Springer Spaniel, Sooty. Lady C named her Tum-Tum after her nickname for James' tummy which she loved resting her head on. Was he so happily married at the time?

I do not condone or belittle what anybody did; I am just repeating the stories as they have been related to me. Lady C seems, if nothing else, and from everyone I have met and spoken to, always ruthlessly to say it as it is, whether you like it or not. She has a reputation for complete honesty. I therefore personally believe her side of her story, if there is a side. Anyway, now it's all in the past, and Lady C says that she understands that James and Irma finally got their marriage back on a good track and she is happy for them.

An aside to this story is my having met during interviews with Lady C down at Castle Goring in December 2015 Tum Tum's two descendants – they were both adorable and exceptionally well-trained, calm and well-behaved dogs. I wish my three Schnauzers were as well behaved – they are a gang that rules the roost! Sadly, as I was preparing this manuscript, one of her adored dogs, Charles (affectionately referred to by Lady C as King Charles), just died, simply of old age. I spoke and wrote to Lady C to tell her how sad I was to hear the news, as

I know, for her too, her dogs are darling family members, and naturally she has been devastated to lose him. I'm glad I had the opportunity to meet him.

A social whirl

Writing a Social Column for *Boardroom* magazine and catching the latest social events meant that the majority of Lady C's social engagements were not purely private. Her engagements were often hosted by members of the Royal Family such as Prince Michael of Kent at a luncheon in his home, or by others in theirs, or cocktail parties with the likes of Margaret Thatcher. One minute she was at Ascot with Heddy Simpson, widow of the founder of Simpsons on the Strand, and the next she was attending the Vienna Ball with chums. She attended many charity balls, which she often helped organize, with the likes of Prince Edward as a guest of honor for the one she held for the St. John's Ambulance fund. In October 2000, as Chairwoman, she helped organize a musical evening under the patronage of the Secretary of State for Scotland, to raise funds for the Adoption Forum and the Scottish Adoption Association, charities close to her heart. At the time, she lived in Bourne Street, in London's exclusive Belgravia.

If it wasn't one thing, it was another. One moment Lady C would be at the Maypole Ball with the Duchess of York as guest of honor, the next at Ivana Trump's engagement party with Riccardo Mazzuchelli. She would pitch up at the Royal Enclosure for The Guards Polo Cup in the presence of The Queen and Prince Philip, or could be found with Greek shipping heir Manoli Mavroleon at one of Andy and Patti Wong's extravagant parties – a very wealthy socialite Hong Kong Chinese couple living between there and London. One of the highlights of her life as a good Catholic girl was being received by His Holiness Pope John-Paul II in a rare private audience at the Vatican, which are usually reserved for heads of government and Royal families.

Lady C came into the orbit of Roddy Llewellyn who was the Queen's sister HRH Princess Margaret's boyfriend at the time, who'd been introduced to her by her best friend Colin Tennant (later Lord Glenconner) when Roddy ran a landscape gardening company with John Rendall and Don Factor.

Lady C had become friends with John after meeting him and Roddy at a glamorous Black & White themed party at The Dorchester Hotel on London's Park Lane. The party's hosts were a dashing Swiss financier, Christopher Dreyfus, and his exotic black American wife, Jewel. *"Hence their humorous Black and White theme,"* John said. People were so less paranoid about political correctness in those days, and Roddy and John were two single chaps around town and had only been asked to balance numbers. Being already married, their friend Don didn't make the 'cut'!

At Tatler magazine Peter Townsend ran the 'list' for Debutante parties for what was then known as 'the Season'. If you were on Peter's list you received wonderfully glamorous invitations from people you didn't know, but who wanted their daughters to meet eligible young men. The invitation concept was the same; ask fun-loving and eligible people!

Georgie was seated at the same table as John, and they had, he said a very jolly evening, with lots of laughter. Following that first meeting Lady C and John subsequently met at other parties, gallery openings, dinner parties and sporting events such as Polo and Royal Ascot, where Georgie had a prime car park place near his own. Frequently their guests overlapped and people strolled from one picnic to another.

John had a great love of animals and had been the owner of the famous lion called Christian who was reintroduced into the wild by George Adamson. He and Georgie shared an interest in their love and appreciation of dogs. When John's daughter Tallulah was about seven years old, Georgie offered her a Springer Spaniel puppy which she had bred. Georgie was then living in the Cundy Street flats owned by the Grosvenor Estate and Tallulah and John were invited around to choose a puppy. The puppy they chose was the best dog he ever owned he said. They called her Bella. When Lady C wrote a book about Bella's mother Tum Tum (*With Love from Pet Heaven by Tum Tum the Springer Spaniel*), the gift she had received from James Buchanan-Jardine, John was delighted to write an endorsement for the book.

Their paths again crossed when John became the Social Editor of *Hello Magazine* in 1998. Georgie was often at the events which he and their photographer covered for the magazine. John told me how delighted he was when he heard that she had adopted her two sons Misha and Dima from Russia, but how he saw less of her then because she had moved to France. This is the period where Lady C had purchased and was renovating her Chateau and had placed the boys into full time education in France. Once when they were back in London visiting and John rang her one of the boys answered the phone and told him: *"Mummy has gone to McDonald's."*

When Georgie returned his call the following day he asked, *"What on earth were you doing at McDonald's?"* She let out a frightful shriek apparently and said that she had been at the terribly glamorous society hotel, Claridges. I suspect that one of the boys got a severe reprimand for that! John said that he was very aware that Georgie has been a wonderful mother to her boys, and that they have beautiful manners and admirably support their mother in all her projects.

As an example of her friendship towards others, John said how he always admired the fact that Georgie was such a loyal friend to Margaret, Duchess of

Argyll. When the Duchess had lost all her money and was ailing in a hospice in Battersea, Georgie was one of her few regular visitors, whereas other erstwhile and so-called 'friends' abandoned the once glamorous Margaret.

I'M A CELEBRITY... Get Me Out Of Here!

The popular TV show's own surveys identified that about half the viewing audience of the 2015 series loved her, and half did not. Well, that's over 5.5 million viewers who don't even know her who loved her feisty performance and touchingly frank, take-no-nonsense approach, even if at times she swore like a trooper.

Of the other 5.5 million, well, maybe if they get to know her through this book they'll change their mind about her. The moment she left the show, just a few days before its end, the viewing audience dropped from 11 million to 6 million. It had started at 5 million and shot up to double that after her first days of feisty comments and one-liner put downs. Some journalists described it as *"The Lady C Show"* and said she was the only reason half the audience were dialing in. That's entertainment, and probably why ITV hired her in April 2016 to do her own reality show in September, *Lady C and the Castle*. Lady C pulls in the audience and ups the ratings!

There's no question, manipulated editing if it was so, as she and others claim, left Lady C *"looking like a real bitch"* as a couple of people said to me about her *I'm A Celebrity... Get Me Out Of Here!* performance. They also asked themselves if her response was the normal her, or was it how many of us would have reacted when pushed to the very limit and under such harrowing conditions? If we could have seen what led up to her outbursts and what created the on-the-edge persona that we saw, I'm asking myself if we would see why? Was being dragged back to the hated bullying days of school just too much to take, as the show's psychiatrist told Lady C, and as she related to me afterwards?

Her cousin Enrique said, *"Nothing sweet ever seemed to have been said by anybody on the show. It was horrendous – and to be vilified in front of the entire nation and all your friends – frightening – and to carry on as she did is stoic."*

For all the hype and bad press for Lady C surrounding the reality show, I note that there was equally good support from many newspapers and on-line media. I myself have witnessed men, women and young people, especially teenage girls, instantly crowding around her at her local Tesco supermarket in Worthing, West Sussex, or at a gas station in Kennington in central London. The *"Love you Lady C"* comments, the *"You told 'em Lady C, you stood up for women being bullied"* remarks, were virtually all expressed in a similar way, while asking for a 'selfie' photograph, comments in my experience offered with universal praise not derision! It was a huge eye opener for me. She gave her time willingly to everyone who asked for a 'selfie' or an autograph, with a ready smile and good humor, staying and chatting with all and showing a genuine interest in each. Even making sure that their 'selfie' came out well, before thanking them for saying hello – not quite the bitch her performance at times in the Jungle implied in some camp mates' eyes and words!

Presenters of the show Ant & Dec thought the 2015 series was: *"One of the best yet – thanks to characters like Lady Colin Campbell."* Speaking ahead of the final, Dec said: *"It's been one of the best series ever I think."* Ant added of Lady C: *"She was up there with the best. She just kept giving day after day. Just brilliant."*

When I interviewed Lady C about how hard it was staying in the Jungle, she said that physically it was like being in the bush in Jamaica. The same plants, trees, fruits, foods, creepy crawlies (except snakes and scorpions) etc., so the physical was not a shock as it was rather like being back home in Jamaica – the temperature and humidity were similar.

Being quoted as saying that she was the star attraction of the show and the best they've ever had – that's called program revenue I think. Which is *why* the producers did not want her to leave the show when she decided to walk out just before the end. Alison Boshoff for the *Daily Mail* newspaper reported: *"Let nobody say they couldn't see this one coming. After an explosive 19 days filled with more insults and spats than even the most fevered producers could have dreamed of, Lady Colin Campbell has left the Australian jungle setting of ITV's I'm A Celebrity... Get Me Out of Here!"*

After bullying of her unraveled, from day one she developed instant attack ability, as agile as a hungry lioness on the Masai Mara plains of Kenya. The show's physical and psychological environment pitched teams and people against each other and unleashed the lioness inside her, delivering at times horrifyingly brutal verbal attacks.

There's no question that as claimed by her later, and witnessed by Kieron Dyer (the England football star and fellow contestant, who watched the play backs after coming out of the Jungle when he got home to England from Australia), selective over-manipulation and editing by the TV show's producers often left her looking like the sole antagonist. If we could have been a bug on a tree and seen everything that led up to her outbursts, maybe we would view her slightly differently.

Her friend Rona, Lady Delves-Broughton, said of her performance: *"I thought she was so brave, it was very hard and testing wasn't it?"* I thought that was a very good, short, and beautifully simple summary of Lady C's performance. Rona's granddaughter, who's just fourteen, watched Lady C in the Jungle and was riveted, along with lots of her pals at boarding school, and would love to meet her; she thought Lady C was brilliant.

In this chapter of the book it's hard to understand Lady C's quotes if they are not printed in full. There are in this section of the book some vulgar or profane words within quotes made by people, to accurately portray exactly what they said and meant. To understand the exact nature of an obscenity, vulgarity or other offensive expression it's essential to the reader's understanding of the context they spoke in. The practice of hinting at the word with asterisks or blanks between the first and last letter, however well meant, is weak and dismissive of reality in the context of what somebody else actually said. People are not stupid and it's how the majority speak 'sometimes', when riled and angry.

Justice John Marshall Harlan — a conservative American judge in the 70s — uttered a phrase that has become First Amendment lore: "One man's vulgarity is another's lyric."

If you do not wish to read any profane or vulgar words, or are underage, please turn away now and jump on to chapter 7.

Everybody talked about Lady C's feistiness, temper and bad language. Well the latter is part of who she is when pushed over the top I'm afraid, and as she once reminded me, Princes Diana's most frequently used words in her presence when talking of others and really upset were *'fuck' and 'cunt'*! Born a lady into an aristocratic family and elevated by marriage to a princess. Oh dear, who would have thought of such words from the Queen of Hearts – but maybe it makes Diana more real to us, that when really upset she used bad language too.

The feistiness and temper we know from Lady C from the reality TV show was something she never had as a child growing up she said to me. It started to develop during her school days of bullying, but it grew, she acknowledges herself, during and after her marriage; she could see it happening from then, and through the suffering at the hands of the Press slating her throughout her divorce case I imagine. Her cousin Enrique told me that, *"Her feistiness and temper only emerged from the time of her marriage and divorce."*

For all the hype and some bad press for Lady C surrounding the reality show, I note again that everyday women who bumped into her in the street, in gas stations and supermarkets or the local pub when I was in her company, saw her as an example for women everywhere of how to stand up for themselves.

As former British World-Middleweight Boxing Champion Chris Eubank, a fellow contestant, said: *"Imagine the loss of revenue when 5 million viewers, half the viewing audience nearly, dropped out after she left the Jungle and they stopped dialing into paid calls to delegate tasks, vote people tasks or vote them out."*

Lady C's great aunt Maud at the
Smedmore family home in Kingston

Lady C's grandpa Lucius Smedmore
on the family tennis court

Georgie's well-connected
parents, Michael Ziadie
and Gloria, nee Smedmore

Lord Colin Campbell in 1897

Lady Colin Campbell in the fabled
Boldini portrait of 1897

11th Duke of Argyll and his third wife Margaret. *Inset:* The stunning young beauty
Margaret Whigham, heiress and future 11th Duchess of Argyll

David Koch around the time he
was courting Lady C

Lord Colin Campbell and Lady C

Lady C's late brother Mickey, who was an eminent barrister then solicitor in
both London and Jamaica

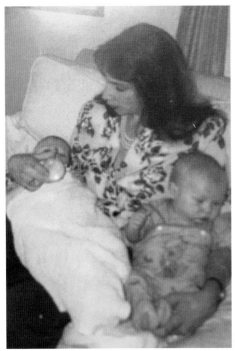

The babies adopted from Russia in 1993
Misha (Michael) and Dima (Dimitri)

At the Château d'Algayrié in France and
the freedom of their own bikes as teenagers

The boys growing up - Misha and Dima with Mummy

Dima photo-bombing Misha!

Lady C out and about with Dima

Lady C's men - Gusband Peter Coleman and eligible bachelor sons Misha and Dima

Lady C's cousin Enrique Ziadie presenting the Gucci Cup at the Royal Windsor Horse Show

Lady C with her two sisters, Fibby (L) and Puss (R), in Grand Cayman

Lady C at her London home

Lady C sparkling with her gusband
Peter Coleman

Lord Colin Campbell 40 years on

Lady C modeling in New York in 1968   Lady C modeling in London in the 1970s

Lady C with Vivienne Westwood the fashion designer

One or two of her friends told me that they were not surprised at anything, but were a bit surprised at how fierce and vicious she was sometimes in reacting to people, but they felt that she was very entertaining. The real Georgie is the best part – someone who's extremely kind-hearted they said. And as others have said of her to me, if your need is genuine, she will do anything for you – but if she suspects you have taken her for a ride or attack her, she will bury you!

She could be shamelessly rude in others' eyes and often pounced upon her unsuspecting victim with fangs out, roaring with language that would shame a sailor!

Lady C was nothing if not controversial throughout her time in the jungle. She shifted from being momentarily stunned at nasty remarks to leaping into attack, from hilarious and memorable one-line put downs to being protective and caring of others when they were attacked. A lioness unleashed, able to attack with stealth one moment and protect and care for her cubs the next.

***

It may be interesting to many if I take a moment to look at her horoscope star sign (The Sun), and her Chinese horoscope animal sign and traits (The Moon).

Not surprisingly this lioness was born a Leo, who tend to be warm, action-oriented and driven by the desire to be loved and admired. The Leo have an air of Royalty about them. They love to be in the limelight, which is why many of them make a career in the performing arts.

The Ganesha astrology guide says that Leos, much like their name, are strong, fierce, bold, courageous and regal in their lifestyles, ways and expression. Amazingly creative in almost all spheres of their lives, Leo individuals are independent and dominant. Known to be the most authoritative amongst all the Signs of Zodiac, Leos or Lions are often brave-hearts, and their confidence ambition and positive thinking are exemplary and unparalleled.

The word 'doubt' or, for that matter, 'self-doubt', is not a part of a Leo's dictionary. Most Leo-born natives are outspoken and brazen – lions are loving, amorous, chivalrous and a joy to behold until you cross their path.

The Chinese Horoscope from the Lau's Handbook describes the Ox (one of the 12 Chinese animal cycles), which is Lady C's Chinese horoscope sign (driven by her birth date and month in that Ox cycle), as symbolizing the attainment of prosperity through fortitude and hard work. They stick to routine and conventions, and whilst generally fair minded, it's difficult to persuade them to change their view as they are stubborn and often have strong prejudice.

They are graceful socially and considerate of others' feelings, and are admired for their integrity and ethics. They will operate within a fixed social system and be quite good showmen. Given the chance and motivation they will embrace new and progressive views. They can climb to great heights and amass great wealth and prominence.

If you merge the Leo and Ox traits together you land up with a warm-hearted yet slightly impersonal character with a dignified appearance. The Leo can also be dramatic and even pompous at times, as the Leo sign does take up a lot of room.

The Ox's sternness and uncompromising outlook will only serve to reinforce this sign's indomitable will. A respected and commanding personality, the Leo Ox will have the ability to lead effortlessly.

***

Among Lady C's burgeoning fan club during the reality TV show was *Downton Abbey*'s creator, Julian Fellowes, who was quoted by the *Daily Mail*'s Sebastian Shakespeare as saying: *"She is such a character. She comes from a small Jamaican family with some pedigree, which I know. Audiences like someone like her, who isn't like anyone else. I back that."*

Her friend and fellow controversial celebrity best-selling author Wendy Leigh said of Lady C's performance in the Jungle that, *"What she thinks is what you get, there's no filter."* Wendy, who wrote biographies of David Bowie, President John F. Kennedy, Patrick Swayze and Arnold Schwarzenegger, sadly died in May 2016.

You have to admire some of Lady C's one-liner instant responses; they are as sharp as a razor blade. I'm sure that many of us wished we had the ability to have a ready quip to throw back at someone putting us down, rather than think of one later when it's too late as we often do? A bit too colorful in her language for some, yes, but she is who she is. As the *Mirror* newspaper said of her time in the jungle, *"She's proving to be a real TV goldmine."*

Here are some of the famous Lady C one-liners from the *I'm A Celebrity... Get Me Out of Here!* TV reality show, which those in the UK watched and heard, and I'll weave them into the events or bush-tucker trials within which they appeared. That puts those comments into context.

Let's look at the first bush-tucker trial of the show which Lady C did, hilarious for the magical show-stopping one-liners that Lady C came out with. These first trials were where contestants had to eat horrid things or live creepy crawlies in order to win points that would see the whole camp getting a good meal that evening - but only if the pair of trial contestants ate everything foul or creepy that was put in front of them!

Lady C and Jorgie Porter, the highly popular British TV soap star of Hollyoaks, sat down for the first bush-tucker trial. They were each presented with 5 different dishes of horrid things to eat, and I can only say, that there is *no way* I'd be eating any of these things. When Ant & Dec explained the trial, Lady C said, to their bursts of laughter, *"I wished I had known that it was definitely food, as I would have worn my pearls!"*

What scrummy delights were to come?

The Spanish-Vomlette: First they were served what was called a Spanish-Vomlette and Jorgie's egg omelette was covered in live cockroaches – Lady C's egg omelette was covered in live crickets!

Poor Jorgie picked up the first cockroach which went scuttling across her hand and she threw it panicked from hand to hand before popping it in her mouth saying, *"Sorry mate, sorry mate. It's looking at me!"* With hands flapping and body convulsing with each one, she bravely ate all three, nearly spitting out the second one. Lady C said, *"What a brick you are,"* and, *"Isn't she wonderful, she deserves champagne."*

Lady C approached her live crickets with her knife and fork, of course, and stabbed and ate one after the other in quick succession whilst Jorgie, holding her hand over her mouth, looked on in astonishment. Lady C, showing not the slightest sign of concern or distress on her face, remained completely poised and said that they were, *"Actually rather good, I hate to disappoint you."* When asked if she wanted to eat some more she said, *"Let's not get carried away, I don't want to ruin your fun!"*

Spaghetti Bollock-nese: Second both were served Spaghetti Bollock-nese, turkey testicles on a bed of live sea worms, which were wiggling and squirming on the plate! Lady C had to eat three turkey testicles, which were at least cooked; whereas poor Jorgie was faced with eating three live, wiggling sea worms! There is no way I would have been even trying the worms, sorry.

Lady C picked up her knife and fork, very lady-like as always, proceeded to eat her three turkey testicles and. And said, *"Delicious actually,"* in an imperious tone of The Queen's English. Then, with a royal hand gesture, she said, *"Ship me some of those over to England please. Scrum, scrum."*

Roasted Camel Lips: The third food test saw Jorgie served cooked ostrich tongue and Lady C a piece of roasted camel lips with the raw and *very* hairy lip sitting on the plate staring at her!

Ant introduced her dish as roasted Pars-lips and explained what they were, which made Dec and Jorgie gasp with raised eyebrows and a look of horror. They all burst out laughing when Lady C said, *"They look rather hairy!"*

Jorgie bravely chewed her ostrich tongue first, and nearly choked on it, however she rather took to it and said that it was *"The best food she'd had so far in camp,""* and ate it! Lady C picked up her knife and fork, very composed, and cut a piece of camel lip and after an initial skinning up of her lips said in answer to Dec's question as to what they tasted like, *"It's just al-dente"* (a culinary term used to refer to food cooked so that it's still 'firm to bite' but not soft), which brought the house down laughing. I was beginning to see a pattern of how Lady C sees the lighter side of life and readily finds humour in most situations, easily making those around her laugh and relax.

Pigs' Eyes: Fourth, Jorgie was served a dish of *really large* fish eyes and mussels, and Lady C a dish of pigs' eyes and mussels, and you can guest what each had to eat! Yes, one *eye* each and Lady C went first and asked, *"Where's the plate?"* which brought hoots of laughter as Dec said that it was finger food. She picked up her eye with two toothpicks and munched it without any sign of distaste whatsoever, but said in a tone of polite admonishment to a restaurant chef that it was, *"Underdone and chewy, and not delicious, the least delectable so far."*

Jorgie commented at how brave Lady C was and Dec said of Lady C's effort, *"No messing about there!"*

I nearly gagged with Jorgie as she flapped her arms about, gagged and yet ate her huge fish eye as it audibly, popped – OMG, what a moment! Talk about gross.

Apri-Croc Tajine: Fifth and last, it was as bad as the first, an Apri-Croc tajine was served and Jorgie got a crocodile penis on a bed of apricots, which looked steamed and Lady C said, *"Ah, lucky girl"!* which caused Jorgie to collapse laughing and say that she was, *"Rather hoping for a penis!"*

Lady C got crocodile anus! It also looked steamed – but, yuck. Lady C said, *"God this is like gristle to cut through, this is not something to recommend – but then I've never liked arses,"* which sent Ant & Dec into tears of laughter.

Jorgie said that she loved crocodile penis and that it tasted like Dim Sum – my having been served pig's penis and all sorts of stuff in China in a Dim Sum house, nothing would surprise me – and no, I wouldn't eat it. Ant asked Jorgie if she was a big fan of the penis then and she said, *"Yes, I'm a big fan of the penis,"* which saw everybody on the set collapse into fits of giggles.

You have to take your hat off to these two women and everyone that does these trials on the show. Chapeau indeed!

In the after trial out-take room that evening Lady C said with a look of dignified noblesse oblige, *"Well, I've been surrounded most of my life by arse-holes, I thought I may as well eat one."*

Her performance in the food trials won her the hearts and minds of a huge viewing audience and drove the word on the street that you have to watch this woman on *I'm A Celebrity... Get Me Out Of Here!* Without doubt, and combined with the first outrageous outburst against Tony Hadley, she drove viewer ratings up into the stratosphere for this show. As the best-selling celebrity author Wendy Leigh said, *"She is not a character, she is a _cast_ of characters!"*

Fellow contestant and lead singer of Spandau Ballet, Tony Hadley, managed to upset Lady C in the first couple of days as the bush-tucker trials got under way. He declared Lady C and the TV presenter Yvette Fielding as the laziest members of camp after settling in with all doing camp cooking and cleaning duties, and he selected both Lady C and Yvette for the first trial after being made the King of Camp himself. Up until then all seemed to be getting on reasonably well with each other, but after this first trial things started to deteriorate badly. Some in the media accused Tony of being sexist as he named all his male colleagues as hard working. One media report suggested that he had placed Lady C at the bottom of the work ability list as she was the oldest member of camp and likely wouldn't be as active as others.

In any event, Tony the King of the Camp sent both Lady C and Yvette to do the task, and when they got into the Jungle trial area, not knowing what was to come, they found they were to be washing up a pile of what looked like eighty plus mess tins with old food baked on. This was in order to discover a letter of the alphabet written on the bottom of just seven of those tins under the baked on food. When the correct tins were hung up on a rope provided, and viewed, they would create a word – winning this game by getting the correct word would result in everyone at camp getting a meal that night, rather than rations of just rice!

However, when Lady C and Yvette arrived at the Jungle site to learn the task, Lady C didn't see it as fair that Tony had selected them, and raged that it was *"Ludicrous"* that they should have been given the task at all by Tony. To Yvette's surprise she refused to take part in it, turning to set off back to camp to confront Tony. Yvette tried her best whilst smiling and chuckling at Lady C's reaction, taking deep breaths and pleading with Lady C to have a go or at least keep her company whilst she did it. Lady C said that nothing would induce her to do this trial and said, *"Do I look unsure?"* as her answer to Yvette asking her to stay, and added *"No, no, no,"* as she stormed off and returned to the camp to confront Tony. And confront him she did.

Tony watched Lady C re-enter camp with an impish grin and blackened face make-up, as many had on while getting into the spirit of the Jungle, but they all looked more akin to animals trying to hide-themselves in a jungle lair and become invisible. Tony was clearly in her sights and was set upon by a very upset Lady C when he asked her what the result of the trial was as she was now back. Remember, he'd selected her for the task, having accused her of being the laziest person in camp. And that was after she had cooked everybody's breakfast the morning before! Quickly the whole bun fight started, with accusations flying back and forth – the viewers were gripped, as I am sure they'd not seen anything quite this volatile on the show before. Ratings almost doubled overnight from 5 million on the show's opening day. The audience were glued to their TV sets, and could hardly wait to see what was going to happen next.

Lady C wasn't standing for it, and the *lioness* was first unleashed!

With the stance of a big-cat, teeth bared indicating her hostility and readiness to fight - she verbally pounced on her Tony prey at an alarming rate, so astonished was she by his decision to choose her for this bush trial, but no more astonished than Tony at her attack. She absolutely let rip and said, *"When you were shoveling food down you the other morning, who do you think prepared it?"*

"I know, I know," he mumbled softly with head somewhat cowered down, suggesting he knew he had been unfair nominating Lady C as one of the laziest in camp, and went on to say, *"It's not personal."*

Chris Eubank the big boxing champion standing between them and watching this exchange could only smile as he put his head in his hand waiting for the victim's throat to be, metaphorically speaking, seized, and she went straight for the kill. With clear annoyance, and a fixed facial expression of sheer determination and anger, she said, *"This is a typical male cop out. Grow up. It is personal. If you're man enough to make the decision, stand by the consequences."*

Tony said that he appreciated what she said, but before he could say more, Lady C interrupted in very grand English tones with, *"Appreciation is a wonderful thing and a lack of it is very noticeable."* He sought to claim that it was not his fault if he was not made aware of the game's consequences, but again, before he could finish his sentence Lady C snarled: *"You're a 55-year-old man and you've not figured out yet that everything has a consequence. Give me a break, what planet are you on?"*

Asked where Yvette was by Duncan Bannatyne, entrepreneur of TV's Dragons Den fame, Lady C explained that Yvette had stayed in the bush to do the task, as she wanted the reward for the camp. Lady C added: *"I have five tiaras, and turned down one of the richest men in the world. Nothing would induce me to sell myself when I think it's wrong."*

All the while Brian Friedman the choreographer was sitting nearby wearing an Australian felt bush hat. He smirked, gently biting his lips whilst turning his head away in amusement at her remarks, but not wanting to be seen to be laughing at her I suspect, and become the lionesses' next kill. She concluded her angry rant at Tony by saying, *"I mean, the whole thing is a God damn farce!"*

Yvette, bless her, carried on, and completed the task on her own and won supper for them all that night. In the out-take room where contestants get to let off steam or just summarize their feelings in private later in the day, Lady C said, *"I'm disgusted by what has happened, but it's damn funny that people who were stuffing their gullets on my labour whilst sitting on their big fat arses, were able to think I'd done nothing."*

Lady C was headline news in all of the British tabloid Press the next morning, and across Britain her hilarious one-liners were the talk of everyone's conversation. A love her or hate her divide was beginning to appear for the first time. When Duncan Bannatyne taunted Lady C in an endless debate that raged about each person's share of a tin of soup, Lady C said, *"Listen darling heart, there's no man tall enough or rich enough to cower me – don't even think of starting. You're a mouse compared to what I'm used to!"* Asked to calm down by Tony Hadley she said, *"Wind bags, you're both used to having your own way and I am more used to it, but I'm sensible, and you're not!"* Caught in the same dispute with something Duncan said, Lady C hit back with, *"You are a little pussy who has not even been voted to do a trial or challenge yet, so keep your cackle to yourself!"*

When Tony interrupted Lady C in another discussion she said, *"Don't interrupt me when I'm speaking; you are nothing near as sensible as you think you are!"* In the out-take room later she said of Tony that, *"He's little better than a buffoon in many ways."*

As Wendy Leigh also said of Lady C whilst the latter was in the Jungle, *"God help anyone who crosses her!"*

In another camp fire discourse Lady C announced to her fellow contestants that, *"The fact of the matter is that most of you, if not all of you, have to consider the effect that you are having on the public; I don't have to, I don't have to, I don't give a fig-fuck what the public thinks of me,"* to an astonished look from most, and gasps from others. As some were celebrities seeking the limelight of the show to bring them back into the public eye, it may have been a raw nerve. In Lady C's case, she had been quite plain when saying up front that she was in it for the money, which would pay to repair the roof on her castle. She wasn't seeking fame, nor did she want infamy out of it. In retrospect I think she obtained both.

One other trial she walked out of was when three contestants each had to stand in an open fronted cubicle side by side, and in Lady C's cubicle a huge python was seen slithering on a tree branch just above her ahead. Yvette Fielding and Susannah Constantine and Lady C started describing what each had in their cubicle. The snake in Lady C's cubicle started moving, quite quickly for a giant snake, towards Lady C, sticking out its tongue to sense its prey, and she said, *"I'm sorry, get me out of here, I'm not prepared to jeopardize my life,"* as Susannah muttered under her breath with rolling eyes, *"What the fuck!"* in annoyance at Lady C walking away. And Lady C walked off.

On another around the camp fire discussion an argument soon broke out over Tony and Jorgie not being willing to put on bell boy hats and serve Lady C, Chris Eubank and Kieron Dyer. The heated discussion went around and around and eventually Lady C said, *"Tossers!* (British, slang for a male who masturbates). *Tossers, the whole bunch of you!"* Told off by Brian the choreographer for talking over Duncan when he tried to share his view, the lioness was unleashed again as she struck out with what has to be one of my favourite put-down lines ever:

"You my dear have verbal diarrhoea. Not only do you have verbal diarrhoea, you are so full of shit that if you were given an enema you'd disappear off the face of this earth without trace," – and added, *"Be careful who you take on, dear, baby, boy, some people actually have sharper tongues than you; self-important little runt – desperate for attention and can't get any."*

When Chris Eubank the world champion boxer tried to make some calming comments Brian remarked that he was segregating the camp, and Lady C shot back: *"Shut up and let somebody else speak, you are always shooting off your God damn motor mouth."*

Duncan piped up that he hadn't yet had and wanted to get a trial and Lady C snapped at him that: *"That's part of the problem, you are desperate for the limelight, you vain old goat,"* said to chuckles from all around.

Brian said to Lady C, *"You're vile,"* and she called him a bitch. He replied that, *"No, you're the bitch"* – which brought a sharp response when Lady C said to him, *"I'm bitchy when I'm speaking the truth about a bitch, and you are a bitch,"* to gasps of shock from Yvette. Kieron put his head in his hands, looking very uncomfortable with this verbal exchange.

When Tony said she's playing a game, Brian commented that, *"She thinks she's superior because her title makes her superior."*

Lady C pounced back with the comment, *"You're an idiot."*

In the out-take room later in the day Lady C said, *"I don't like being surrounded by false creatures, posing as the real McCoy, and I hate to say it, but there are far too* many of them in this camp." She added, *"I'm not prepared to reward people who have ganged up against me, been abusive to me. Apples will grow on lilac trees before that happens! They have destroyed my team spirit and they will endure the consequences, that's all there is to it."*

In another out-take room moment, talking of Brian again, she said, *"I think he's a bitch, I've thought it for some time. I think he's manipulative, I think he's divisive, I think he's the choreographer of many of the dance moves that have been taking place here."*

Told by Yvette that they were all sick of hearing her voice and to be quiet, Lady C replied, *"Well if you are sick of it, remove yourself!"* and she added when told that she could be a lovely woman but that she ruins it by being so rude, *"I'm rude when the occasion warrants it!"*

Sitting around the camp bed area and fireplace one evening Tony asked what was creeping towards his bed and Lady C learned forward and scooped up a giant beetle in her cup - and threw it on the fire. Tony screamed: *"Don't put it on the fire, that's really cruel,"* and Lady C responded calmly saying, *"I did what any sensible person would do, I threw it on the fire"* – and added with a tone of annoyance now, *"You are a chippy oik and I've had a belly full of you."*

After Tony said that she should not have done it she laid into him with: *"You are a hypocrite, a typical pretentious up yourself arsehole, that's what you are, I've had enough of you,"* and added, *"You arch hypocrite, you pretentious piffle, you chippy oik with the brains of a pea and a mouth of diarrhoea!"*

There's not much you can say after that, is there. (The old English word piffle means to talk or act in a trivial, inept or ineffective way.).

Tony said that if she was any kind of lady she wouldn't have a tongue like that and apart from telling him that he wouldn't know the definition of a lady, and that he'd probably never met one she added, *"I couldn't care less what your opinion of me is. My opinion of you is that you are the lowest of the low, aside from being a God damn bore."*

She continued her attack saying, *"Let me tell you something boy* (said with a Jamaican tone and pronounced, Bwoy), *you are of no significance to me. You may be very impressed with who you are, but as far as I'm concerned, you are a total zilch – you are so used to creeps and dolly birds and tarts in awe of you, because you can sing, and you don't even have a particularly good voice; you aren't a Carreras that's for sure!"* That would be José Carreras, the famous opera tenor.

In the out-take room later she said of Tony in private to the camera that, *"As I have an IQ of 154 and he most likely has an IQ of 54, if that, I don't think there's* anything wrong with my powers of discernment, whilst there's clearly a lot wrong with his. Aside from anything else, he's a blasted liar and a gutless creep!"

More trials!

The Mealy Worms and live crickets: Wearing a scarf over her head and protective plastic goggles over her eyes, a glass globe shaped helmet with a hole in the top was placed on Lady C's head. The trial was to stay in the helmet for two minutes after 'things' were poured inside from the top - and there were going to be three such trials all in one go!

First they poured in a tub of mealy worm grubs that wiggled around her neck and chin, and then a tub of live crickets were poured in on top of the grubs, who ran around her head and face, seeking to crawl in her ears, nose, mouth, everywhere! She made the two minutes and after they were all brushed off her she was asked what she thought of the challenge.

Lady C said in a reflective tone, *"It was tiresome but darling, I've had <u>real</u> challenges in my life. This was not one of them,"* with an air of feigned haughtiness.

Green biting ants: Second, with a fresh jacket, headscarf and goggles back on, a square glass box was placed over her head and an entire box of green biting ants was poured in through the top.. This really looked difficult to cope with as they were trying to get up her nose and into her mouth, and with gritted teeth she kept snorting through her nose to stop them climbing up – it must have felt horrid and I find myself itching just writing about it! But the two minutes she did and the glass box was taken off her head and all the ants brushed off!

"I'm fine," was the only comment.

The last of these critter trials was a glass box fixed to a bench with a hole in one side for her to place her head, and a hole in the top to pour in whatever dastardly creatures were coming next!

Helmet of hell challenge: Fresh jacket, head scarf and goggles back on again, she lay down on the bench and placed her head into the box. About twenty scorpions and as many big black spiders were poured into the box on her head, and crawled, to most viewers' horror, across her head and face as she remained tight lipped and motionless.

Her remark coming out, as experts were still picking off scorpions attached to her jacket around her neck, was, *"Very tiresome, but I meditated and was calm."*

The unseen crabs: Another separate trial was when three of the ladies, Jorgie, Yvette and Lady C, sat on a bench and had to place their bare feet into a large glass box on the floor with a blindfold on; and with their feet 'feel' how may objects were in the box – and Lady C guessed correctly at four live crabs, of which one bit her!

The Panic-Pit: There was one trial that Lady C refused to do once it became clear what was expected of her, and it took the show's hosts by surprise when she explained why. The trial was called the Panic-Pit and consisted of crawling down into an underground narrow tunnel and maneuvering into a small underground room with no room to stand, and to shut the door and remain under there for a set amount of time, no doubt with all sorts of other horrible creatures being introduced, before coming back up.

Lady said, *"I am not starting it, sorry. I had a cousin who was murdered by being buried alive – this is a matter of record. I'd said I was not doing anything that involved a coffin or coffin-like burial – it's an absolute no, not a chance."* Ant & Dec fully understood.

In fact, as she said later, the cousin had been buried alive but actually survived, and in the heat of the traumatic memory being brought back to mind during the Jungle, she misspoke about his dying buried alive – not that it made such a memory of being buried alive easier – nor the memory of having an aunt shot to death and a grandfather murdered.

Summary of the Jungle.

She handled everything the Jungle and the show threw at her except the snake den and she refused to do the mess tin washing up for being unfairly selected as a point of principle, and the Panic-Pit due to traumatic family memories – but she did nine or more other trials and she ate live crickets, turkey's testicles, roasted hairy camel lip, and she ate a pig's eye and a crocodile's anus – does a menu get any more varied? It's just lucky that she isn't a vegan!

She suffered all sorts of creepy crawly things climbing over her head and face, from mealy worm grubs and crickets, to biting green ants, scorpions and spiders, and even a biting crab on her toe, and she took it all in her stride!

She certainly proved at times to be a divisive member of the community and moved from vicious remarks and some unforgettable put downs given to those who upset her, to genuine care and concern for others. Elected to do so by paying viewers, she took part in virtually all trials and all the food ones, which was a stellar example to the other contestants.

She left behind some contestants who loved her and some who literally hated her and some who sat on the wall. Kieron Dyer, the celebrity ex-England football star, and Chris Eubank, the former World Middleweight Boxing Champion, are two people whose hearts Lady C won over and who have remained good friends since leaving the Jungle. When I interviewed Kieron about what he thought of

Lady C's time in the Jungle he said: *"If I had to go to war, I'd want her by my side, as she'd die for you; she is exceptionally loyal once you become friends."*

That's certainly a comment echoed by virtually everyone I have spoken to who's a friend of Lady C. They all say that she is exceptionally loyal. I'm sure Chris Eubank would say the same. Both he and Kieron were very generous in giving me time to interview them and both described Lady C as someone they had squabbles with early on in the show. Kieron found her akin to a mother lioness figure, who started defending him and looking out for him, and Chris found himself being very protective of her as a true King of the Ring, recognizing that she was a woman who deserved being cared for. She was certainly opinionated and stubborn, admittedly, and as Kieron said: *"You can't win an argument with her!"*

She is a very, very knowledgeable woman too, as most of those connected to the reality TV show with whom I spoke expressed, and *"Someone, who knows a lot of well-known names personally,"* as Chris said. Yet when she and Chris Eubank got chatting, out would come their Jamaican patois as Kieron recalled from their Jungle moments, and with which Chris smilingly remembered such conversations. Lady C speaks perfect English and does not usually speak in Jamaican patois, but when she wants to turn it on she can, as I've witnessed in my home many years ago and in her company this last year. Chris said, *"She takes a negative remark as 'piffle' and doesn't usually bite – if they are part of a bullying process she'll respond, and sharply,"* and added, *"She lives life, is wealthy, intellectual, worldly, sharp-witted; truth stands out and she speaks her mind."*

Whatever problems were put to her in the Jungle she always had a solution. Lady C has what Chris called: *"A magic energy and a capacity to do things."* No matter what the tasks, she'd take on anything for anyone it seems, and was seen by those who warmed to her as a matriarchal figure and good fun in and out of the Jungle. Kieron knows already that he's made a friend for life and talked of his family's love for the woman who's thirty years his senior, and how his mum and his kids aged 4 – 16 all adore her. Since the show she has invited Kieron and his whole family to Castle Goring and took them on a tour (during renovations) and savored taking care of them and building on their budding friendship.

Chris rather boldly said to me: *"As, I see it, she has a form of genius."* That might sound strange, but he was talking about her energy and what he described as her *"Majestic personality."* Proof of that is that she was the person most talked about by 11 million viewers. *"It's her energy that's genius, and her intellect, and her ignoring political correctness and just being who she is,"* Chris said.

Wendy Leigh for the Mail on Sunday summed up Lady C well when she said that her performance in the Jungle, *"Conducted a scorched earth policy… roasting her opponents with some of the most searing, soul-destroying and, at times, hilarious put-downs ever heard on British television."*

Oiks!

The UK's *Daily Mirror* newspaper said during the reality TV show, *"The super-posh celeb is fast becoming the darling of the Jungle, despite branding viewers oiks."*

I must address this, as it is a term much misunderstood by most people, and may not be known at all to many readers. The Oxford English Dictionary definition of an oik gives the meaning as: *an uncouth, unpleasant or obnoxious person.* An oik therefore can refer to a Duke or a working man in the street. Her remark was *not* aimed at every working class person as some in the media then implied and as she immediately confirmed when I asked; it was aimed at a certain *type* of person in the viewing audience.

If I have learned nothing else from spending time with Lady C, it is that she has an amazing command and use of the English language and she chooses her words well, even when under attack. Words do not slip out in the wrong context. They are selected and spoken with purpose and meaning, and she is no snob. Oik was chosen to describe *any* uncouth, unpleasant or obnoxious person watching.

'I'm a Celebrity' stories told by old hacks attacking her afresh.

I've read stories, admittedly by only one or two journalists, reminding us in every single article that they write of how Lady C was born. They write every time in intimate sexual detail of how she was raised a boy and tell us the gory details of her marriage and divorce. For thirty plus years she's been over her divorce and became a multiple *New York Times* best-selling author and now a regular TV personality, having had a second reality TV show and been on stage with her own show at The Edinburgh fringe festival - isn't *that* who she is today?

It's rather like journalists talking about Roger Federer, seven times Wimbledon Men's Singles tennis champion, and every time he wins another major title reminding readers that he lost the opening match in the ATP Tournament in Shanghai in 2013 when reigning champion to qualifier Alberto Ramos, ranked 70 in the world! Why would you bring it up every time you wrote about him – you wouldn't would you – and they don't!

In fact Lady C tends to talk openly about her birth, and the circumstances of her upbringing, and her divorce frequently too, but only because she is still constantly asked about it. But I believe she no longer needs to explain or justify anything, as she has risen above all of that history and is now a highly successful woman and a celebrity, and that's all that matters now.

I also realized that Lady C must still make some in the media nervous because, when your whole life has been laid bare across tabloid newspapers for the entire world to read for 40 plus years, there is a certain amount of fearlessness about your behavior. There is nothing to hide and she'll take anybody on face to face; and yet some try to drag up old news and cause fresh hurt. I find that sad.

I think it's about time that journalists stop repeating her birth circumstances and how she was raised as a boy every single time they write about her. We know. It's not news anymore! They don't have to like her and can write what they want about her, but let's move on with the birth and upbringing thing - please guys.

Claims of being bullied in the Jungle.

Lady C claimed after she came out of the Jungle that much of the bullying hurled at her, which resulted in her quick, sharp retorts, was edited out, leaving just her responses and creating a false image of her as the sole antagonist. I must admit that's all I saw too, so the complaints seemed to me justified, but I wanted to hear from others.

She realizes herself that editing must happen on all reality TV shows; *"to create tension and excite viewers"* is what she said to me. It's obvious that tension on reality TV shows is the staple diet without which they cannot thrive or drive viewer ratings and advertising dollars up, but she felt this series was too one sided.

And let's remember, the show itself acknowledged that their usual ratings of over 5 million viewers a day shot up with Lady C's presence and behavior to over 10 and sometimes 11 million a day. To maintain those ratings I'd be very surprised if the producers did not, consciously or unconsciously at least, edit more aggressively than usual, to show their main attraction's more outlandish side - knowing that with her they were onto a viewer rating and advertising dollar winner. Maybe I'm wrong, but it just seems logical.

"She may have felt that she was being bullied, but viewers can make up their minds from what they have seen," said an ITV source to the media after her suggestion that they had unfairly edited the daily program. *"We feel we have accurately represented what has happened on the campsite,"* and, *"It is bizarre for her to claim she was bullied."*

Well, was it bullying or not?

The two fellow jungle camp-mates not involved in bullying her are probably the best to ask as to what they felt about her claims of being bullied. Kieron Dyer the famous former England, Newcastle United, Ipswich Town and West Ham footballer, and a fellow contestant had this to say to me when I interviewed him: *"Georgie called it bullying, and they (Bannatyne and Hadley) antagonized her constantly."*

It was clear to me in chatting with him that Kieron would personally not call it bullying. He saw it as more like aggressive teasing, and pushing her hot buttons to get a reaction. He saw it as her *'antagonists'* seeking to show her in a negative light to the viewers, who might then vote her out quick.

He felt that Tony and Duncan especially antagonized her a lot, and he said of her responses, *"Her vocabulary is brilliant, and you don't even know some of the words – she can be brutal with her tongue if you have a go at her."*

Chris Eubank, the former World Middleweight Boxing Champion said about claims of bullying: *"I was well aware that she was being bullied by Duncan and Tony, and she was targeted and felt threatened."*

When it comes to defending herself as we've all seen, she clearly needed no help, though I'm sure no one who laid into her for the first time realized what a lioness they were unleashing! As we've all seen, once she was shaken from her calm, jovial demeanor, she remained poised in self-defense, ready to strike at the slightest provocation thereafter.

Well, I'm not sure about you, but I'm not sure I agree with the producers of the program when they said she was not bullied. Whether it was seen as bullying by some or teasing by others is immaterial. It was by definition of The Oxford Dictionary correctly perceived by Lady C as sheer bullying!

If she was being bullied and reacted by giving as good as she got, then *"Nuff respect!"* to her, as they'd say in Jamaica.

Let's not forget her time at an all-boys school as a child; Lady C was bullied without mercy throughout her school days as we've read, and she knows what bullying is. I think she developed a survivor instinct as a grown-up, when, for the first time, she could defend herself against such bullying. She learned to use her wit and her words to strike at people seeking to put her down. She has learned to hit back quick and hard at the slightest onset of bullying, to stop it in its tracks, and not to demur from her task.

We heard in chapter two from her classmates that she was indeed mercilessly bullied at school, and was right to believe that years of horrid fear would explode emotionally in the Jungle if she carried on taking any more and as someone in her mid-sixties, just to amuse an audience.

What did the reality show's own psychiatrist say about bullying in the Jungle?

Lady C says that when she paid a visit to the show psychiatrist on behalf of fellow contestant George Shelley (The Union J boy band lead singer whom she was worried about and how he was coping), she found the psychiatrist had already reached the same conclusion regarding herself. It turned out that the doctor had made the connection. She had been bullied as a child and, *"She was now being bullied again. This would bring it all back."*

Did the TV producers over manipulate the editing to drive ratings, as Lady C says they did, but they say they didn't?

Editing is clearly not easy for producers who have to condense 24 hours of filming into a one hour show every day. Obviously a lot of what happens doesn't make it to the final cut, as Kieron highlighted to me. In this case they seem to show a lot more of her responses to being teased and not the trigger remarks made to her, and most of the attacks on her didn't appear in the final cut. Having reviewed all the recorded shows after he came out of the Jungle and got back to England, Kieron said to me during our interview that, *"They could have easily shown most of the attacks made on Lady C too. I know it's hard editing, but they did her an injustice."*

H.H. Princess Olga Romanoff, great niece of the last Tsar of Russia, who's known Lady C for over 25 years and been a dear friend for over 14 years, said that Lady C was: *"Incredibly brave and the two guys who constantly berated her were nasty."*

"One thing is for sure," she said when I interviewed Her Highness regarding Lady C, *"she takes no shit from anybody and gives it back."* She clearly became so tired and drawn from exhaustion, but as Her Highness said: *"Goodness, she just got on with it."*

What did the 'man in the street' think of Lady C in the Jungle?

I jumped in the car with Lady C the afternoon that we arrived at Castle Goring after we had dumped our bags and picked up her beloved dogs, and we drove down to the local Tesco supermarket. We went to simply buy eggs and milk for breakfast in the morning. However, we took *90 minutes* to get out, as everybody recognized her and wanted a 'selfie' photograph with her. She'd only been out of the televised reality show two weeks and Christmas 2015 was just a couple of weeks away. We must have stopped for scores of photos and every. Every single 'selfie' request was met with a genuine smile as Lady C chatted and asked about them and their family.

Just the day before I had seen a media article from her past by a journalist who seemed clearly not to like her at all; the tone was almost venomous. The article made nothing but negative remarks, as some journalists had done over any incident in her life over the decades. This was a double-take moment. Here were 'ordinary people', so to speak, virtually all delighted to see her and approaching her with enthusiasm at Tesco's. The two experiences seemed very at odds with each other. I was not aware of a single person in that crowded supermarket that was negative toward her; everybody was very much pro-Lady C, and pro her honest, in-your-face behavior, her colourful language and all. Isn't it the 'ordinary people' and what they think that matters in these situations? She's very much *The People's Lady*. As a few have since said to me, she is an unexpected British treasure to ordinary Britons, especially to young women.

When it comes to mingling with 'the man in the street' Lady C has no airs and graces; she chats to anyone, anytime, and if she owns a castle and you are a car mechanic for a living it doesn't seem to matter to her from my experience and from listening to scores of people talking about her. I honestly feel that she either likes you as a person, or she doesn't. There's no grey area, it's a very black and white decision, which she makes. Your upbringing, celebrity or obscurity, wealth or otherwise has nothing to do with it. Mind you, woe betide someone who is disrespectful or rude to her, because they are going to get an earful for sure, no matter who they are!

My favorite surprise encounter:

We were astonished when one lovely Lady Came up to Lady C when I was with her in Tesco's supermarket in Worthing, and showed Lady C a photograph on her iPhone of a tattoo on her brother's arm, which he had just had done. It was a tattoo of Lady C!! – wow!!!! That's what you call a fan! ! About a week later it became a major news story in *The Sun* national newspaper.

Back in London, we stopped at the local post office in Kennington the following day and out popped some ladies who lived opposite in a housing shelter for battered women, as they told us. They had recognized her from their balcony and wanted a 'selfie', and a 'selfie' they got, whilst she happily chatted away to them and asked how they were doing, and were they okay? It wasn't a show, or to impress me. It was, I found consistently, just who she is. She genuinely cares about other people, and those worse off she cares about all the more.

How her heritage links to her character today as we saw in the Jungle

Now we see emerge her heritage of Lebanon and Jamaica culture that I talked about at the beginning of this book. The link to the personality forged in the fires of her life of schoolboy bullying, the trauma of how she was raised, the violent marriage and the hounding by the Press afterwards – it came out in who we saw in this reality TV show, even if at times she was over the top and often profane. When attacked, she responds by going on the attack, but I have found in her company in all sorts of situations that she doesn't swear at all, it's just not part of her day-to-day vocabulary until someone or something really ticks her off. Then she's quick to resort to some profane words - but so are an awful lot of people both you and I know when they are truly upset, if we're honest.

I asked her about that temper and she said: *"I'm the first to admit that I have a feisty temper, like my mother's, but at least I say what I feel and am honest about it."*

Of her feisty temper, I think it's because she's fearless, as I've said earlier and she doesn't give a damn; she says it as it is. Is she entitled to such behavior? I'm not sure, but her life experiences have shaped her to be defensive and have made her what she is. She's someone who thinks of others before herself I've experienced. But she's also someone who, if attacked, offended or upset by your action, will go straight for the kill. This lady takes no prisoners, hands flailing and often with raucous words flying. It's who she is, and that's unlikely to change.

Her friend H.R.H. Princess Katarina, who's a member of both the Yugoslav Royal Family and the British Royal Family, said to me of the show that: *"I did not watch it on TV and find all such shows, especially the likes of the Kardashians, ghastly!"* I have to agree with Her Royal Highness, even I generally do not watch reality shows because of all the false drama *created* which takes its participants through degrading events for the amusement of a watching audience. However, there is no denying millions do watch such shows, so it must be what a lot of people want and enjoy. Night after night eleven million British viewers watched this show that Lady C was in, to see what happened next.

Rather like the result of the British 2016 EU referendum, you may not like the result but you have to respect the will of the people. If it wasn't for the 5 million plus people during the reality TV show *I'm A Celebrity... Get Me Out of Here!* who really loved Lady C, then Lady C would not today be enjoying such a massive increase in national celebrity and recognition as she is, nor be in such demand by the public. So I willingly recognize such shows and their great success.

Chapter 7

Lady C's books

Diana in Private: The Princess Nobody Knows.

IN 1992, LADY C wrote the book *Diana in Private*, which saw her as the *first* person to break the news to the world that Diana, Princess of Wales, felt trapped in an unhappy marriage and wanted a divorce. Andrew Morton's book came after Lady C's, but because Diana fully cooperated with him as was revealed later, it is the one most remembered. Without Lady C's book, there may never have even been a Morton book.

Lady C's book told a shocked world of the Princess's battle with bulimia and her affair with Major James Hewitt, which had been going on for five years. It wasn't just Prince Charles who carried on an old love affair, as Diana had left the world assuming – they already lived separate lives and both saw other people.

Everyone, the media and establishment combined, called Lady C a fantasist, and dismissed her book's claims! But her claims were corroborated by Diana herself in her Panorama interview and in events as they unfolded, including her desire for a separation; the divorce; her loss of her royal status; and her belief that her bodyguard Barry Mannakee had been killed. It was explosive news, and Lady C broke the story of Hewitt and Diana's affair six months before the world knew, and before Morton published his book. Because he had Diana's blessing, as he wrote the story she wanted told, everybody assumes Morton broke the news to the world of Diana's unhappy marriage, but he didn't, did he? Lady C's book hit the global market six months earlier, something most of the Press seems to forget also.

How did *Diana in Private* come about? The first book on Diana was started by Lady C because she approached the palace and gained an appointment with Diana to consider writing her authorized biography. Diana was someone that Lady C had met before, as she had many contacts within royal circles at the time. The arrangement broke down, as Lady C says, because Diana, after multiple private interviews with her, wanted to use the book to trash The Prince of Wales. Lady C felt such a partisan attack was not fair. Neither party was innocent she assumed, and both bore blame, and while seeking to support Diana's story Lady C felt that she needed to write a more balanced one. She says that she told Diana that she could not write such a one sided attack, and Diana withdrew her cooperation. Lady C went ahead and wrote what she felt was the truth in *Diana in Private*.

Why Lord Colin Campbell felt he needed to apologize to Prince Charles for the book, as he said in his 2015 Press interview, is a mystery to me. I have read the book and found it balanced and quite sympathetic to Prince Charles, exposing the other sides of Diana that the public had not seen.

Lady C's friend Mark Sykes commented that he thought her book on Princess Diana: *"nailed it. And a delicate reference to my mother's affair with King George VI."*

In 1995, at the same time as the *Diana in Private* biography propelled Lady C into the media's spotlight, she went to the Royal Courts of Justice over a *Daily Mirror* newspaper article that wrongly said she was transsexual and born a male. Lady C said to me that she accepted undisclosed libel damages and the *Daily Mirror* newspaper apologized, and she withdrew her lawsuit; but only after a long drawn out battle, which she felt was designed to drain her financially and make her give up.

Lady C's cousin Enrique remembered what people were saying when Lady C's book on Diana came out, and said to me: *"I was in Miami at the time and friends were calling from England saying that it must all be lies."* Friends and family rang him astonished that Georgie or anyone could write such things of Diana. Morton's later book, as we've said, and events, validated virtually everything Georgie had said and proved her right.

Enrique knew Georgie would be stoic and would not care, as she knew what she had written was true as she's only ever dealt with facts, as various members of her family and numerous friends have told me. *"We learned as kids that Georgie never told lies,"* he said, so he had no doubt that what she had written was all true. A few years later, he recalled sadly going to the British Consulate in Miami to sign the book of condolence when Princess Diana died, and as he said, *"Everyone in the queue was by then talking about Georgie as the only one who told the truth about Diana."*

Lady C wrote this first book on Diana's struggles to shed light on the fact that the Princess was not just a captivating world personality, a beautiful woman and a caring and devoted mother suffering from an eating disorder and needing help, but that she was not quite such an innocent either. That she was in Lady C's mind, from all of her private interviews with her, also a cool, calculating woman who set out to destroy Charles by any means, fair or foul. When Lady C would not play ball Diana turned to Morton, Lady C believes. That Diana had been having affairs at the same time as claiming Charles had not dropped Camilla was validated too – but Diana wanted to make it look as if all the problems with the marriage were down to Charles. That she was in a loveless marriage is accepted, and did it start because of Charles' continuing affair with Camilla after he married, maybe – or as she said in the now famous 1995 TV interview, way after Lady C's book came out, *"There were three people in this marriage."* But it was six of one and half a dozen of the other in reality it seems when we know all the facts, and if we seek to look beyond the legend. Charles may not be an innocent but as Lady C saw it Diana greatly, and unfairly, maligned him in Morton's book.

Major James Hewitt

At the time that Lady C's book *Diana in Private* hit the world headlines and caused a sensation, none the less so over the news that she had been having an affair for some time with Major James Hewitt, my wife and I owned a small boutique country house hotel down in Devon. We specialized during the seasons for salmon and trout fishing, and for shooting days for which we kept kennels for guests' gun dogs, and we had a lovely little gourmet restaurant and an oaked beamed village pub.

One afternoon, (I was in Hong Kong at the time), a woman checked in and announced in confidence to my wife that she was a journalist from a national newspaper and wanted to book a room for the night for Major James Hewitt. She asked for absolute confidentiality and said that she was going to interview him late evening, and for my wife, when he arrived, to please slip him unnoticed up to his bedroom suite, and once he'd settled in to let her know, she'd be in the bar.

We knew of the headline news of course and that representatives of the Press were staking out his family home, which wasn't more than half an hour from us, if I recall correctly, and she knew his arrival meant that he'd be bound to be noticed by my wife – so she may as well fess up and seek confidentiality in advance.

Over time we'd had numerous celebrities and well-known people staying with us, from Sir Time Rice the lyricist and Andrew Lloyd Webber's musical partner for many years, Craig Charles, a TV soap star of Coronation Street, Noel Edmonds, who lived nearby and ate in our restaurant regularly, to the Duke of Wellington's family coming for a shoot, to High Court Judges, to members of the Royal household and many others. So maintaining the confidentiality of high profile guests was second nature for us.

We didn't have a check-in desk counter as most hotels do, but a discreet, small partners' desk and chair in the double-height entrance hall, where my wife sat waiting for Major Hewitt. As he arrived she took him unnoticed straight up to his bedroom suite, and he ordered a drink. After he'd settled in she quietly advised the journalist who was at the bar, and she in turn asked for a bottle of champagne on ice and two glasses to be sent up to his suite where she could conduct her interview undisturbed in its sitting room.

Somewhere around 6 a.m. the next morning, before my wife came over from our home in the grounds of the hotel, he had quietly checked out before the other guests arose and left a note with his mobile number for my wife with a message. The message was for her to please call him so that he could give his credit card details and pay his bill, which he promptly did when she called him.

Only after his interview appeared in the newspapers did my wife mention to our staff that he'd been staying with us, and one of our housekeepers said, how funny, as she cleaned part time for the Hewitt family home! My wife Mary requested her to ask him the next time she saw him, whether he'd be kind enough to sign her copy of *Diana in Private*, Lady C's book, which he very kindly did and had it delivered back to my wife through our 'mutual' housekeeper. He was, my wife said, a very charming man and an absolute gentleman.

Here we are decades later, and I am writing a book about the woman who broke that story to the world of Diana's affair with Major Hewitt; it's one of life's little twists of fate isn't it.

Diana's desired separation story in Lady C's book rocked the establishment, and the media vilified her at the time for talking rubbish. The media later wrote of how Lady C was the first to predict the Wales's separation and divorce, and that she brought startling new revelations around their relationship and affairs.

Lady C strongly believes from her multiple meetings with Diana in private, that she was flawed psychologically, damaged she believes from her childhood parental issues. She feels that Diana is still seen in America and much of England through rose tinted glasses, but that in truth she was not a wounded angel who could do no wrong, nor an innocent, but someone who had multiple love affairs and who was an arch-manipulator, whilst being an amazing humanitarian and wonderful mother.

The Real Diana

Lady C later wrote her second book on Diana, *The Real Diana* (1998), which exposed for the first time some of Lady C's royal sources and was a definitive story of Diana's life up to her death in August 1997. The book became her second *New York Times* bestselling biography.

She shared with us that the reason she knew so much about what went on behind palace walls was because Diana herself was the early main source, through a series of some thirty private meetings and conversations, as well as having spoken to many who knew Diana first hand. Lady C said that they spoke a number of times again in what were to be the last few years of Diana's life. The media wrote of how Lady C brought Diana's story to life through intimate and sensitive insight, creating a fuller picture of Diana than had ever been read before.

Lady C tried to show the real Diana across her entire life's spectrum, and how she could be opposite things to different people. A woman from a privileged aristocratic background who married into the Royal Family but never settled in it, it seems. Diana was someone who nevertheless had the common touch and who did much to bring the Royal Family into modern times, whilst showing huge compassion in immersing herself with genuine vigor into multiple charitable causes.

From before her marriage to Prince Charles and up until her tragic death alongside Dodi Fayed, her Egyptian lover and son of Harrods owner Mohamed Fayed, this book grabbed the imagination of the world, just as Diana had done in life, and tragically in death.

Upon Lady C's second Diana book's release, Fleet Street news editors went into in a spin with its in-depth details about a side of Diana's life that, as with Lady C's first book, the late Princess would most likely have sought to hide from the public. Lady C was having no part of Diana's attempt to attack Charles and the Royal Family itself she said, and that as much as she respected Diana and her good works, she held and holds Prince Charles and the monarchy in high esteem, and these motives above all others drove her to write her two books on Diana.

Her publishers Macmillan Publishers and St. Martin's Press said: *"Royal insider Lady Colin Campbell sets the record straight on many of the most controversial aspects of Diana's turbulent life."*

Setting the record straight was one of Lady C's goals with this book and as she said herself at this time of Princess Diana, that, when she met Diana at a mutual friend's house in 1990, she was astonished by her conduct. Up to this point, the Diana she had encountered was a Princess in her manners and in what she said, and one who had behaved very much in keeping with the norm and traditions of Royalty. In social situations, she was as circumspect as the rest of them. Now, however, she was the antithesis of circumspection. Throwing caution and reserve to the wind, she had said to Lady C that she wanted her to write the truth about her life because she felt as if: *"The whole fairy tale is crushing whatever's left of the real me.... If you'd just write about the real Diana, it would make all the difference."*

The Royal Marriages

In 1993, two years before her second book on Diana, Lady C wrote a book entitled: *The Royal Marriages*.

She may hold the monarchy in high esteem, but news is news, and insider knowledge news for those in the full glare of the public eye cannot necessarily be private if the participants flaunt their issues or the establishment is awash from years of infidelity. It was an exposé where she talked about the affairs in the marriages of Charles and Diana; of Prince Andrew and Sarah and their marital issues; of Princess Anne and her first marriage – and talked about Lord Plunket, and the paternity questions she claims were sometimes raised by others of some of the Royals and The Queen. Lady C also wrote in this book about Princess Margaret's marriage to Antony Armstrong-Jones, the 1ˢᵗ Earl of Snowdon, and about Prince Philip's alleged affairs, and of some of the figures around those rumors.

Empress Bianca

Empress Bianca was intended to be published in 2005 through Arcadia Books. It was Lady C's first novel and certainly was not expected to create a legal storm. I suspect that in the end, that helped sell many more copies of the book once it was approved for publishing and after some major editing, way beyond what it might have sold before everyone talked about it. Every cloud has a silver lining as they say.

The *Daily Mail* wrote at the time that Lady C's book was first due to be launched: **'Pulped Fiction: World's richest widow at war with royal novelist.'**

The book was meant to be a fictional story of an ultra-rich woman who'd survived a number of billionaire husbands, with the latest and others, who died in suspicious circumstances – suggesting that she had murdered them and got away with it. In a lawsuit Lily Safra claimed that this book described her and her husband, and was not a work of fiction, but a poorly masked attack and accusation against her as a murderess and as such was pure libel. She threatened to sue the publisher for libel and stated that there were a number of striking similarities between her and her husband's real life, and the fictional book's characters too. Her last husband and the book's main character's last husband both died in fires in their apartments in Monaco. Mr. Safra's male nurse in fact was found guilty of starting the fire and served 8 years in prison for it.

Lily Safra chose as her lawyer Anthony Julius, who was the lawyer Princess Diana used to divorce from Prince Charles. Arcadia Books the publisher was under pressure and decided to withdraw the then limited run of some 2,000 books it already sent out to book shops in the UK, and cancel its planned print run in the USA. They said at the time: *"We've asked the bookshops to return the books to us, and then we'll destroy the copies."*

Lady C insisted that her book wasn't about the Safras, but was based on one of her relatives, and that so many Lebanese families have similar stories and similar losses and twists to their tales.

After Lady C sued Lily Safra and the matter was concluded, the UK's Dynasty Press published a version of Lady C's *Empress Bianca* in 2008 in America, and had issued copies in advance to Lily Safra's lawyers removing any suggestions of similarity to anyone in real life, including the Safras, and asking if their client or they had objection, before going to print, and after some months of receipt and no reply, printed. The book sold well – as Lady C had intended, as pure fiction.

The Queen Mother: The Untold Story of Elizabeth Bowes-Lyon, Who Became Queen Elizabeth the Queen Mother

Lady C wrote *The Queen Mother: the Untold Life of Queen Elizabeth* in 2012, a decade after Her Majesty's death at the age of 101.

The book wrote about the late Queen Mother with what most whom I spoke to thought was with warm reverence and respect for the debt owed by the nation to her enormous achievements; many believing that after the abdication crisis of Edward VIII, she had through her will power, influence, leadership and common touch, saved the monarchy. Lady C however aimed to tell her whole story, not through rose tinted glasses and misty hindsight, but as she understood reality from all that she had learned from Royal insider circles.

Two pieces of the late Queen's life story written by Lady C caused pandemonium and shockwaves upon reading. Lady C made claims firstly that she was told by those that knew that Lady Elizabeth Bowes-Lyon (the future Queen Elizabeth, queen consort to King George VI), the 9th child and 4th daughter of the 14th Earl of Strathmore & Kinghorne, Lord of Glamis, was not in fact the daughter of the Countess, but of a French cook in their household employ.

The book alarmed the establishment and was a shock to the nation too as the late Queen was and is held in the highest of esteem by the nation and its people, and the Press vilified Lady C over these allegations. As she says, it is based on what she had learned from Royal insiders, and was rumored wider within the establishment for decades.

Secondly, Lady C's book talks of The Queen Mother having *an asexual* approach to marriage, so when it came to producing an heir, and as The Queen Mother preferred not to have sex, they chose artificial insemination. In so far as the conception of a legitimate heir to the throne was concerned, using the King's sperm and his wife's womb was quite acceptable and retained the true Royal line without having to have sex. Other European Royals had done it as she explains in her book.

Lady C said that the sources for these claims came directly from the Duke of Windsor, Margaret, Duchess of Argyll, Lord Beaverbrook the newspaper empire giant, through his granddaughter Lady Jeanne Campbell (Lord Colin Campbell's stepsister) and lastly, the Marquise de Casa Maury, as Freda Dudley Ward became when she divorced her MP Liberal husband and remarried. She was of course one of the women who had an affair with the then Prince of Wales, David, the Queen Mother's brother-in-law who abdicated his throne as Edward VIII, bringing her and her husband to it. It was apparently an open secret in circles in which Elizabeth and Bertie (as King George VI was known in family circles) mixed that theirs was a '*Marriage Blanche*', but a very happy one Lady C said. She wrote that The Queen and Princess Margaret were born by this same legitimate method.

The establishment and many Royal authors have called the story all poppycock without any hard evidence, but she is adamant about her multiple Royal insider sources on this, admittedly without hard 'written' proof. As multiple of her claims based on other insider Royal sources in Diana's books were all similarly ridiculed but later proved correct by Diana herself confirming them, one cannot help but fall on the side of Lady C in believing that her separate and multiple sources *may* be right on these two shocking claims also, as unpleasant a taste as they may have to most of us, including me. However, we may never know the truth.

Lady Colin Campbell's, *A Guide to being a Modern Lady*

In October 1986, the book launch took place at the Foreign Press Association. A good friend, Paul Sidney and a successful editor of Random House at the time, had suggested she capitalize upon her background and write such a guide. She started writing and had met Graham Lea, who published some top books, in the winter of 1985 at a dinner party given by Anne Hodson-Pressinger. He asked her to send a sample of what she was working on, liked it and offered her a contract.

The Press had a field day of excitement at the book launch because the aging Margaret, Duchess of Argyll came, and she and Lady C enjoyed posing together for photographs. A number of Lady C's personal friends came along to support her book launch too, such as Princess Katarina of Yugoslavia, Prince Philip's great niece; Prince and Princess Lew Sapieha (of the Polish Royal House of Sapieha, originally of Lithuania), as well other friends such as Lord and Lady Pennock, Rona Lady Delves Broughton who is one of Lady C's best friends still today, Sir James and Lady Mancham; her ex, the actor Larry Lamb came, and her cousin Peter Jonas, then Managing Director of the English National Opera.

Daughter of Narcissus

Lady C wrote this book about her mother and in it she addresses the common but rarely tackled problem of narcissist personality disorder from the view of a family member. In this case a daughter suffering under a mother. It opened up discussion for countless thousands of people who felt able to speak about it now it was more out in the open from a high profile writer. As she talked about this part of her life at the Edinburgh Fringe Festival this last August, a number of people at each audience decided to go buy her book and better understand their own suffering, and hear of ways that Lady C had coped with it.

Lady C's published books in chronological order:

Lady C wrote *Lady Colin Campbell's, A Guide to being a Modern Lady* published by Heterodox in 1986.

In 1992 she wrote *Diana in Private* with St. Martin's Press, New York – a *New York Times* best seller!

Then came *The Royal Marriages* in 1993 also by St. Martin's Press, New York.

Her autobiography *A Life Worth Living* 1997 issued by Little, Brown and Company, and has recently been republished by Dynasty Press.

With St. Martin's Press, New York, she wrote *The Real Diana* 1998, which exploded the story of the Diana myth and was another *New York Times* bestseller!

She wrote *Empress Bianca* her only novel in 2008.

Daughter of Narcissus in 2009 was followed by *With Love from Pet Heaven: By Tum Tum the Springer Spaniel* in 2011.

She wrote her equally shocking but sympathetic book *The Untold Life of Queen Elizabeth, The Queen Mother*, which was published by Dynasty Press in the UK and St. Martin's Press in New York in 2012 - which became her third *New York Times* bestseller!

As Anthea Redmond, an American based Public Relations, Media & Hollywood Publicity Consultant said to me, Lady C's style of writing is that she does not labour every word or phrase. She just tells the truth bluntly and straightforwardly – the reader gets the message immediately: *"No gilding the lily, no implying, which is so refreshing."*

Chapter 8
Charitable causes and a hectic life

Charitable causes

WE'VE READ EARLIER THAT as a young person in Jamaica, Lady C was raised in a family which did much charity work, particularly the women, and so she grew up constantly helping with events as a child. Her cousin Enrique remembered that, *"Our mothers, who were childhood friends, did a tremendous amount of charity work."*

The children of the family had to help set up and serve people at functions, generally held in their own family homes on immaculately groomed lawns. Typically staff in such households all lent a hand beyond just helping to set up and clear away too, and enjoyed being part of giving back to their local communities. You can just see the kids wincing at being asked to help out yet again when all they want to do is go out and play. However, in the long run it has rubbed off on them all I discovered. I suppose that's how Lady C got her lifetime bug of being involved with charities. All of this charity work by their parents without a doubt influenced the kids and their behavior too; charity work is second nature to them all.

When Social and Personal Secretary to the Libyan Ambassador in London as we read earlier, Lady C organized a charity function which they hosted that the Press went wild over, especially over the eminence of the guests such as the socialist Labour Peer the Earl of Longford, and Prince Paul of Romania, and Sir James Goldsmith and Lady Annabel Birley. The years working as Social Secretary to the Libyan Ambassador, for which she brought her already sizeable social contacts and her ability to reach people to the fore, enabled her to build even more social, business and government contacts.

She helped channel donations from Libya to some of the needy British charities, and those she felt most deserved help. Everybody gained. The Libyans' reputation at the time needed enhancing as caring, and the generous donations enabled charities to help those most in need in Britain. Remember too, that this was a time when Libya had lukewarm relations with the West, but had not yet had the cataclysmic breakup with it. Gaddafi's atrocities were yet to come to the fore of the Western world.

Her whole life has seen Lady C involved one way or another with charities and raising money and she could have a direct personal impact to help many at once. Lady C used to chair, joint chair or serve on numerous Charity Ball committees to help organize events and raised serious amounts of money for the charities, which often have members of the British Royal Family as guests of honour, such as:

The St. John's Ambulance Ball supported and raised significant money for the association dedicated to the teaching and practice of medical first aid founded in the UK in 1877, which also supplies ambulances and community volunteers.

The Poppy Ball was a prestigious event held once every two years, with serving members of the Armed Forces in attendance, culminating in an after Ball party in an exclusive private London club. A silent auction conducted by a Sotheby's auctioneer sees proceeds go towards the many vital and urgent causes and projects supported by The Royal British Legion.

The Maypole Ball was a charity fund-raiser for major charities and Lady C chaired the ball and raised funds for SSAFA (the Soldiers, Sailors, Airmen and Families Association) and the Chemical Dependency Fund.

The Spring Ball in aid of the Hospice of St Francis in Hertfordshire and Buckinghamshire which care for the terminally ill.

The Rainbow Ball in aid of the Rainbow Trust Children's Charity which provides emotional and practical support to hundreds of families who have a seriously or terminally ill child.

The Russian Ball, passionate about Russian culture and history, and whose Patron is H.H. Princess Olga Romanoff, descendent and great-niece of the last Tsar of Russia, and personal friend of Lady C. Their Balls in recent years have attracted the likes of H.R.H. Princess Michael of Kent as guest of honour.

In 1978 Lady C sat on the charity committee of **KIDS,** which unites retailers, manufacturers, foundations and individuals to support people affected by poverty and tragedy through donated new clothing, and **Crusaid's children charity** and the **AIDS Foundation charity.**

In 1979 she recalls Joan Collins being very genuine when she and her husband Ron Kass attended the premier of *Oklahoma* to help raise money for the KIDS committee Lady C sat on. Lady C was delegated to take care of Joan for the evening and ensure that she was introduced to everyone, including Prince and Princess Michael of Kent, the guests of honour. She said that, *"Joan was wonderful with everybody,"* and, *"She charmed everybody and went out of her way to show interest."*

Her most personal moments of pride in seeking to 'give back' have been performed for the **International Organisation for a Just Peace in the Middle East**; a pressure group, which operates in strict privacy. It supports established organizations like the UN and governments and has three aims: 1) To see Israel recognize Palestine and Palestine to recognize Israel. 2) To see a peace process which at the time she joined them, was again underway and 3) To see the creation of the State of Palestine. To help in their own way to make people see the glass as half full rather than half empty in regard to all three aims, the agreed approach for Lady C was to have her talking to journalists to encourage them to write positively about the possibilities of peace, and asking newspaper publishers to do so also. The hurdles were that the Palestinians' reputation right then in the West was very negative, and the Zionist hostility to any peace settlement involving the Palestinians in discussions was very strong.

She felt that in doing her small bit to help with contacts and requests was at least doing something, and hoped that one day their goals and work would contribute toward a solution. Sadly twenty years on we seem no closer to seeing a State of Palestine and Israel and Palestine coexisting than we were then. Both sides continue their rhetoric and intransigence sadly whilst wanting us to believe that they alone have been trying to compromise. I hope as Lady C clearly does, that one day both sides will find a way to bridge their mutual hatred and mistrust, and that the separate States of Israel and Palestine will exist in harmony. Having lived and worked in the Middle East myself, covering a period of over thirty-four years on and off (and having some understanding of the multiple cultures, religious sensitivities and different branches of Islam and Christianity), it's time for both Israel *and a* Palestine State to exist. Now of course with far-greater dark regional forces at play, even a Palestinian State will not change the region's volatility.

By 1998 Lady C had for some time sat on the committee of The **Red Cross Ball**, but she began to recognize, *"that such committees were going from all members being committed by personal conviction, to some, basically becoming a cutthroat business."* It seems that a number of show-biz types were coming onto the scene in those days who were genuine in wanting to use their fame to help raise money; they were altruistic about helping without seeking publicity, but some were only interested in the publicity it gave them and the photo opportunities. She very much shied away from that approach and decided to step back from such committees, and in future would take tables at events and fill them with friends she knew would be supportive in raising money and be of value that way.

I was astonished but not surprised to read of her support for an individual worthy cause in the springtime of 2016. A young bowel cancer survivor, who was only 26 when diagnosed, knowing that their father had died of the disease. An e-Bay auction was run to raise money for treatment, and Lady C had come across it and donated "an opportunity to have afternoon tea with Lady C" in return for a hefty donation to the fund by the winner. A lovely twist to this story is that Lady C's son Dima, who was following bidding on Twitter, very proudly told her that her item was bid for higher than anyone else's donation. In fact, one of the bidders complained on Twitter that she'd really, really like to meet Lady C but was priced out of the market!

What did Lady C do? She told her son to tell the charity that she would host afternoon tea for this lady who got dumped out as well; as long as she donated the price she fell out at during the bidding. *"That way much needed medical treatment got two bites of the cherry,"* she said to me. She never seems to miss an opportunity to help others.

Lady C and a busy life

We're beginning to know one side of Lady C, the woman who one minute may have been at events with The Queen, hosting Prince Edward or Prince and Princess Michael of Kent at a Charity Ball – and the next minute is relaxing at home with personal friends such as Mark and Alexander Sykes or Rona, Lady Delves-Broughton – or popping out to dinner or the opera.

However, there's also another side of Lady C who's just an ordinary woman, mother and friend, who's as happy sweeping the floor or cleaning up behind her dogs or fixing a leaky tap! She's someone surprisingly down to earth and self-reliant, someone who thinks of others before herself.

When I spent a week in London and Goring with Lady C and her sons at the beginning of my research, just before Christmas 2015, I unknowingly was about to do a lot of the local UK traveling and see a lot of people. Not long out of the Jungle, Lady C was suddenly in high demand by the media, but she would not hear of it when I asked if she'd like me to come at a later date as her literary agent had suggested to my publisher. He rightly was concerned not to over-tax her with the media clambering to speak to her. She said she had made an appointment with me, and I had booked my tickets from the US before this all unfolded, and she was going to keep the appointment, as long as I was flexible to conduct interviews around her having to attend certain media events and interviews – she would not hear of me canceling or delaying my trip, period.

You learn quickly with Lady C what are suggestions, and what are statements not to be questioned!

Mind you, so many demands were being put on her time that many of our interview sessions were held in the car between London and Goring, or late at night into the wee hours, or in-between journalists coming or going in the daytime whilst she was beetling about. I'm a great believer in whatever will be, will be, and went with the flow, asking questions and taking notes whenever I could. I love the Jamaican countryside version of this saying, which my mother-in-law told me: *"What is for you, cannot be un-for-you!"*

One evening before we went out to dinner at a local pub I found myself sitting on a chaise longue which was covered in a thick layer of cat and dog hair and placed at the foot of Lady C's bed. I was sitting on the chaise covered in cats whilst the dogs tried to get my attention, as Lady C sat at her dressing table putting on make-up for the evening. It was just like many animal lovers' homes and she was very unpretentious – somehow sitting at the bottom of the bed in this lady's bedroom seemed very normal, as one would feel with any old friend. Her ability to put people at ease through her unassuming manner is very natural.

I sought to balance my notebook on my lap or at one stage, a cat's back, to take notes, as he was not going to be put off his usual spot just because I had got there first! He simply pushed his head under my notebook and wedged himself between it and my lap! By the way, the dogs came to the pub with us (and got a bone each from the barman), and were as good as gold.

What was interesting for me was to watch this busy socialite move from an informal to a formal appointment, and onto an even more formal evening one, numerous times a week. Each day's multiple events required a change of clothes, and she did so with ease and calm. Well, calm most of the time.

Looking back now, those interviews in the car, sitting at the kitchen table or sitting on her chaise whilst she sat at her dressing table doing her make-up, proved to be perfect moments to talk with Lady C, as she was undisturbed by others. It was up to me to vie with the cats and dogs for her attention (in the car too!), but they were times that at least allowed me to ask questions uninterrupted. I found it fascinating that she never hesitated or prevaricated over her answers. She responded straight away to each, and spoke meaningfully, succinctly and with conviction. Listening to her answers to my various questions often left me momentarily speechless and in fits of laughter at what she had to say. I hadn't laughed so much in ages, and she just says it as it is without strained political correctness, which is so refreshing.

There's too much political correctness in the world today from people who think it makes them more important to be 'seen' to be politically correct, when actually they are just masking their true feelings and are often the ones that stab others in the back, which is the ultimate prejudice. Being overly politically correct to me is a sign of weak, false people, not sensitive, inclusive people.

Those moments alone with Lady C were gaps of quiet in her day where her mind refocused and flowed openly with stories and memories – nothing was held back and her opinions were to the point and always with humor. Sometimes looking up stories in her biography as an additional reference point, I found that she had almost word-perfectly repeated them as answers to the questions I was posing twenty plus years later as she had written in the book, and she really was saying it as she had consistently said it and believes it to be.

While she has two housekeepers living-in at Castle Goring and a weekly cleaner in London, and hires chefs and a butler from Royal service whenever she throws more formal dinner parties in London, and now for the Castle Goring wedding business has a specialist catering team, she tends to muck-in at home when things need doing, and like the rest of us does it herself. She was preparing supper for us one evening at the castle, and there was no way that I as her guest was being allowed to help or wash up. I was quickly put in my place and told to relax and fire off my questions for the next part of my research for the book. When I got up in the morning to find Lady C busy mopping the kitchen floor and corridor – as it needed doing – I discovered this was typical of her day. The next moment she's off across the fields giving the dogs a walk before creating serene calm ahead of another hectic day by sliding away for thirty minutes to do her meditation. She meditates twice a day and swears by it to keep her balanced and energized. The level of energy that she has is phenomenal, so maybe I should start taking up meditation again!

A typical day in the life of Lady C goes a little bit like this:

At her London home, we get up and we breakfast, which she insists on preparing herself, then she bathes and dresses. She does her meditation and an early morning of work, correspondence, email and phone calls – creating time to sit and take my endless interview questions in-between. A change of clothes for a formal interview with a journalist from the *Sun* newspaper coming to the house, and then a photographic session with her boys for their Christmas special 2015 magazine. A rapid change of clothes as they leave (the third today), and a follow up call is made to the TV company's limousine office, checking what time their car and driver is arriving to take us off for her show attendance tonight. Then we rush off to the ITV studios, her sons and me in tow. We arrive at their Thames embankment studios for a live charity show, which she has committed to lending her support to. *Text Santa*, with a massive live audience, one minute manning phones with other celebrities and the next, on stage. A take-away style bite to eat is kindly provided by ITV in the celebrity side room before the show, and a nibble is achieved in the after-event room – then the limo back to her house around midnight and to bed. Tomorrow's another day and another packed schedule, always! I'm tired just remembering it all.

At the *Text Santa* charity evening fellow celebrities such as Amanda Holden the TV presenter and Nicole Scherzinger, pop star, singer and former girl group Pussycat Dolls, joined Lady C. Olly Murs the songwriter, pop-idol and 2009 winner of the UK X-Factor was there, as well as George Shelley, boy band Union J's lead singer. When George arrived into the ITV studio's celebrity holding lounge and spotted Lady C, he gave her a huge hug and kiss. Lady C's son Dima got to know George's mum in Australia during the Jungle reality show when they were their supporting their son and mother respectively, and he got on very well with George. A lot of laughter and banter followed!

On top of all this, we were in London at her lovely Kennington home where she has four floors, beautifully laid out and packed with fabulous antique furniture and stunning paintings (but the stairs certainly would keep anyone fit) one minute, and the next minute we'd motor down to Castle Goring on the South Coast of England and might be back in London before midnight on the same day – *or* back up to London the next morning in time for a newspaper interview, then back to Goring to meet with the restoration team that afternoon, and be back in London again that evening. I mention all of this as it's her reality, and it's seriously hectic.

A hectic life, but still time to care about others

Paul Issa's son, Jude arrived in London to study a couple of years ago when he was 19, to do an internship with a major City firm. Whilst her sons were still, most of the time in France, Lady C insisted he stay with her and have one of their rooms and Jude remembered that, *"She took great care of me and I hardly saw her with her hectic schedule, but am forever grateful to her."*

Nicola Croswell-Muir recalled how, going through her own divorce, Lady C was always there for her as someone with a sympathetic ear and wise counsel. So too did Princess Katarina, the granddaughter of King Alexander I of Yugoslavia and great-niece of the Duke of Edinburgh, and how Lady C stood by her during her own divorce in 2010. She's known Lady C for over 30 years and she said, *"Georgie will always help anybody and was always there for me, she's an open-ended story."*

Another old friend of Lady C for 25 years, from his youth in London, is Count Manuel de Pino Montano. The Count is heir to the ancient Spanish Dukedom of Cardona and his title of Count granted to his ancestors is a noble Papal one. When he was just 20 and in London he was going through a very personal and conflicting emotional time, trying to work out who he was, and Lady C took him under her wing and gave him sage counsel. It was for him a moving and pivotal time in his life, in which she helped him to navigate. It was a time when he would discover who were his real friends and who were friends who'd disappear when you most needed them and who had only been there because he was titled. He said that Lady C, *"was always there for me with wise words of support, and many have let her down over the years, yet she still welcomes new people into her life with an open heart."*

When I visited Castle Goring in December 2015 it was thick into the restoration phase, both inside and out, and she was chatting with her English electrician one minute and asking after his mother (his late father had been a British Ambassador) and speaking to her Jamaican contractors the next moment and laughing with them (Carlyle and his son both have broad Jamaican accents and are absolutely top professionals in their trades).

Do have a look at some of the photographs in the book. If you want to see what it looks like now and look at renting it for a private party, wedding or corporate event, please go to: *http://www.castlegoring.com/*

The restoration of Castle Goring came at a time when there were too few qualified heritage tradespeople available in England, and too many projects underway, and Lady C did not want to delay six to twelve months waiting and waiting. She knew that there were great artisans working on heritage Georgian buildings in Jamaica too, and that this problem may be an opportunity to have a mix or local British and Jamaican artisans; people she would know after her French restoration experience, who would 'get' what she was trying to do with a sensitive restoration. In hiring some Jamaicans she could also give those artisans a massive career opportunity of going back to Jamaica having worked on an English heritage restoration project approved by English Heritage, and give them an earnings opportunity and exposure to European restoration techniques that would benefit them and their careers in Jamaica when they returned home.

She wanted to look overseas for some of the tradespeople but, as she said, she had hell with the board of English Heritage. She totally understood and supports their aim and role, but felt that they or the individuals involved, if they meant it or not, seemed to be racially prejudiced because she sought some Jamaican workers, as well as English and EU ones. A short, sharp conversation about her not wanting to go down the route of suing the board for racial discrimination seemed to free up the paperwork approval much quicker and gain approval to bring those people in from Jamaica who she wanted to close the gap of insufficient heritage workers being available in England at the time. Most people would be afraid to take on such a major government body, whereas they I am sure learnt that you do not want to take on Lady C if you can avoid it.

Carlyle is the Jamaican Project Manager who has managed, as an accomplished carpenter of heritage Georgian buildings, the whole restoration of woodwork, plumbing and general stone masonry. The main staircase was a perfect example of stunning restoration, which he carried out. I witnessed his extraordinary craftsmanship, which Lady C said was approved by the heritage board, applied to a staircase that had been left under a broken and badly leaking glass cupola for decades, and which had deteriorated into a rotting dangerous condition. He totally restored it to its former glory it seemed to me.

Carlyle's son Johnny P is an accomplished painter, artist and general contractor, and there were endless miles of high ceiling corridors, rooms and halls, over multiple floors, that all needed painting, and were by the time of the castle's grand "house-warming" Ball held in June 2016, as was the stucco and railings of the Palladian rear of the castle. But Lady C's great pride and joy is the chapel, which was restored by a young artist named Fabiola Umar, and which she intends to use for Mass.

Complemented by an Englishman called John, who was an approved electrician, whose late father was a British Ambassador, Sir Richard Best, all of them were hard working and very professional, and were clearly committed to the heritage goals that needed to be met. Mind you, when Lady C wants something done or thinks things are not spot on, she gives clear, concise directions and follows up to see that everything is done properly. There's little room for misunderstanding with her or any job not quite right going unnoticed. She is fastidious about detail and adhering to English Heritage rules, which she wholly supports.

The Jamaican crew were paid the going rate for the job and got free accommodation provided by Lady C as well. She used specialist UK companies exclusively to do works such as roof replacement and as much as she could through local tradespeople when the skilled craftsman were available. Thanks to being part of the *I'm a Celebrity… Get Me Out of Here!* reality TV show in 2015, she earned just enough fees to pay for the entire roof repair and replacement at the castle.

When somebody asked her what she was doing for Christmas, she said that she had a bunch of pals coming down to stay a few days and a big Christmas day lunch. Asked if her staff would be working or she'd hire her usual cook and butler she said, *"Absolutely not."* In Jamaica Christmas was always a time when all the staff had the day off, and Lady C has always felt the same way. Christmas day is when she and her guests all muck in, and she prepares Christmas dinner for them.

Chapter 9

The private world of Lady C

What has inspired her throughout life?

AS A TEENAGER LADY C WAS influenced - rather than inspired as she explained to me - by Ayn Rand, the Russian born American writer and philosopher who was from the objective school of philosophy. Now if we're honest, most of us will not be quite sure what that means, and so I looked it up for myself and for those who wouldn't mind clarification! In the broader meaning of the term it refers to the ability in any context to judge fairly, without partiality or external influence.

As a child Georgie was seen by many as a gifted painter and whilst she did love to paint – with so much expectation put on her shoulders, she felt that it became off-putting and lost the desire to become a painter. She still loves the visual arts and said something quite prosaic to me, which I think speaks volumes about her craft as a writer; *"I suppose I now paint with words."*

When at school and a model in New York, Lady C wanted to be a dress designer. However, what's sad in a way for someone who has such flair and style is that the whole hysteria thing around fashion as she saw it was off-putting to her. She found that an article of clothing's destiny rose and fell on an inch of hemline – life seemed too important to her to be surrounded by such trivia. That side of things became *such* a bore for her and it drove her away from fashion design and drove her to want to write.

Fashion and the world of everyone being well-dressed influenced Lady C from the very beginning. During her parent's era in Jamaica, *society* dressed well, people turned out *"groomed to an inch of their lives every day"* – fashion itself was not *intellectually* challenging to Lady C though, and *this* was the crux of the problem as she saw it. Whereas writing was just what she needed to challenge her intellectually and it excited and motivated her.

Interestingly, Lady C's father's family has a history of intellectuals, headed by Mai Ziadeh, the Middle East's foremost female writer for the first half of the 20th century in Arabic and French. She wrote about matters of great import in her time – so part of Lady C's heritage is from such a female ancestor and it must be in her genes. Lady C is herself one of a number of cousins who write, and one is Antony C. Winkler, a first cousin and a fellow Jamaican writer. His first novel was *The Painted Canoe* (1986), and maybe his best-known book is *The Lunatic* (1987), which earned him a spot on the bestsellers list and it became a movie in 1991. He wrote two plays and a number of short stories, one of which *The Annihilation of Fish* was made into a film starring Lynn Redgrave and James Earl Gray.

Lady C was inspired to write her first book as she felt born to write, and she felt a burning need to communicate if something was worth saying. She wrote a book of philosophy at the age of 23 and was modeling to pay the rent when she wasn't out on the town partying. When she discovered that her mother had finally gone mad, she realized that she needed to write "substance and shadow" of that story, to name it all so to speak, all her inner suffering, to talk from what she'd been through and what she had faced. She had called her book "*The Substance and the Shadow*" and she wrote its manuscript which was about false values. But the publishers told her that they wanted more material on her herself in the book, and what *she* went through to reach age 25, and to write the book from that perspective. They said that she didn't have a Doctorate in Philosophy to be listened to seriously otherwise, so the peg to hang a buyer's interest on would come from her writing about her own life under her mother, her birth circumstances and how she was raised, and show readers how she came to her conclusions in her book about her mother. It never happened, as she was not ready, nor willing to talk about that publicly at the time. Much, I suspect, from that story landed up in Lady C's later and highly successful book on her mother *Daughter of Narcissus*.

She has said that no one has inspired her so much as *influenced* her. But if anyone influenced her above all others it was, surprisingly due to their relationship, her mother. She was her mother's favorite in the early years despite everything, and whilst as a child that must have been wonderful, after her mother became an alcoholic it all changed and their relationship became horrific – that *influences* people for sure! Her younger sister was sent away by their father to boarding school aged 5, to protect her from the mother, so we're talking serious issues here from the mother. Something I learned in the world of corporate leadership is that poor behavior by others is itself a massive learning on what not to do or how not to behave. In that respect Lady C took away invaluable lessons from this life which she was forced to lead all the same.

Who is Lady C and what's she like in private, as a mother, family, friend?

She is in my opinion and from those whom I have spoken to a very intellectual, *street-smart* and well-educated woman. She literally *hates* saying no to people and is consequently pulled left and right by so many requests for her time and attention. However, she is highly organized and efficient and generally copes well with the strains of her life. Lady C has a memory like an elephant I discovered, and a tremendous capacity to remember names, places, dates, and numbers. I don't know how she does it. I sometimes can't remember what I came into the kitchen for!

Lady C is happy to be curled up with a book in a pair of old jeans, wearing a favorite old sweater and having a cup of tea in the country; her dogs and her cats surrounding her – bed or sofa, either will do for all of them. Like Cinderella going to the ball, the next minute she is in a stunning *haute couture* ball gown with a diamond tiara and matching necklace, leaving her London residence for a glamorous white-tie Ball. Most of the Balls that she attends end in the early hours of the morning, but I don't think any handsome Princes have been chasing her in the following days with glass slippers.

An interesting thing is that she is just as at ease in the company of Royalty at a white-tie Ball as she is walking in the East End of London chatting to local shopkeepers, or nosing around a favorite auction house to buy unique pieces of antique furniture at a knock down bargain price. She may sometimes appear distant and haughty by her stature and demeanor, and her accent might frighten some people off, because they assume she is going to be aloof or arrogant. But to their surprise when they engage in conversation with her, they find her very down to earth, chatty and humorous; she's in her element and people take to her quickly. She is just as at ease in both worlds, and loves both. She loves being peacefully alone as much as she loves being in the company of others.

Let me tell you a lovely quick story that speaks to her ease with people, as it was enlightening at the time for me and does speak volumes as to who she is. We were dashing down the main Lambeth road in London in her car, and *had* to stop in a local garage to get oil – the oil indicator's red warning light had come on accompanied by a few choice words from Lady C when spotted! We hadn't pulled in for more than ten seconds when the guys in the garage recognized Lady C and were excitedly chatting to her; almost simultaneously a lady passing by on the adjoining footpath spotted who it was and dashed up and asked for a 'selfie' photograph – and, as always, Lady C enthusiastically obliged with a genuinely ready smile and asked how the woman was doing. The woman's broad grin and laugh lines around her eyes lit up her face, and the message was unspoken and clear: she was really excited to have taken a photo with Lady C and to have met her. Everyday people just love her feisty reality!

It doesn't get more private than to hear from her sons, sister and cousins, to hear from close personal friends and hear stories and anecdotes about her from them. We're going to hear about her private homes and there are some lovely pictures in the book of some of them too, and you can see those fabulous tiaras and necklaces everybody has been asking about as well, and some of her spectacular couture clothes and ball gowns. We'll talk about her hobbies and habits, and what she's passionate about in life – it all takes us into her *private* world.

You get an introduction and sense of who she is and some of her habits when witnessing as I did, a *Sun* newspaper interview and photo session held at her London home, whilst I was visiting with Lady C and her sons. It was almost Christmas when the session took place, and the journalist and his photographer had arrived over an hour late, and Lady C had a car coming in a couple of hours to whisk her off to the ITV studios on the Thames Embankment for a live show, and she'd have to change beforehand. She was to take part in the live UK nationwide TV *Text-Santa phone-a-thon* charity event, to raise money for three children's charities, all dear to her heart. These were Macmillan Cancer Support, ensuring that no one should face cancer alone, Make-A-Wish, granting wishes to enrich the lives of children and young people fighting life threatening health problems and Save the Children, working in 120 countries to save children's lives. There's a theme around charity support in her life as we've read, from a child to successful adult, she's always the first to lend a hand when asked and she did not hesitate when asked to lend a hand to this evening too.

Needless to say, the journalist got a bit of a ticking off when he arrived profusely apologizing about traffic and a lack of legal parking in the area, for which he was absolutely right. He was reminded about good time-keeping as was his photographer who arrived late too – but traffic and a lack of public parking spaces in London were sufficient to keep Lady C's comments as light-hearted banter more than anything else. They got a good amount of teasing all the same, with the slightly mock tone of a teacher berating children for being late for a class.

She was asked about her fabulous one-liners or quips and whether they were planned and she said with a cheeky grin: *"No, they just come out!"*

The journalist mentioned to Lady C's surprise that she had just been tagged as the second-most Googled person in Great Britain in 2015, and this was the week before Christmas! The most Googled was Cilla Black, the Liverpool born British pop star and TV host, an old personal friend of the Beatles and a British favorite who had sadly just died. What an unusual phenomenon Lady C has become. Not meaning to be the slightest disparaging or rude at all to Cilla's memory, as she greatly admired her, but just commenting on her own position of being the 'second' most Googled person in 2015, she said: *"Goodness, the lengths celebrities will go to, to be number one."*

She talked with the *Sun* journalist about Christmas in her world, and explained that of course she was buying gifts for her grown up sons, things that they needed, as well as giving them some money to go and buy things *they* want, which usually meant clothes. The boys chipped in, when asked, and said that they liked to shop in places like Jermyn Street and Zara for Men for clothes. I learned that she's not someone who really enjoys shopping at all, she generally finds it boring, but she loves getting things like antique furniture and *objets d'art* bargains at auctions. Even so, that's a go in, look at what you want, go for it and walk away. I've been to a few auction houses with her and she has an uncanny eye and sharp bidding skill - having lived and worked in the Middle East over a thirty-six years period I learned to negotiate and barter well, and I could see that innate skill coming out from her Lebanese heritage.

When asked where she buys her clothes she said, *"I have forty-eight years of couture clothes slowly accumulated and have virtually not changed my size. I can still get great wear out of them."* That's the thing with quality classics - they stand the test of time don't they, and what starts off as a high price, in reality is the most low cost long-term value. Lady C is very careful how she spends her money and spends it wisely. For everyday dressing and running around, if she likes something, she might buy it in two or three different colors and pair with jeans and a cashmere sweater.

She always shops in the sales and buys classic clothes in them too I discovered. It's not surprising really coming from a family that owned department stores that she knows the retail merchant business and buys wholesale wherever possible, not retail. She let us into a secret when she said that for most of her life designers have loaned her clothes to be seen in. Otherwise she has bought couture from their 'samples' or items of 'catwalk worn'. When you reach your mid-sixties and you can still get into clothes from your 20s and 30s, lucky you, most women would say I'm sure!

I learned that she's not a shopaholic and that she writes things down that she needs and sticks to it, deciding what she needs up front; she goes into a shop, gets them and gets out. She never buys things she can't afford and is never seduced by advertising! She said to me, *"People like us spend our money sensibly."*

Talking of Christmas, as we sat in the drawing room of her Kennington, London house, it had a beautifully dressed and lit Christmas tree in one corner, nothing else cluttering the room, just the one elegant tree. Christmas for Lady C is always spent with family and dear friends around her, who typically come and spend the night or certainly don't leave lunch until 3 a.m. the next day! She tries not to over indulge, which is probably why she still has a sylph-like body in her sixties and she eats sensibly.

As for food shopping for Christmas, I think I was as surprised as Lady C when she was asked if she did her food shopping at Harrods. She was very clear.

"No, a fool and his money are easily parted!" She buys most of her foodstuffs for Christmas from Tesco's and I can only tell you, she does so for her everyday food shopping too as I have experienced multiple times. At Christmas she adores their ordinary Christmas puddings and mince pies (not the luxury ones, the ordinary ones), *"They are both the very best,"* she said. She may buy gifts for other people at Christmas from Fortnum & Mason I discovered, but she's a Tesco shopper at heart.

The *Sun* journalist seemed quite surprised to learn that she shops at Tesco's supermarket, because like most people who shop there she finds that the food is great value for money. As I have been with her dashing into Tesco both in London and Worthing multiple times, it was no glib comment for a Sunday newspaper. *"People like us don't have to follow rulebooks or what others expect of us. Being well-bred means that you do not have to follow trends,"* she said.

She believes that you should have what you want, when you want it, *'if'* you can afford it. One item that does not come from Tesco is brandy butter, she's always made her own; otherwise, Tesco it is for everything. She goes to Aldi's supermarket but only to buy champagne, nothing else, as they have such great deals on champagne at Christmas she said, as she adjusted her scarf and how she was sitting in a delightful arm chair for the camera angle the photographer desired for the next shot.

Lady C believes that Christmas should not be about money and how much you spend, but it should solely be about having loved ones around you if you can, having guests stay for an excellent Christmas lunch if you can, and celebrate Christ's day. She felt strongly that you should have as good a day as you can afford, no matter how much or how little you can spare. She doesn't count money when she spends it; but that does not mean that she is not careful with her money, she is. It became clear to me that she likes to be generous to others, and spend sensibly and within her means for herself.

And what is Christmas fare typically in the Lady C household? It follows the same pattern year in year out, *"It's always turkey,"* and she has chestnut stuffing, gravy, potatoes and of course a tilt to Jamaica, sweet potatoes; Brussels sprouts for those that want them, but she loathes them like me, and prefers broccoli. Then of course there is Christmas pudding and mince pies, and *everything* comes from Tesco. Pudding is served with her handmade brandy butter, followed by fresh fruits and a selection of cheeses, all from Tesco too, of course. Goodness the woman should be hired by Tesco as an Ambassador, or make their Christmas TV adds, as she is a real Tesco devotee!

When the journalist was wrapping up to leave, he noticed amongst a myriad of silver framed photographs on a sofa table a picture of Lady C with Pope Paul

II and asked about that experience. She explained to us that as a Catholic family, a friend whose family had been ennobled by the Papal See had arranged a private audience for her and His Holiness. It was quite unique as His Holiness normally only saw Heads of State in complete private. Madame 007.5 wouldn't tell me anything else or explain why!

Let's look at what her family and friends have to say about Lady C

So many of her friends are such fascinating people themselves, and her story in the eyes of her friends brings who she is in her private world to life.

When it comes to friends, I know from interviewing people most of my life that somehow in sharing a little of who the interviewee is helps make them more real when reading their views. Telling you such vignettes, as I shall occasionally, with the odd one line quote, is not intended to distract from Lady C's story and what her friends say about her, but to expand it. Each friend's story adds another layer of who Lady C is, from those with whom she chooses to surround herself. They bring the *real* Lady C to life, talking of who Lady C is as a friend. First though, let's get to know her sons a little and what they think of their Mummy, and also some of her family.

Family matters, and no less so to Lady C; especially as her beloved sons drive her to be a success, in order to always provide and care for them. They are young men in their early twenties now and she knows that they are soon to make their own way in the world. Whenever one talks to her about her sons, a glint of unmistakable pride appears in her eyes. It's her time now to prepare to take care of herself for the gentler years ahead, which seems as I write these words a contradiction in terms! Lady C and gentler years somehow do not go together, as I'm not sure in reality she's ever going to stop living at a full gallop and walk calmly through the balance of her life!

Her beloved sons

After huge bureaucratic nightmares and thanks to her friendship with the then Russian Ambassador in London, who opened the right doors for her in Russia, Lady C finally adopted two little boys, Misha (Michael) and Dima (Dmitri). They were given the family name Ziadie-Campbell.

She adopted these two separately orphaned boys from Russia on her own in 1993. She had almost completed the adoption of one boy, only one had been envisaged, when she was told he was no longer available and how about this other one. So she shifted her application to that child. Later, when coming to conclusion for that child's paper work, she was told that the first child was available after all – so she made the decision to adopt both, and did!

She said to me that: *"I've always been maternal and Russia was a country where it was possible to adopt babies."* What had taken her aback when she first dealt with English social services about adopting children was that they told her not to even to waste her time trying in England. Imagine, she was someone who had the commitment, passion, love and financial means to give a normal family life to two abandoned children and take them away from an orphanage, and the British authorities in those days would rather leave them in a home. And this was the 1990s!

At the time, everywhere it seemed, being single was a barrier. It's quite the done thing to adopt as a single mother now, as the likes of Angelina Jolie have, but when Lady C did it, twenty-three years ago, she was breaking new ground; and what a great job she has made of it as we'll hear later from those closest to her. It cannot have been easy all the same and there are some wonderful anecdotes from friends of Lady C about her coping with two strong willed little people when they were small. I suspect when they were bigger too!

Over the early years of the boys' lives the family had lived between a house in Belgravia in London and her Château d'Algayrié in France, both now sold. They currently live at their London home in Kennington, near the famous Oval cricket ground, and Castle Goring in West Sussex on the south coast of England. The boys each have their own rooms at both residences, and in Castle Goring have their own 'wing' with a massive entertaining come sitting room, dramatically decorated for young guys. Lady C has always said in every interview when asked, and told me the same, that everything she has ever done since she adopted them was and is geared to giving her boys a better life.

Misha (Michael Ziadie-Campbell) is photographed in the book with Dima "photo bombing" in the background, which is a great photo and shows their fun-loving approach to life, and the fact that they are so incredibly close. They are both very genuine, lovely young men who have been raised with great manners and consideration for others, who have been well educated and who have to work for what they want. Household chores are a must, and knowing how fortunate they are in life is something that's been second nature to them too.

Misha hopes to get experience in the hospitality industry in running events, learning the industry's ropes and gaining bar and nightclub experience too. Right now his goal is long term either to own and run his own nightclub one day, or when his mother feels he's ready at some time, he'd like to take over the running of the business at Castle Goring in a few years – which he sees himself helping at from day one, all the time – *"Can you see us not being roped in?"* he said!

Dima (Dmitri Ziadie-Campbell) in my discussions for this book, like his brother was very genuine and open with his comments and is looking at career and media options at this time, and has been approached by a number of TV program directors, so let's see how they pan out over time. Both boys have huge hearts. Like his brother Misha, Dima is fluent in both French and English. The brothers enjoy traveling; New York, Paris, South of France and Mexico have all been on the agenda this last year or two.

The three of them are a strong and close team who have fun and like any household with two young twenty somethings, still get told off when things get too much for Mum. I was a guest at Lady C's house one evening for a drinks party and informal dinner with some of her friends in town, invited to come and meet me. We'd ordered a Chinese take-away and were sitting down in the dining room unpacking it. The boys were doing their own thing two storeys up in Misha's room and taking care of their own supper. Lady C's London house's kitchen is aside her dining room on the ground floor (one enters the house up a flight of steps from the garden and outside, on the 1st floor above) and Lady C was about to put empty take-away boxes in the trashcan, when she realized it was overfull. She let off an almighty scream up the staircase which is at one end of the dining table, and demanded both boys came down immediately; whilst letting off a round of expletives that they boys had filled the bin just before a dinner party and not emptied the trashcan. A number of smiles appeared around the table, some raised eyebrows at the expletives and polite attempts were made to carry on the conversation as if nothing had happened. It made me smile because which of us with grown up kids have not lost the plot sometimes with something they have done that ticked us off?

The boys, arriving with thunderous clamor coming down six flights of wooden stairs from the third floor, were harangued mercilessly and - in silence almost - removed the trash and replaced it with a clean empty bin. As Misha was passing me, as I sat right at one end of the table by the bottom of the stairs, he leaned towards me and whispered, *"It's easier when you're wrong just to admit it with Mum. Be quiet, and get on with it."*

What's also worth noting is that when Lady C is with old friends, she is simply who she is, and she behaves as she would if no one was there. I saw from the looks on friends' faces that they love her for being who she is, for being honest and open.

Childhood and schooldays in England

Looking back to their childhood and growing up, the boys have early memories of living in Belgravia in London and around 1996 going to their local kindergarten at St. Peter's in Eaton Square. Later Lady C sent them to Hill House Preparatory School in Knightsbridge, which was close by. Hill House has the distinctive old-fashioned school uniform of burgundy knickerbockers for boys, tan shirts and more often than not the pupils can be seen wearing the uniform's mustard-colored, round-neck sweaters. They can be spotted in little packs walking with their teachers around Knightsbridge. When I used to work in Knightsbridge myself in the 90's small packs of these students could be seen bustling around with their teachers and were a regular sight. This was Prince Charles's first school too. Both boys now appreciate how privileged they are and what their mother sacrificed to give them such a good educational start in life.

Some of their favorite memories are happy holidays with just the three of them. As kids and adults in London or France, or traveling all over, despite how busy their Mum's schedule became, she always made time for them and this they remember and appreciate immensely. She's always busy, and they sometimes see less of her, but on holidays she relaxes with them completely and that's what they value most.

Lady C bought the Chateau in France to renovate and use as a peaceful retreat for holidays and possibly to do some writing there. The boys remember living in a habitable part during the restoration works, and thought they were there for the summer. Lady C wasn't happy with Tony Blair's England and wanted her boys to learn French, and before they knew it, what they thought was a summer holiday became their new long-term home!

Going to a local rural school in France could not have been easy aged 9 with English schoolboy French. Provincial French people were not kind or welcoming either to these *Anglais* kids. *"We were made to feel outsiders immediately."*

When they moved to France and then stayed for school, they had to integrate with kids from the village and many it turned out were quite rough and violent – they learned to shut-up quick, as they were not liked as outsiders. It was their first take on French culture – and they automatically had to band together and be strong up front as a defensive mechanism – the local kids learned quickly that when they tried to pick on one of the *Anglais* brothers they had to take them both on, and that helped them survive those first months as they settled in. It must have been quite frightening after the decorum and genteel behavior of Hill House in London, an upper crust school teaching correct behavior and good manners. The boys quickly learnt street smarts.

The French kids were not very friendly at this stage, but it's not just France is it, maybe it's every country where if you are completely different you are at first kept at a distance. They were taught early on to stand on their own two feet by this experience which is little different to going full time to boarding school, you have to learn to stand up on your own two feet pretty quickly. They did chores like doing their own laundry by age 10, as Lady C needed to board them mid-week and be in London, and yet some of their by now local friends had no idea how to do laundry or get a meal ready. But they did - as they said, *"You learn quickly to do things yourself when obliged to."*

Slowly and over time they felt that they got to make a few friends in France and treasure them, and realize now that it's easier for kids than adults. They love France, but prefer to live in England. They'd been to Hill House prep school in London first as we know and their Mother's friends whom they grew up around are mainly based in London, so there was nothing in France historically for them when the Chateau was sold. They always knew they would return to France frequently to visit the many dear friends they had made over the years, and they do, regularly. Dima for example went on to do his degree at college in France. He didn't think he'd ever graduate, but he did in early 2016 at the Toulouse Business School where he got his degree. Misha is moving now towards getting the further education he wants for the hospitality industry as we read earlier.

Memories of Jamaica and family

Thinking of their Jamaican heritage through their mother, some of the boys' earliest memories of Jamaica were when we they were quite young, and when they had spent time with relatives getting to know everyone and seeing Jamaica. It may have its crime and social issues, but it is still a tropical paradise and for kids would have been a magical introduction to their heritage.

I remember my first visit to Jamaica in the early 1970s. After my flight had landed, I was driven after dark by my best pal's father Don Garcia up to their home at Guava Ridge, way up in the Blue Mountains. I awoke the next morning at the crack of dawn literally, mainly from jet lag. I dressed and wandered through the open French windows of my bedroom across to the edge of a manicured lawn. I sat on a bench seat under a tree which was perched on the edge, as that part of the mountain dropped away hundreds of feet to the valley below. In the distance I could see the enclave of villas at Newcastle, where British troops would retreat in the stifling heat in the summers in the 1800s and 1900s to avoid mosquitoes and malaria. In the far distance I could just see the capital city of Kingston. It was slightly chilly, the clouds were for me strangely pink from the rising sun over the mountains, unusual tropical bird sounds greeted me and the bleating of goats from the valley below echoed upward. I was surrounded visually, close and at great distance, by tropical foliage and sweet smells. I am sure that the boys had their own unique first morning in Jamaica too, despite being little at the time, as it really is a special and unique heritage.

Dima recalled one trip to Jamaica when they were still not yet teenagers and that their Mum's friend Nicola Crosswell-Mair, who was at the time building a new home up in Jack's Hill in Kingston, had taken them to look at the house. She has come to visit them in London frequently over the years since and she flew over to England for Castle Goring's house-warming Ball this last summer.

When they were aged 17 they went to Ocho Rios in Jamaica for two weeks holiday, swam with the dolphins, zip-wired and spent lots of time with their Mum's family, getting to know everybody now as young adults; going to Polo matches, which they've always done, and just relaxing on this tropical island.

In London they have found it easy making friends with people from the Jamaican community, and always find that they are people that 'give openly' to others, who instantly welcome strangers and try and make them feel at home. Some may not be very well off, but as Dima noted, *"what they have they'd share with you."* They love the influence Jamaica has had on them from their mother's heritage, and her family and friends, and their own visits there. Jamaicans they agreed are nice; they are respectful people, wealthy or poor. Their Jamaican roots through their mother transferred to their upbringing for sure. They learned, as I could have told them, that Jamaican women are strong – they are typically highly influential figures in the family. Misha's favorite Jamaican food had to be oxtail stew with rice and peas, which just happens to be one of my favorites! Now there's a man after my own heart! Reader, if you have never enjoyed the delights of an oxtail stew with Jamaican rice and peas and a lovely gravy, you have not lived!

The boys also recalled a lovely holiday they'd enjoyed in Turkey one year. A number of Lady C's friends who'd been invited as her guests on a gullet cruise in the Turkish Aegean Sea sailed around the islands and the boys greatly enjoyed the whole experience, and thought it a memorable and magical trip. One interesting story that emerged tells us a lot about Lady C's character. It's a story a couple of her friends who were her guests recalled too…. One of the lady guests had a few too many drinks one day it seems, and one of the Turkish crew got a bit too familiar with her and another female guest; he crossed the line in his behavior toward them basically. Lady C from all accounts put a stop to that straight away and put him in his place very sharply. The crew and this particular chap were not unsurprisingly a little subdued in their behavior after that. When they had docked one evening and the crew had gone ashore for a break and after some time it had become very late, guests wondered if they'd ever come back, but they did, nothing said. At the end of the holiday the crew member in question, by his demeanor and subdued look, assumed that he was going to be in serious trouble when Lady C surely would report the incident to the boat's operator as they docked. To his surprise, she said nothing to the boat's owners. *"That's her really, she doesn't hold grudges,"* Misha said. The crew member made a mistake; he got it in the ear from Lady C (and Tony Hadley knows what that's like) and it was forgotten.

They seem very thankful for their mother's determination and strength to never back down from a fight brought to her either. She's always strong, she never gives in, and gets back up when she's knocked down they felt. *"It's easier for us boys to take her on and manage her as we know her the best."* Lady C has her ups and downs like everybody, but overall she is a happy person, and she loves clowning around and can be very humorous; *"She's such a teaser,"* Dima said.

Apparently she's notoriously five or ten minutes late for everything - but if the boys are late by just one minute you'll see her limited patience coming out, and she's going to cuss them – but woe betide them if they tell her she's late. Sounds like many a parent to me!

Her time in *I'M A CELEBRITY… Get Me Out of Here!*

Dima had flown down to Australia during his mother's time in the *I'm a Celebrity... Get Me Out of Here!* reality TV show, shot in the Australian tropical bush. I wondered what he had learned from the experience of going to his mother's defense. He sadly found out that a lot of people are two-faced as he described them and start to show their real intentions over time and under such pressure. He learned too that others wanted to use his mother's fame and sidle up to him to get close to her. He could not help anyone like that he felt and was not seeking attention for himself. *"A lot of show business bull,"* as he said. But then he made some genuine friends from the experience, as did Lady C, so I think on balance he got much out of the experience.

As he'd said of Lady C during a number of Australian and international newspaper and TV interviews at the time, she was an inspiration to him and Misha. With age and the passage of time he realized that many youthful errors could have been prevented by listening to her advice. He said of her performance in the Jungle that he was, *"intensely proud of her."* Of her behavior at times during the show, he admitted: *"She gives as good as she gets and loves controversy."*

He told me that he was not surprised by what happened in the show, or attacks on his Mum, but what was interesting for him to see was how some of his friends' attitudes changed towards him because of how they perceived his mother's behavior in the show. It was shocking for him to see some peoples' real colors, people he thought were true friends. He learned quickly then as to who stood up for them as a family and who didn't: *"It sorted the wood from the trees of who was a genuine friend of mine or not, and I said goodbye to some."*

Their mother's books

When asked what they think of some of their mother's books Dima said, *"I've never read them."* When people talk about them or their mother, they just talk about the woman they know and the fact that she always tells it as it is, whether talking to her own sons or a stranger. They admitted that they both have to look up words she writes or says sometimes, as she often uses big words; only because she has such a grasp of the English language and they know that they learn so much from her as she really is someone who knows how to use words.

I have noticed that she is very deliberate with her choice of words and means exactly what she says. She hates being paraphrased, and if she uses particular words within a particular phrase, God forbid the journalist who quotes her out of context. I hope both boys decide to read my book of their mother and find it fair and engaging, a history of their mother's life to-date, and approve of it.

Her boys reflected on how, *"Mum has to frequently deal with crap from people,"* and that she writes it off generally, but can dish it back and yet usually maintains calm. If you have a go at her, she is going to have a go back, make no mistake. They were clear that they don't always agree with her, but that's family isn't it? They know that their mother has always given them what they need, and if you want something from her, she'll expect them to be as kind and supportive when she needs something. *"We are a very tight family unit, the three of us,"* Dima said.

The boys' view of family and those in their mother's circle.

Of everyone in their life they have felt closest not unnaturally to their wider family as well as their Godparents. Lady C's cousin Enrique and her sister Margaret (Lady C's sister Puss) are especially valued; they live near each other in Boca Raton, in Florida.

They also feel close to numerous of their mother's friends, some of which of course are also Godparents or honoree Godparents. People such as Peter Coleman, Count Manuel de Pino Montano, David Hornsby and Rupert Dixon and many others they feel close to also. They said they had so many who cared about them and were around them growing up, that they lose count of them all but value each and every one of them.

Peter Coleman, Lady C's famous "Gusband" and a Godfather, has always enabled them to feel that they can open up to him and tell him anything. He does not judge them, but gives his advice and has no motive in doing so – he's very relaxed and so loyal to Lady C they felt. Some friends in her past have not been faithful, as both her sons and one or two friends shared with me, and some have taken advantage of her and been a negative influence.

As we were concluding our last chat together Dima was being approached by an American TV company about doing a reality show, and was in talks with Britain's ITV 2's producers for the reality-show *Love Island*. A slightly raunchy show where a guy who's single retreats to a villa with a sexy Lady Chosen for him I believe, and they are left, hopefully sometimes off camera, to discover each other.

The fun part for Dima would be the show's habit of bringing the mother of the single guy to view the prospective woman he's taken up with and give her view! I can only imagine the verbal battering any particular young woman would get if Lady C took against her – the viewer ratings would surely be double that night in anticipation! Any reality TV show featuring Lady C's boys would hit the jackpot on viewer ratings without doubt.

The future for both these boys looks good. Of course, they will have had walk-on parts in *Lady C and the Castle* reality TV show this past summer too, the UK reality show of Lady C renovating her castle and topped off with a house-warming Ball for friends and the glitterati. The boys have been well educated with Lady C's foresight, and they know how much they are loved – she gives them a lot of freedom and trust, and treats them as the young men that they are. They are absolute gentlemen in their manners and behavior, are typical lads about town, appreciative of the advantages they have been given in life, dress well, adore their mother, love fast cars *and* the ladies, and they know how to have fun. Girls, as at the time of writing, they are available and only ever speak of women with respect as they've been raised!

Sibling and Cousins of Lady C proved charming and refreshingly honest:

I found Lady C's sister Margaret (Puss) and Lady C's cousin Enrique quite delightful. My wife was thrilled that I had been in touch with her old school friend Puss and we plan to pop in for a "gals reunion" and meet Enrique the next time we're down in Boca Raton, which is usually a couple of times a year.

I learned so much about Lady C from these bosom members of her family, and both seemed to show a genuine and great closeness beyond the norm of siblings and cousins without making a point to try to, it was just obvious. One of Margaret's early memories was that they never carried cash around as children in Jamaica, they just signed for things anywhere, a shop, a restaurant etc. as, *"Everybody knew we were Ziadie girls and they would send the bill to Daddy, who would promptly pay. I had a sweet and delightful upbringing as the youngest child."*

Talking of family, Margaret related that Georgie was her Mummy's favorite and that Georgie had always said that it was not easy as their Mummy expected so much from her. Whereas it became clear in talking to Margaret after a while that she wasn't close to their Mummy at all, far from it, but was very close to her Daddy and his sister.

She always felt closer to their Ziadie relatives than her Mummy's side of the family. Sadly Lady C and Margaret's Mummy had a major alcohol problem, and Margaret only found out years later that her mother was a complete alcoholic at the time, when aged 5 she was sent to boarding school. She didn't understand at the time why her Daddy was sending her away, but she learned many years later that it was the best way he could protect her. Goodness, how hard it must have been for such a wee little soul. It was hard enough for both my wife and I and our three children when they each went off to boarding school in England aged 11. We were living in Hong Kong or England, but I cannot imagine how a 5 year old copes, or how her father coped. It must have been a huge heartbreaking wrench for him too. One cannot help but think what affect it must have had on her mother also, despite her alcoholic issues; during lucid moments, she must have been aware that her baby child had been taken away from her.

When Margaret and my wife were at Servite Convent there were people of every background and race, from Lebanese like the Hammatys, Marzoucas, Ziadies, etc. and those of colonial British heritage like Mary and Cathy McConnell, and those of Chinese heritage like the Lynns, and African and Indian Jamaican heritage. They were just one group. There were no racial barriers or racial thoughts of any kind and it truly was to follow Jamaica's national motto, *Out of Many, One People.* If there was any distinguishing by the nuns at this school, it was not because of race, or color; it was because of economics. The Ziadies, like the Harveys, were seen as a well-to-do family and seemed to get looked after that much better by the nuns than the less well-off, Margaret recalled – that was something evident even to a small child.

Georgie was in the eyes of her sister Margaret like a mother figure during her school days in Jamaica, and also at college in England; Lady C had a flat in London at the time that Margaret was in senior education there. She took care of everything for Margaret it seems. Margaret remembered that once when the driver was not around for some reason in Jamaica to bring her home for a weekend, Lady C took responsibility. If there were no family driver, no one would have picked Puss up on the Friday evening as her Daddy would have been working, and mother plastered most likely. So her sister Georgie, without permission, simply took their Daddy's car and went and picked Margaret up, and no one was any the wiser. Her big sister was just there, and was to be there on many such occasions for her little sister.

Lady C from various accounts always drove fast and as Puss said, *"We'd fly around the roads over Mount Diablo like a lunatic to get me back to school on time after a weekend break or a holiday. She's always been a fast driver."*

Something that came out strongly from both Lady C and her sister Margaret was that they both loved their brother Mickey. Anyone who knew him commented to me how lovely a man he was, and he was someone that always loved his family and protected Lady C. Margaret remembers that, *"Georgie could be very mischievous,"* and recalled how she had one time come to pick her up from school using their Mummy's car without permission. When their parents asked how on earth Margaret had got home as they'd not sent the car and driver yet, she only said, *"Oh I got a lift with someone to save you worrying."*

After the Servite Convent, Margaret was sent to The Priory School and then to school in England. Later when she worked in America she naturally gravitated to the Jamaican community – suddenly she found herself not being invited to parties or people's homes because she was white – the first time she had come across racial discrimination and she was shocked. She recognized that their father's generation were very snobbish, and when she was home from boarding school he might take an afternoon off and take her to one of his clubs – but there were no barriers that she was aware of because they were of Lebanese heritage rather than British. Certainly she felt no difference because of their race. When she was growing up, most of the past barriers of race or colour were rapidly coming down.

Her cousin Enrique, looking back to childhood and growing up with Lady C through the years, remembered that as first cousins they were unusually close and always had fun. As Lady C became more and more feminine in other people's eyes, nothing changed for Enrique, Margaret or the family and friends of their age groups around Lady C. They just knew her the way she was and as kids, it was who she was. Was she effeminate? Looking back, yes but no one close to her thought of that at the time. She was just a favorite cousin for Enrique for example, and Georgie was Georgie, and they were very close. *"Our mothers were very close, so we became very close too,"* Enrique said.

At aged 10 Enrique was sent off to boarding school so he only saw Lady C when back in Jamaica on vacation from school in England. He remembered that on one such trip they were taken to a Chinese restaurant near Lady C's home. It was owned by a very wealthy Chinese man and they'd all sit together, both families, and no one thought of race or ethnic or cultural differences, parents and kids, all were friends.

Losing people at this time of high murder rates in Jamaica affected every family and it affected Lady C's too. When Georgie's grandfather Lucius Smedmore was murdered Enrique was at school in England, and he wasn't told about it until much later. It was in May 1963, alone in the house at the time as his daughter and her husband were on vacation, that Lucius was brutally murdered by a thief who broke into the house Lady C said, and as I've reviewed in *The Daily Gleaner* newspaper. Lucius was battered by a plank of wood with nails driven in it, and later clubbed to death as the thief came back. The thief was eventually caught and found guilty of murder and was hanged. However, Lady C never got over the horrendous loss of her beloved grandfather and of having seen his body and blood in the house, shortly after the murder.

There was also 'cousin Bobby', who had been burned to death. Bobby was not really family, but his parents were close family friends of the Ziadies, and they were referred to as aunt, uncle, etc. out of respect by the small kids – Lady C shared a flat with Bobby at one stage, so Enrique felt it was very traumatic for her to lose him. Another aunt was murdered whilst sitting in her car at the traffic lights.

The 70s were a very tough time for Jamaica as they were for Lady C in her own life, whereas cousin Enrique and Lady C's sister Margaret were both away at boarding school so were sheltered from everyday reality. Margaret might have to walk a mile from the school's main building at Servite to the tennis courts, but she felt safe. Michael Manley was then Prime Minister and his daughter Rachel was a friend of Lady C and Mickey and was often in the Ziadie family home. Unfortunately, as Margaret said, *"Michael Manley may have been good to bring greater education to the masses in Jamaica, but he did so much damage to the economy that we're still trying to recover."*

When Georgie was in New York she always wrote to her little sister Margaret, something Margaret remembers well. She'd send her Sonny & Cher records and Margaret saw a lot of Lady C's New York friends who she'd bring down to Jamaica on holiday.

Enrique's mother bought a house in London so she could be with him in England during his vacations and visiting weekends off from boarding school, and so sometimes it could be two or three years before Enrique came back to Jamaica, as he'd spend holidays with his mother in England.

Both Margaret and Enrique would say that anyone who spends a few days with Lady C knows how intelligent and bright she is. At age 17 and in New York, her level of intelligence was way off the charts in IQ terms Margaret recalled. Lady C really can talk with knowledge about almost any subject as Enrique and his friends found, and she has an excellent memory for facts, dates and names.

Neither Margaret nor Enrique had gone to Lady C's wedding, as one was in Canada and the other in London and neither could get away at such short notice as it all happened so fast. They met afterwards however when Lady C and Colin Campbell came to Jamaica for the wedding reception which her parents organized at the family home. Enrique remembered that they seemed well suited and all seemed relatively okay.

A day or two after the wedding reception a small bunch of them went to Devon House for lunch, Margaret, Lady C and Colin included. Devon House is a fabulous old plantation house set in stunning lawns and grounds in the center of Kingston, and is retained as an example of Jamaican colonial heritage. It has from the 70s had little boutique restaurants; shops and ice cream parlors set in some of the adjoining courtyard buildings, which are all very popular with both locals and tourists. Margaret was a bit taken aback when Colin turned to her at lunch, unprovoked, and said that she was a spoiled brat! She was just 18 and excited for her sister and Colin, and chatty, and he was so obnoxious to her she recalled. Lady C apparently jumped down his throat for having a go at her little sister so uncalled for and for no real reason. Needless to say, Margaret from that moment onward took a dislike to him, as he, *"rubbed most people and me the wrong way; he seemed to offend everyone so easily."*

The whole family remembered with disbelief when Lady C came back to Jamaica from England some time later to recover from having her jaw broken by Colin, and having to be hospitalized. She was scarred and bruised and they simply could not believe what had happened and how any man could do that to his wife, let alone a so called gentleman. Lady C's father never said much about it so I don't know what he thought as no one recalled anything he ever said about it, whereas they said her mother liked Colin as he was a Lord and she said little about him negatively to the children, now young adults themselves. Maybe Colin and Lady C's mother shared something by both being alcoholics, as Lady C has said.

Margaret remembered a nice anecdote from when she was around 19 and she went with Lady C and a few others up to Newcastle when she was home from college in Canada (Newcastle is a hill station up in the Blue Mountains above Kingston in Jamaica I mentioned earlier, and one of my personal absolute favorite places, where many of those who can afford a second home have houses up in the cooler air to retreat to at weekends or during summer holidays). The sisters were having a philosophical discussion, and Margaret said something or other philosophical to the listening group of friends. She remembered that Lady C said, *"Out of the mouths of babes comes wisdom, don't dismiss her."* I think listening to Margaret and having spoken with Enrique, they still hold Lady C in the highest regard, and see her as someone who is super intelligent, smart, sweet and very perceptive. *"She's quick to pick up on things and she listens,"* was another comment made to me.

Margaret remembered another anecdote that speaks to who she sees her sister is. At the time that Margaret was working in the US and earning very little and renting a flat, she could barely afford to get sick; but unfortunately she did. Margaret needed medicine, but didn't have the money to buy it and did not want to ask her parents. Lady C found out she was ill from one of her friends, and the next day rang Margaret and told her that she had just wire transferred $500 to her bank account and to go buy the medicine she needed. She always took care of her little sister growing up. Margaret remembered that if she were home from school for a weekend, her sister Lady C would often, *"spoil me and buy me some dried, bittersweet sour plums as a treat."* My wife had a passion for these bittersweet sour plums from boarding school days too and still does, it seems to be a Jamaican thing, and no doubt hailed from the ethnic Chinese families. I saw that because when we lived in Hong Kong in the 80s and 90s we found the same dried, bittersweet sour plums all over Asia, but especially in Hong Kong and Singapore.

Lady C's Gusband

I'd like to share his story of a special friendship with you, separate from the other friends of Lady C, as after all he is her Gusband, Gay Husband so to speak, and very close to her. I think that merits talking about him separately and I remember very well the enjoyable interview which I had with Peter Coleman.

In a TV interview at the end of the reality TV show in Australia, Lady C was described as having 'a secret' 35-year relationship with a gay man she calls her 'Gusband', Peter Coleman. They had first met back in 1981 in England and became close friends and remain so to today. Peter has often said in newspaper interviews over the years that the term 'Gusband' perfectly sums up their unconventional relationship, and that many of their mutual friends have adopted the term to describe their 'dancing partners', who partner them in the dance of life, but not in bed.

"Georgie may have been born an aristocrat and then married into the British aristocracy but she doesn't care about where someone comes from or what they do," according to Coleman. *"She cares about good manners and fairness above all things."*

On the subject of snobbery, he revealed that Lady C wears Ugg boots and jeans around the house and loves to eat McDonalds, so what's snobbish about that?

"Above all, deep down my Lady C is a very kind, and extremely sensitive woman, who has been severely hurt throughout her life," Peter said.

The media may not have known about Peter Coleman and assumed his relationship as a 'Gusband' was a secret which they were now exposing, but everyone who knew Lady C knew of her special friendship with her 'Gusband', it was no secret to any of them, nor has their relationship ever been hidden.

Peter is from an old Irish family and whilst he does not live with Lady C, they frequently will stay over at each other's homes after late night events, often travel together, and he is her main dance partner. Like her Peter loves to dance, and is a dear friend to Lady C and both her sons.

I spent quite some time chatting with Peter, who comes across as a hell of a nice person. He's charming and humorous and very loyal to Lady C. Peter told me that Lady C and he met in 1981 in Tetbury, Gloucestershire at the home of Lady Edith Foxwell. Talking of meeting Lady C, he said that as soon as they met they hit it off and realized that they knew many of the same people. Lady Edith Foxwell was a rather high profile socialite from the 1940s – 70s; it was at a House Party that Lady Edith was throwing that they met. She was a colorful British eccentric known as "The Queen of London Cafe Society" in the 1970s and early 80s. In the 1970s she began running the Embassy Club in *Mayfair*, which was London's first modern *New York*-style nightclub and which attracted many celebrities, including *Marvin Gaye*, who became a frequent guest at Lady Edith's estate (and her lover at one time it's been said by some). She was one of the few members of London society who remained close friends with Margaret, Duchess of Argyll, who was a dear friend of Lady C's.

From Peter's various comments it was clear that he recognizes in Lady C an extremely strong character who is who she is, and who is someone in her own right. Some people fail to understand her and look at her from a British point of view he felt, and fail to see the Jamaican and Lebanese bias built into her character – that's the key to understanding her we both agreed.

A great commonality of their relationship is that they both love dancing.

With her boys, even when they were very young he made a conscious effort to never talk down to them. When they went to live in France and he saw much less of them, he famously bought them crossbows when he visited Lady C's estate there. I'm not sure if that was for target practice on the locals, bearing in mind what Lady C has to say about the rural French later in the book! Over the years he's taken the boys to watch Polo matches at Cirencester Park in Gloucestershire and when the Princes Harry and William were also small the four boys landed up playing football on the sidelines together.

As Peter says, Lady C has, *"a good sense of home."* He talked about Lady C's appreciation for the arts and fine furniture, saying that she has a good eye for colonial and British antiques, and reminded me that she's had to work very hard to get where she is and is a great example to the boys. He said that a great expression that sums up Lady C would be that she has, *"sophistication without the snobbery."*

I must tell you a little side story on furniture and antiques when talking about Lady C. When I was with Lady C bobbing up and down on the road between London and Goring Castle, we twice stopped by at rural and London auction houses. On this occasion Lady C had to have a quick look at what was coming up that might fit well with both her décor and the period of Goring Castle to help fill some of the vast new rooms which she had acquired. She's very tech savvy and while I was busy interviewing her after supper the next evening at the Castle she was keeping an eye on the auctioneer's website on her laptop, on her lap, watching live for her 'lots' to come up. She managed to buy two or three pieces which she wanted at the price limit she'd set herself.

She lost one set of antique French needlepoint chairs – a few expletives let rip, a few times! Relentless and tenacious, she called up the auction house and asked them to offer the buyer X% more to get the chairs off them, as she suspected they were bought by a dealer who, for a price, would let them go. They were, and she was right, and in the morning they accepted her offer and she got the set of antique chairs she wanted! Six French needlepoint armchairs if I recall correctly.

Peter talked of Lady C being splendid with the boys, teaching them to be gentlemen. They are growing up fast and now in their mid-twenties, capable, knowledgeable and they managed in France much of the time on their own, boarding mid-week locally as I've said earlier. Peter said as I have that, "*They work as a team, the boys.*" Peter felt in conversation that the boys appreciated France and their rural community and eventually blended in with the local kids. They learned to be fluent in French and English at the same time, which was Georgie's goal for educating them in France; they became fluent in French by only speaking French at school and when boarding, and only speaking English at home at weekends with Lady C. They can deal with kings or the man in the street, are assertive yet polite, and Peter said they will be very successful aids to the business venture of Castle Goring.

We talked about Lady C's work with various charities over the years, and Peter said, "*She has a great understanding of European aristocracy and knows a lot of the families personally, and their relatives.*" Having sat on various charity ball committees and chaired many, her commitment as we've read has been constant since a child. She doesn't need the glory and doesn't seek it when it comes to charity work.

I asked Peter about his special relationship as 'Gusband' of Lady C as he sees it. He said that Lady C bounces ideas off him. He tells her what he thinks and tells her if she is wrong – he floats alternate ideas until she comes around basically. He felt that he was a calming influence on her. He was smiling in his voice as he told me a story about Lady C hating his driving, as he is a slow driver, whereas she drives fast. She apparently hates taking directions and snaps at Peter when he tries to guide her. He said, "*I'll tell her stop the car and go do her trans-meditation and be calm – few can talk back to her as I do and get away with it.*"

Talking about her time in the Jungle reality TV show, he said that to call her a snob as 'the boys' did in the show is so far from the truth, as she's as easily found in McDonald's in a pair of old jeans and Ugg boots as she is at a ball. He said this explained her public fury at her jungle campmates, including Tony Hadley, who if anything is guilty of inverted snobbery. I've accompanied Lady C myself shopping at Tesco on a number of occasions when interviewing her for this book, and she's been in a pair of old jeans, an old sweater, Ugg boots and an old coat covered in dog and cat hair, and trust me, she is no snob! You have to take her as you find her, but she brushes up well!

Speaking of Lady C's clothes and jewelry he felt that she has great dress sense but for Ascot one year he remembered that she put on one of her Chanel couture suits before leaving her home, which he did not think suited her. He said to Lady C, *"It looks awful,"* but she was determined to wear it and ignored him. So he added, *"It looks like an old woman's clothes,"* and said nothing else. There was silence, but his remark seems to have done it, as apparently she took it off immediately and changed into another outfit without another word being said!

She does have wonderful jewelry and Peter spoke about her jewels as one of his favorites from her five glorious tiaras is the Gold Citrine one. *"It makes her eyes light up,"* he said. The emerald one and a sapphire one are admittedly very special, whereas the rubies are just spectacular in his opinion.

Speaking about her quick wit, Peter gave me an example of driving in a car with her in Jamaica when someone shouted out to Lady C from the roadside, *"Go back to your country!"* And she shouted back, *"Some of my ancestors came here in the 1500s. Yours came later. This is more my country than yours, so if anyone is leaving it should be you!"*

He talked about her loyalty to individuals with a charming anecdote. They had gone together to a Polo match at Cirencester Park with another friend, Lady Anna Brocklebank. Lady C had arranged to stay the night at Peter's flat. After the Polo, they were all invited to a cocktail party at Lady Apsley's house. The Earl and Countess own Cirencester Park. Lady Apsley upon hearing that Lady C was to stay in Peter's one-bedroom flat immediately and thoughtfully suggested to Lady C that she must stay at Cirencester Park house instead. But Lady C said, *"Thank you so much, but I've already arranged to stay with Peter."* She's very loyal Peter felt and there she was giving up the opportunity to stay the night in grand style, and no doubt a rather grander breakfast Peter speculated, to stay in his one bedroom flat, because she had said she would and didn't want to offend him.

He sees it as terrific that a major trait of hers is loyalty to people, and that she only expects that in return, which came out strongly in my multiple interviews of her friends who virtually all said the exact same thing. She's terribly hurt by individuals who take advantage of her and has become wary of people sometimes.

She is, in reality, believe it or not, a very soft person," Peter said. "So many take advantage of her, and when people have and let her down, it deeply upsets her."

He remembered once when they were in the South of France together with lots of people – mostly his friends who didn't know who Lady C was – she just fitted in, and clearly from all we read and hear from many, she simply gets on with people very easily. She has a fundamental interest in music, classical particularly, and she has her meditation as Peter reminded me. Meditation gives her time to reflect and gather her thoughts, and she meditates twice a day without fail, morning, and evening. Peter said, "I think it helps her cope with so much; she's always bright and engaged for everyone."

What some of her friends and those that knows her say about Lady C?

I asked myself the question, why print what her friends think about her, as surely it will all be similar praise anyway and a collection of *how wonderful she is.*

However, I realized that most know a lot about Lady C from childhood and through decades of negative press and right up unto today. Hearing what Lady C's friends had to say about her, the private Lady C, and hearing personal anecdotes of her from her friends would bring who she is to life. It would also give us a balance of opinion too – against the past years of often, negative comments from those that actually do not know her on a personal basis. So talking to a spectrum of her friends was valuable, and it became obvious to me as I began to track down and interview some of Lady C's friends, that they were a fascinating group of people in their own right. Hence, I have given a very short history of each person or their family background where appropriate.

There are of course countless more friends of Georgie who I did not get to interview, so apologies that I didn't get to you had you wanted me to, *mea culpa.*

Many of her friends' remarks pointed to one identical thing; that she was a very loyal and decent friend who always stuck by people, especially in times of need. Literally all were independently unanimous in this comment, or that she was, as many have witnessed over the years, an amazing and successful single mom.

As part of my research for the book, many people's quotes were captured, including Lord Colin Campbell from his press statements made late last year. What 'everyone' has to say about her adds up to the collective layers of stories that built in front of me as I concluded my research and interviews, and enables you to see holistically who she is as a person today – that's why I tell their stories too – they add to and do not detract from Lady C's story. We'll hear from members of Royal families and friends from around the world, including from her new friends made on her Jungle Reality TV show.

A subtle tensing around the eyes suggested that the mention of Lady C's name did not sit well with the former Jamaican Prime Minister, Eddie Seaga, when I interviewed him at his office in Jamaica. Eddie became the *Prime Minister of Jamaica* following the General Election of October 30, 1980, when the *JLP* won a landslide victory over the incumbent *People's National Party* (PNP) and Michael Manley, with the largest mandate ever in Jamaica's history. A mutual friend Nicola Crosswell-Mair had kindly obtained the appointment with him for me, mainly for me to understand the history of Lebanese migration, about which he was very knowledgeable. He was clearly momentarily uncomfortable in his older generation mindset with the concept of someone of gender adjustment, but respected the woman and the family. He said to me that he knew Lady C's mother Gloria well, and that his family the Seagas were quite close with them as friends. However, he never really knew Lady C who was a child in those days (he's a generation older and is 86 now), until getting to know of her and her life story in the 1970s when her marriage and divorce hit the headlines.

"As multiple Lebanese families in Jamaica," he said, *"this sister married that person, that brother married this sister, and in the end many of us are related as cousins, as we, the Hannas and Ziadies are. Often, distant cousins but nevertheless, related. At the top of the Lebanese society tree were the Issas and Hannas and then the rest of us."*

Some of Georgie's friends I interviewed over breakfast in local restaurants, others I interviewed in their offices or their homes, often times morning or evening being offered drinks and food as is so the custom in Jamaica and indeed in Middle East communities too. Pop over for a drink and chat may land up as dinner, as it did with Bruce Terrier and his lovely wife! Some of Lady C's friends fell into both categories, being Jamaican and of Middle Eastern heritage.

A number, like Cookie Kinkead who has known Georgie since aged 12, talked of Georgie's mother being a very challenging woman and mother, and many remembered her acerbic nature and drunkenness. Lady C's mother was known by Cookie, Suzanne Chin, and some others who prefer not to be mentioned, to always be sitting on the back verandah of the house, cigarette in one hand, drink in the other, and worse for wear. The front door invariably in these slightly insecure crime laden times kept shut, and the front of the house seemingly closed up and too much trouble to have a go at, Cookie remembers that you could never leave the house unnoticed as you had to go out via that rear verandah and there was the formidable Mrs. Ziadie – and she missed nothing!

Cookie is a famous Jamaican photographer known for using natural light who lives in Kingston, Jamaica. Her first official assignment was in the early 70s with Bob Marley and The Wailers for their album *Catch a Fire*. She has done work for most glamor magazines globally, like Vogue and Elle, and photographed

Royalty (Prince Charles is just one) and celebrities (Bono, Naomi Campbell, Ralph Lauren, Kate Moss, Bob Marley, Quincy Jones – you name them, she's photographed them), and is engaged in multiple projects at any given time.

A number of people recalled how Lady C can be very tough but that she's very genuine and kind-hearted at the same time, again oft repeated comments made by multiple people who know her. Many remarked that whilst having sex changes or adjustments is today common place news and no big deal, even transgender surgery, in the 70s having surgery to fully realize becoming a woman was not commonplace and frightened many who did not understand it. Paul Issa said to me, *"She constantly reinvented herself from that day onwards and has remained sincere, real, warm and to be honest, what you see is what you get."* Paul asked his early twenty-something son to come and chat with me as how he had been treated by Lady C in London, and what he said typified who she was.

Paul Issa is from one of the two most prominent and first pair of Middle Eastern families to migrate to Jamaica in the mid-1800s. Paul's forefathers are Palestinian and from whom half of all Lebanese/Syrian migrants to Jamaica got their helping hand to start business. His father went on to found a hotel chain of which *Couple's Resorts* is most famous today in the Caribbean. He and his brother also run the Issa Foundation, a major charity in Jamaica.

Many, many of Lady C's friends commented at how she has always had and always retained a huge sense of humor, and how she has risen to every challenge and met it head on. Most felt that yes, she has a feisty temper, but then it's impossible they thought not to have scars with everything she has had to face in life, and not respond to a life of attacks as she has.

Lady C's friend Gloria Seigert, an eminent psychologist, helped and encouraged her throughout the writing of her book *Daughter of Narcissus*. Gloria said to me about Lady C that, *"She is so entertaining, with an ability to laugh at herself, which is an enjoyable quality."*

Her dear friend Nicola Crosswell-Mair said of Lady C that she charts her own life's course with her own hands. She may snap when pushed, but otherwise is a very calm and poised person.

Almost all I spoke to described Lady C's cleverness at turning out immaculately dressed every time, glamorous and stunning. Nicola said of Lady C that, *"She has a great sense of style."*

Another empathic theme that evolved as I spoke to people in Jamaica, England, America, Mexico, the USA and elsewhere, was that of divorce. A number of Lady C's friends have over the years sadly divorced and like her dear friend Nicola, Lady C was there for them to help them go through such a personal and

Lady C looking fine on the staircase of her château

Lady C in a couture gown by Murray Arbeid
one of Princes Diana's favourite designers

Lady C stunning in couture

Lady C's sapphires,
diamonds and pearls

Clockwise from top left: Lady C's emeralds and diamonds, old cut diamonds tiara, rubies and diamonds, pearls and amethysts; *centre:* diamonds and citrines

Bianca Jagger, Charles Delavigne and Mark Shand in 1978

Peter Batkin, Princess Olga, Lady C, Mrs Batkin, Michael Ziadie, and gusband Peter
Coleman at the Russian Ball, Lancaster House 2015

Lady C at The Oldie

Lady C every day style

Larry Lamb the actor and TV star with Lady C in Grasse, France in the early 80s

Lady C's elegant drawing room in her London home

The Grand Salon of Lady C's Château d'Algayrié

Lady C joins TextSanta

Lady C with Misha and Dima at TextSanta

Lady C with Ferne McCann and presenters Ant & Dec. I'm a Celebrity
Get Me Out of Here! 2015

Dima in Australia
supporting Mum during
I'm a Celebrity Get Me
Out of Here!

Lady C admires Chris Eubank's six-pack in the Jungle! *Inset*: The very dapper Chris Eubank, former World-boxing champion

In the Jungle Lady C hugs Kieron coping with the stress. *Inset*: Kieron Dyer professional footballer

In the Jungle with Jorgie Porter, Lady C eating camel's lip, with her knife and fork of course!

The castellated gothic front of Lady C's Castle Goring

The Palladian rear elevation of Castle Goring

Restoration work on the West Wing at
Castle Goring 2015

The new roof on the West Wing of
Castle Goring

The Grand Staircase at Castle Goring
under renovation after decades of water
damage from the glass dome

1st floor balcony beneath the glass
dome, looking into the family chapel at
Castle Goring

Lady C with her fans in Tesco

Another fan of Lady C takes a selfie

With fans in Tesco after coming out
of the Jungle

The young love her

Fan has Lady C's tattoo on his leg – his
sister proudly shows us on her phone

Portrait of Lady C by Cookie Kinkead

traumatic stage of their lives. What's special about her in these women's minds is that, *"she was there for me when I went through divorce and at other difficult times in my life,"* as Nicola said.

Nicola Crosswell-Mair whose father was the last Commissioner of Police of Jamaica up to Independence, is a dear close friend of Lady C. She is a Jamaican socialite who runs a holistic medical practice in Kingston and has at various times in her career been PR Manager for Air Jamaica in London, run her pal Diana Marley's Travel Agency and had her own Art Gallery. She was at Lady C's house-warming Castle Ball this last summer in England, dressed in a stunning gown for the Ball and wearing a glorious tiara.

I love a phrase Nicola used to describe Lady C, which is pure Jamaican: *"She's tallower!"* It means someone who is strong and wiry!

Just to side-track on the circles and how they complete, Cathy McConnell (who became Cathy Christopher) mentioned earlier, was at school with my wife Mary in Jamaica and Lady C's sister Margaret, and Cathy at one time shared a flat in Reddington Road in London's Hampstead district in the early seventies with Nicola Crosswell-Mair and Diana Marley, when she was Diana Cooper. I did not know my wife Mary then, nor Lady C, but knew these gals well!

These girls were part of my circle of mainly Jamaican friends in London in the 70s, my being a Buckinghamshire boy. Many of the guys had been sent to London to study for their degrees, and many of the girls were sent to finishing schools in London, like St. Godric's College in Hampstead. These are schools for young women that focus on teaching social graces and etiquette, and, by the 70s, culinary and secretarial skills, as cultural rites and preparation for entry into society.

The likes of Nicola Croswell as she then was, Diana Cooper and Cathy McConnell; Max Garcia, Joanne Couper, Margaret Hebden and Donna and Marilyn Cadien; Paul Travis, Donnie and Dianna Souter (his sister Carolyn), Clive Huish, Chris and Lillian Foreman; Richard Bayley and Becky Aspinall, Pippa Bogle, Johnny Mafood; Nicola's sister Jane Crosswell, Michael Lewis and Anthony Cooke – a great crowd of primarily Jamaicans in London in the 70s. That's the link that saw me meet my Jamaican wife, and thirty plus years later saw me meet Lady C in London through Nicola, hence why I mention 'the gang'. They taught me about Jamaica and Jamaicans, introduced me to Rum and Reggae and introduced me to Jamaica itself.

Most of Lady C's friends who I spoke to would agree that Lady C is an accomplished hostess who takes putting on a lunch or formal dinner seriously. She's often described by her friends as someone who's a very generous hostess and very down to earth. She is seen as someone who is independent minded. It seems that despite her celebrity and fame, she keeps close ties with family and friends.

Charles Hanna, a dear friend of Lady C's in Jamaica, said to me as I interviewed him in his private theatrical library that, *"She may come across as brash sometimes, but in reality she is very much herself. She is very soulful and marvelous."* He talked about growing up, and his being himself somewhat of a socialite in the community when Georgie was just coming into her own; and now, as he slows down in age as he said, their roles have switched and Lady C has become a great hostess. From what I gather, Charles is still quite a socialite and famous for entertaining in great style. He loves to travel and is admired for his extraordinary home and collection of antiques, and his support of the opera, ballet and the arts. Charles is an opera and ballet buff.

Charles Hanna is the scion of the other founding Lebanese family who were the first to migrate to Jamaica in the 1800s, and whose forefathers built up a huge retail and property empire in Jamaica, which at one stage covered nine city blocks in the capital. It was from the Hannas that the Ziadies got their helping hand when they migrated to Jamaica, a wheeled cart and fabric material, financial loans and then their first shop to rent. He lives at the amazing family estate *The Knole*, Stony Hill, up in the hills above Kingston in Jamaica, set in acres of pristine grounds.

Yet another common trend in talking about Lady C is her friends perceiving that she is one of the most frank, honest persons that they know. Never telling a lie and telling you as it is, whether you like it or not was frequently repeated. As Rona, Lady Delves-Broughton, said to me, Lady C does not suffer fools gladly and being positive seems to be her secret in life. She added, *"Honesty can be tough to take. You may not like what she is going to say, but it's always the truth."*

Rona and Lady C met at the Berkeley Hotel and she said that in those days she and her husband might eat out three or four nights a week. As London was very cosmopolitan, you'd know half the people in the restaurant. Nowadays because London's housing market has meant that a great proportion has been bought up over the years by Arabs, Chinese and Russian, *"most people one knows have moved further out, so you can go to old haunts and recognize virtually nobody!"* she said.

Rona, Lady Delves-Broughton, who is Godmother of Misha (one of Lady C's two sons), is known as the First Lady of Lloyd's of London. She's also Managing Director of The House of Britannia luxury goods shopping web site and lives on the family's 800-acre estate in Cheshire or her home in Kensington in London. She is very close to Lady C and talks to her almost daily, and they frequently attend the theater, ballet and opera together.

Lloyd's of London for our non-British readers is generally known simply as Lloyd's, and is an insurance market located in London's primary financial district, the City of London. It is not a company but rather a corporate body governed by the Lloyd's Act of 1871 and subsequent Acts of Parliament. Lloyd's serves as a marketplace within which multiple financial backers come together to pool and spread risk. These underwriters, or "Members of Lloyd's", are a collection of both corporations and private individuals, the latter being traditionally known as "Names".

Quite a number of Lady C's friends, not unsurprisingly keeping in mind her own earlier career, were famous models in their day, and they had all met in London or New York on the catwalk circuit or through the Ford Agency. Those ladies remember Lady C being generous to the extreme, being very human and absolutely one off, especially when many reflected on what she had to climb through in life to get to where she is.

Just as many women friends recalled personal horrid experiences in their life and how Lady C would appear out of nowhere to help, Lorraine Vidal is one of those. She recalled how when her daughter was taken deeply unwell from depression in London after giving birth, social services took the baby away and despite a long battle to request custody of their granddaughter until its mother was well, they seemed hell bent on denying them that right and placed her in foster care. They even flew at UK taxpayer's expense someone to their Long-Island home in New York, and determined their lifestyle was too grand and not conducive to raising a baby! Lady C swung into action and helped them with legal precedents which finally saw them win a court case and the right to care for their granddaughter, but Lorraine will never forget what a nightmare it all was and as she said to me, she has no idea how they would have coped if it wasn't for Lady C's help and support.

Lorraine told me a lovely story that speaks directly to Lady C being so down to earth. They were entertaining dear friends, Elizabeth Taylor and Tony Curtis when Lady C was visiting her and her husband's Beverly Hills home. Elizabeth Taylor sat on her own for ages in her husband Bernie's private home movie theater watching an old film. Lorraine found her slightly intimidating and said that she would often just turn up at their house and want to be on her own and watch old films in their theater. Well this one evening when Lady C was there, Bernie said after dinner that he was taking everybody for drinks in downtown Beverley Hills, and took off with Tony Curtis and Elizabeth Taylor in Bernie's Excalibur car, and told Lorraine to take Lady C in his Rolls Royce and follow. Bernie took off, but embarrassingly the Rolls would not start. Whilst Lorraine was fumbling around trying to find the number for AAA to call the breakdown service, Lady C jumped out of the car and asked her to open up the hood and she started fiddling with the engine, then shouted to try it again, and it started! Lorraine said, *"She is so resourceful – she literally will do and try anything."* No wonder then that she did not blink at joining the Jungle reality TV show.

Lorraine who lives in Long Island, New York, was a Christian Dior model and cover girl in 1976 when she first met Georgie in London. She became Lorraine Cornfeld when marrying Bernie Cornfeld at his Beverly Hills Mansion *Grayhall*, which sold in 2015 for US$29 million. Cornfeld is the late billionaire best known sadly for the IOS mutual fund collapse in the US in the early 1970s. They were personal friends of Vidal Sassoon, Warren Beatty and Victor Lownes, to name but a few of the big Hollywood names, as well as Tony Curtis and Elizabeth Taylor who were very close personal friends.

Lady C seems to have a well-earned reputation amongst her friends as being someone who is willing to try anything, anytime and as one of her friends Princess Katarina of Yugoslavia described her to me, *"She is an open-ended story and has always been kind to me."* HRH met Lady C around forty years ago and commented how Lady C would help anybody and recalled how she came to her support during the divorce that HRH went through herself. She explained how many of her and her former husband's friends kept their friendship with her, and while some did not Lady C was always there for her.

HRH Princess Katarina lives in England and is by birth a member of both the Serbian Yugoslavia Royal Family and of the British Royal Family; her father was HRH Prince Tomislav, the second son of HM King Alexander I of Yugoslavia, her great uncle is HRH Prince Philip (HM The Queen of England's husband), and his mother was Princess Alice of Battenberg, being HRH Princess Katarina's maternal great-grandmother.

Common amongst friends remarks were that she is certainly feisty but speaks her mind, plainly and with well-chosen words. Just as frequent a common remark was that she makes people laugh. Princess Olga Romanoff said to me that, *"We always make each other laugh, and you can't ask for more than that in a friend can you?"*

During the UK TV program, Channel 4's *You Can't Get The Staff*, Princess Olga was filmed trying to hire a new assistant for her gardener whilst Lady C was filmed holding a grand dinner party at her home in London with a butler and chef whom she regularly retained for such events.

Princess Olga Andreevna Romanoff was born in England and is a descendent of the House of Romanoff, Tsar Nicolas II's great-niece, the daughter of Prince Andrei Alexandrovich of Russia, the last Tsar's nephew and her great-grandfather was Tsar Alexander III. Her father was the son of Grand Duchess Xenia

Alexandrovna, sister of the last Tsar, her father's uncle. She is a leading member of The Romanoff Family Association Committee and lives in Faversham in Kent, England in her 13th century, 33 room home - and has known Lady C since 1971, and became a close personal friend from 2000.

Sticking with that sense of humour, another friend, Baron Marc Burca mentioned that what he loves about Lady C is her slightly naughty sense of humour, which he sees as her Jamaican personality coming out; and he loves the European colonial coyness he thought. He added, *"She's very much a product of her age, of liberty and freedom, as the 70s were."*

I remember seeing the TV program that he next referred to, which was the same one mentioned above, Channel 4's *You Can't Get the Staff*, in which Lady C was having a dinner party at home and the program was filming it. She had an ex-butler of the Prince of Wales called Grant Harrold helping organize the evening and serve her guests. Grant now runs his own butler training agency and etiquette consultancy. Lady C had a great private dinner party with a chef she had used before in the kitchen as well. Fellow guests were the likes of her friends Princess Katarina, John Rendall, David and Rupert and others, making eight guests in all with Baron Burca.

Somebody present mentioned that they were non-domiciled to the UK and whilst they did keep to the rules, anyone seeing them might think they had broken the amount of days rule that they are allowed in the UK without paying income tax, so they didn't want to be caught on camera. Marc said, *"Of course, they were in virtually in ever camera shot to everyone's great amusement when we later saw the show on TV."*

Marc Burca was the founder, and previously owner and publisher of the City of London's *Boardroom* magazine until 1994 (a bit like the Harpers & Queen of the corporate world in the UK as he described it). They ran a Social Column which as I mentioned earlier Lady C wrote for some years. He's been a good friend of Lady C's of many years standing, and a fellow Ascot racing enthusiast who lives in England.

Hardly anyone failed to mention Lady C's passion for her cats and dogs, always Springer Spaniels ever since Tum Tum, her gift from James Buchanan-Jardine. Like Muffi Hiss they flagged Lady C for her warmth of friendship and as Muffi uniquely described her: *"Lady C is like a mosaic with her intriguing background and life."*

Muffi Hiss, I just love her name, lives in Sarasota, Florida, has known Lady C for some thirty plus years from when she was working in London. She is a well-known artist and went through Lady C's adoption of her boys with her when living in England and had many a story to tell of the fun times they all had, which contributes to the below story from her friends.

Apart from concurring like many others that Lady C makes her and others laugh all the time, Mary Michele Rutherfurd said that she's a real tease too, very Jamaican she discovered, and a great romantic, which she felt they had in common. She described Lady C as someone who had femininity that just rolls out of her, more than any woman she knew. She felt that Lady C's story and the life distress that she has been through, as a woman, meant that you feel it; "*She is the ultimate female friend,*" was her personal take on Lady C.

Mary Michele mentioned that Lady C had stayed with her and her parents for a while whilst she recovered after being hospitalized by Colin, and how she had dropped an enormous amount of weight at the time, and understandably was a wreck; and yet look at her today.

Mary Michele Rutherfurd is a Metaphysical Consultant who lives in Miami and Connecticut, and is the great granddaughter of former American Vice President Levi Morton. He's the man who accepted the Statue of Liberty on behalf of the United States from the people of France. She was educated in Manhattan and Gstaad, Switzerland, while her parents were immersed in the studies of Hinduism, Vedanta and Carl Jung and she later attended the Sorbonne, the school of literature at the University of Paris. Lady C had met her in their modeling days when Mary-Michelle was with the Ford Modeling Agency and did work for virtually every magazine and label such as Vogue, Elle etc., was the face of Miss Selfridge and performed on runways in London with Lady C.

I've talked earlier in the book about my amazement at the level of energy Lady C has at her age, and how through her meditational recharges twice daily, she just keeps going. It was Chris Eubank who said to me during our interview that her energy is her genius combined with her intellect. He added, "*She is not afraid to be non-politically-correct, which has all gone too far.*" I absolutely agree with Chris and it is sad that too many people hide behind a pretense of being correct and mask their negative true feelings to others, or use any potential as an excuse to attack and bury people. Such a corporate behavior which I have witnessed and whilst it is absolutely right to have no prejudice on race, color, size, gender or anything like that, even light banter humor can be seized on, typically not by the individuals themselves being talked to, but by over-zealous PC bystanders to score brownie points against another behind their back – a 'no smoke without fire' whispering occurs, a bit like brown nosing! The world needs more Chris Eubanks and Lady Cs who say it as it is, without intending to offend unless they are attacked first.

Chris Eubank is a British former professional boxer who held the World Boxing Organisation middleweight and super-middleweight titles for five years, scoring victories over six world champions in a career that spanned thirteen years. He was born in the UK of Jamaican parents, a country he spent his early childhood in and then tough teenage years in The Bronx, New York. In the 90s he won Britain's Best Dressed Man award, and the Best Dressed Sportsman award 2001. He is an anti-war campaigner, Ambassador for the gambling charity Gam Care, has designed clothes for the Savile Row tailors Cad & Dandy. He now coaches his son who's commenced an international boxing career like his father.

As for Lady C being different as she grew up, her friends like Suzanne Chin who was a neighbor and Cookie just saw "Georgie", they didn't see somebody who was different as her cousin Enrique said earlier. Georgie was just Georgie and they all loved her. Georgie was their Georgie; there were no questions to ask.

Susie remembered that Lady C was brilliant at making clothes, which supposedly being a boy shocked some people. One New Year as teenagers Susie asked Lady C to make her a dress and she didn't want to, so she threatened to sit on her until she did, and laughing I am sure, she did, and Susie remembers how brilliant she looked in it. I could sense the laughter in her voice as she recalled this story as if it were yesterday.

Susie also knew all about Lady C's birth circumstances and how she was raised, as they spoke about everything together as teenagers. She described Georgie as holding a cigarette in a long white cigarette holder, head held high, and sashaying through a crowd with great elegance and self-confidence!

When I spoke to many of Lady C's friends about her days in New York and broken marriage and divorce, they brought much support and empathy. Susie remembers Lady C when going up to New York on her own aged just 17, and having a successful modeling career. She felt that she lived a high pressure life to some degree and that when she came home for vacations to Jamaica she often would spend time in Susie's home to just get-away from it all and unwind. No pressures, no family, nothing to explain to anybody.

Roll forward a few years and she remembers all too well when Georgie appeared with her new husband Colin for a wedding reception in Jamaica. She remembers vividly being by their pool one-day relaxing and Colin was there. She noticed that he was heavily drinking and that his mouth and face were frequently fixed in a very negative, aggressive demeanor, which she found very odd; she could see that he had drifted off, apparently thinking of something which clearly made him cross. It struck her as odd she said, *"For someone who had just got married and I instinctively felt he was bad news."*

Colin's first meeting with many in Jamaica seemed to leave mixed emotions. Nicola Crosswell-Mair remembered at the wedding reception in Jamaica that Colin was very good looking, attractive, tall, but not overtly social. Her tone of voice and facial look of slightly raised eyebrows indicated to me that Lord Colin's behavior was certainly not appreciated by her. Words were not necessary, her face said it all.

She was happy for Lady C, but felt sad a few years later seeing that Lady C's life seemed to be one step forward and two back, as someone sooner rather than later would seek to hurt her, husband or the Press. Yet she witnessed Lady C take all these knocks head on and come out the other side stronger.

Charles Hanna recalled being in New York at an art gallery in 2005 and met Colin Campbell for the first time, obviously long after the divorce. He said that, *"I found him by now unattractive in looks and behavior, not a nice person at all."*

Lady C's heady London days of the 70s were remembered by quite a few, especially her modeling friends. Rona, Lady Delves-Broughton, remembers meeting Lady C in the main restaurant at the Berkeley Hotel. Lady C was with Janet, the Dowager Marchioness of Milford-Haven, whose late husband the 3rd Marquess was cousin to Prince Philip. She met her again shortly afterwards in the company of her friend the Duchess of St Albans's annual pre-Ascot party. She explained how many of the group had a set calendar and routine. She also said how London was affordable then and that most people lived in Mayfair, Kensington, Chelsea and so on, but that her children's generation can't afford to and most of her pals live outside those districts now, as everything is so expensive.

Muffi Hiss remembered that the London of the 70s was so different to what it is now too. She recalled them as carefree times where no one was out to impress anybody; they just enjoyed life, and lived it large. People were good sports and fun, and if you were fun and amusing you could go anywhere and were invited to hordes of parties, as Marc Burca has said to me too.

Muffi who now lives back in the States, in Florida, at the time lived in Cheyne Walk in Chelsea. She was a member of the Chelsea Arts Club, and Lady C and Muffi would often pop down and might stay the whole afternoon drinking and chatting. She remembered one occasion when they were so engrossed in conversation that they suddenly noticed everything quiet and still and everybody staring at them as they laughed out loud; only to discover that lunch was long over and a funeral reception was about to take place!

She mentioned to me that Lady C's long time antagonist Nigel Dempster, the *Daily Mail* social columnist who seemed to hate her and wrote nothing but negative reports on her, once accused Lady C by rumor mill of hitting her children. Muffi said how could he know, and all of us who knew her well had witnessed nothing but brilliant parenting from this single mom which would put most mothers to shame. Marc Bruca thought Nigel hated her because he fought to get tittle-tattle from the outskirts of society as a journalist, whereas Lady C was 'in' society so knew things first hand.

Of her time in the Jungle her friends either had or hadn't seen the reality TV show in England, but those that did had interesting comments to make. Rona believed that there clearly was over-editing, causing unnecessary tension beyond that needed to grip an audience and drive viewer ratings. She thought it excessive as she only ever saw Lady C attacking and never being attacked, and yet as fellow participants in the show said, it was usually her responding to an attack that came first against her. Lorraine in the States saw YouTube clips of the best parts, as the British TV was not available outside the UK. She said that Lady C looked like she woke every day ready to do battle, *"And I thought yes, she's on top of it!"* She added, *"Let's face it, her life has been one challenge after another since birth, and she has pulled through it all."*

Princess Olga thought Lady C did splendidly in the Jungle and took her hat off to her, she thought her an amazing women for going into it. She had herself been approached about going in the Jungle and was considering it when they must have found Lady C she said, as the next thing she knew, Lady C was arriving in Australia!

Mark Sykes thought Lady C was hilarious in the TV reality show and said that he and his wife Alexandra voted non-stop for her! He said, *"She was the only person worth watching!"* Mark and Alexandra Sykes are a fascinating couple not just because they are lovely people, but because of their families. Mark's family due to the Sykes-Picot line and his own ownership of a string of gambling casinos, and Alexandra's late father a retired President of Ecuador.

Annette Balfour-Lynn went on the Eamonn Holmes TV talk show to defend Lady C and complained that she thought there was clear evidence of ITV over-editing which was very unfair, making Lady C out to be the sole antagonist. Something, remember, that Kieron Dyer the England footballer and fellow contestant agreed had happened. She added her experience of being with Lady C after she returned from Australia, and said everybody recognized her in the street and wanted a 'selfie' photograph with her, and crowds gathered around her wherever they tried to go. But do you know what she said, *"She was completely at ease with her new-found celebrity status and happily took part in every 'selfie' request."*

Annette Balfour-Lynn is an English socialite and former editor of *Now* magazine for Sir James Goldsmith, and met Lady C some thirty-five years ago. When she worked for *Now* magazine they'd met at the Savoy Hotel, just clicked, and became life-long friends.

Kieron Dyer, the former England and Ipswich professional football player, has continued to build his friendship with Lady C after leaving the jungle and the reality TV show as we read earlier. In July this year, Lady C opened his wife Holly's new beauty salon in West Bergholt, Essex, *Beauty at the Byes House* during its official opening weekend. Lady C said, *"I know Holly is going to make a big success of it."*

What are Lady C's hobbies and most loved activities?

She loves the ballet, recitals, concerts, and piano music, violin and orchestra music – a wide swathe of visual and musical genres. Lady C likes a broad selection of composers such as Bach, Brahms, Schubert, Liszt, and Beethoven. Her taste in music is classical clearly and I discovered that she also likes Alexander Scriabin, Rachmaninoff and Rimsky-Korsakov.

Asked what she loves the most if she could only follow one thing, it was the ballet. Lady C recalled a story she's told before, that when with her boys, who must have been no more than aged three at the time, she took them to see the ballet, *Nutcracker*. It was being played in the original production, which is magical and enchanting. *"Misha was so transported he jumped up and down with joy,"* she said of the ballet that the boys witnessed for the first time.

The next year she took them to another performance of the same ballet. Aged four now, they could still go into the ladies powder room with Mummy being toddlers and were in the powder room when little Misha said to his Mummy: *"It's boring and last year was good."* She replied, *"Darling, you have just received a lesson in the difference between the truly great and the second rate."* A woman behind her, as only the English can be she said, interrupted and took strong exception and ticked Lady C off for her child's comment and hers. Into the unknown the brave go when they know not with whom they enter battle! I was poised, waiting for Lady C's response when she was telling me the story, as it would surely be a Lady C classic. She had replied to the woman, *"Just because you don't know the difference doesn't mean my children have to be kept ignorant – please butt out of our conversation, thank you very much."* At which point the woman was dismissed, with a flurry of petticoats no doubt, as Lady C left the powder room with her sons in tow.

She is very passionate about attending good art exhibitions and has many friends in the theater world. Her friend Rona, Lady Delves-Broughton, supports many events herself, which they frequently attend together. In February 2015 she went to a Carol King gala, and she took Rona, and she loved the musical, as indeed she loves all musicals. She loves some operas – but doesn't stretch much beyond Italian composers, some Mozart and some Wagner maybe – but she is not into heavy opera and not modern opera. Lady C has many friends who are artists too and is often to be seen in art galleries supporting the display of friend's works.

Chapter 10
Her jewelry, homes and the French!

LADY C HAS A FABULOUS SELECTION of jewelry including her famous collection of five tiaras. She also has a collection of matching necklaces, earrings, bracelets and rings, which are kept in a London bank's safety deposit vault! I have included photographs in the book of some of this collection as so many people viewing the reality TV show have asked about those famous five tiaras; not to share them with you would have been a sin.

They include a wonderfully decadent tiara set with rubies and diamonds, and ones with sapphires, diamonds and pearls, with emeralds and diamonds, with old cut diamonds and one with gold citrine and yellow rose and white diamonds. Enjoy the photographs please.

There are a number of photos in the book too of Lady C's couture, which I know a lot of the ladies asked about also. I've chosen some of Lady C's charming outfits and ball-gowns, which show her with multiple hairstyles to suit the occasion. She always styles her hair herself.

Because she's a sample model size, she has collected some of her clothes over the years from different couture houses. I thought the ladies reading this book would like to know which designers she's favored over the years. She has commissioned outfits and ball gowns from the likes of Tomasz Starzewsky (Princess Diana had a number of outfits designed by him), Givenchy, Valentino, and Dior. Balmain and Balenciaga sit in her wardrobe, as do a few outfits from Murray Arbeid (Diana used him too), Lanvin, Luis Féraud and of course Christopher Lynch, an English-West Indian designer who she likes.

Personal wealth

The net-worth.com celebrity-watch earnings and wealth site lists Lady Colin Campbell as: an English author and socialite, with incredible wealth. A huge chunk of her fortune originates from her books, such as Diana In Private; The Real Diana; The Royal Marriages; and The Queen Mother, the Untold Story. As of 2015, Lady Colin Campbell's net worth was *estimated* by this tracking site to be slightly over £6 million (around $8.6 million), plus her property portfolio.

Her private homes over the years

There's a photograph in the book of her childhood home in an exclusive residential area of Kingston, Jamaica. No longer the family home, nor as grand as it was when she grew up and now modernized, but it gives you a sense of what it once was. It formerly had over five acres of lawns and its gardens and flowers which her mother was so proud of were fabled, Lady C said.

I decided to list Lady C's homes here for you, for which there are photographs of some in the book. There's a lovely photo of Lady C's former home, the Château d'Algayrié, in the Domaine d'Algayrié, Teillet, within the Languedoc-Roussillon-Midi-Pyrénées region of southern France - and a lovely shot of the beautiful drawing room or Petit Salon of the Château furnished by Lady C, which is off the magnificent ballroom or Grand Salon. The local village only had around 450 inhabitants. The Château was built in 1820 by the prominent Foulché-Delbosc family and has twelve bedrooms. In 2001 it became her summer residence and having conducted major restoration work she put the Château up for sale in 2008. She gave up on France.

Lady C had this to say about living with the rural French.

"The French are arrogant, impertinent and nasty!"

Clearly from that statement Lady C decided that in the end she did not like the French and yet she had started her venture of living in France with such respect and enthusiasm for the French and living there. Maybe she's typical of her generation and those of Lebanese heritage households in particular, as most Lebanese of good families that I know were brought up to speak French and to believe that French style and culture led the world. She was taught that they were *the* most civilized race, the leaders of global fashion who had *the* best cuisine – she went to a fashion school with close links to that French industry too – it all made sense that she should see a Château in rural France as a summer residence when she reached that stage in life where she could make such a dream come true.

But when she lived there and owned the chateau, it was a nation in crisis. All the old expectations which she had were gone, and as she said of France, *"After 35 years of socialism they were all but destroyed and certainly, no longer the leaders in anything."* She was sad to find that the French people were bitter and nasty towards each other, and said that, *"To know them is to loathe them."* Clearly an early Brexit warning was being shared.

Lady C's Château was set within a farming community with sheep everywhere and marvelous local cheese production. Her neighbors, with whom she tried hard to become friends, were mainly hard working honest people; however they spoke 'appalling' French she said – so it was not easy for any of them to communicate with or accept even each other I suspect. Wealth and class played no part in it she was quite sure; *"It was pure ignorant French behavior on their part."*

She eventually found a few who became friendly over time and *"one couple"* who became good friends, but they had led a very international life so were not your average locals it seems. No French friends then otherwise, over seven plus years of trying. After much effort trying to make friends in rural France, Lady C found that, *"The French were not worth the effort."* So, in the end, she decided not to keep trying to assimilate with such people. She had nothing in common with most French farmers – who only talked about sheep and cows – so to be fair to them, she realizes that she was not an easy neighbor to have, but most made no effort to welcome her either, and her tone in making that comment to me was one of regret, as I suspect she had truly hoped to have found a niche in that country.

I have a very dear English friend from the days when we lived in Bahrain in the Arabian Gulf, who moved with her French husband to a small village outside Paris, twenty plus years ago it must be now. She said that despite all her efforts she was made to feel very unwelcome for the first five years, and that it took ten years and having taught English to most of the village's children for almost all of that time just to be accepted. *"However,"* she said, *"I am still 'the' outsider."* It reminds me of some English villages with the same attitude. Country folk generally do not welcome outsiders, no matter where they are in the world, which is their sad loss.

For Lady C her home in France was a place to go and chill and be happy in her own company at least. Despite local people, it proved a good place to unwind and rest, so it worked for her, and she didn't need to worry about people outside of her Château walls; shades of revolutionary France?

To restore the Château after she had purchased it, she used English artisans initially so as to have no issues over language with detailed restoration work, which she thought could be a nightmare of misunderstandings. However, they proved somewhat lazy and ripped her off she felt, so she got rid of them. She called in local French artisans, wanting to put her money into the local community, but they were *so* arrogant and sought every opportunity to rip her off and were even worse than the English apparently. Wealthy English aristocrat and Chateau names may have come together to create a "Caching" opportunity, which is sad, as whoever did a great job at a fair price would, with a Château from the 1800s, likely have a long-term repetitive source of income. Heritage buildings need constant repair, as I well know, as my wife and I owned a 17th and 18th century property in the English countryside at one stage of our lives, and it constantly needed something doing. Lady C gave an example of the Château needing a quote for a new boiler. The local builder quoted Euro 26,000 and she got it done by a local English builder she found living in Southern France for Euro 6,000! That sort of greed does embitter people, and it doesn't lend itself to honor nor trusting local tradesmen either does it?

The French system is so regulated, locals will charge top dollar and do other jobs at the same time as yours she discovered, so nobody gets proper service. She felt that this was not ethical and meant that your simple job of say, two days, can take nine months to complete. *"It's a senseless system and a classic socialist system collapsing,"* she commented.

France's economic indicators this last year of 2016 suggest that the economy has lost some steam, in part due to the ongoing strikes over a controversial labor reform bill, to increase the work-week from only 35 hours, and make it easier to hire and dismiss people. The standoff between the government and hardline national labor unions continues, despite the French parliament pushing the new laws through, with neither side willing to compromise; there seems no end in sight ahead of the 2017 French Presidential elections.

All is not well in the French Garden of Eden it seems. Unemployment is high (France's figure is the second highest among the G7 leading developed economies) and the government's finances are weak. The cost of labour to employers in France also includes social security contributions that are higher than in most other countries, which means borrowing money to pay benefits to an ever-increasing number of unemployed. I'm reminded of Maggie Thatcher's wonderful statement on socialism: *"The only problem with socialism is that eventually you run out of other people's money!"* In the end, Lady C brought in a Polish building company to help restore her French home, and they did everything at a very reasonable price, quickly, and delivered good quality work within building code!

Lady C bought the chateau as a summerhouse to retreat to really – but the children's Hill House School's French mistress said it would be good if the boys could spend a year full time in France so as to learn good French. Lady C felt in hindsight that she was herself ignorant as to how France today had become, and how the French have dropped away from power, and naïve not to realize that no one needs to learn to speak French anymore. At the time she thought it would be a good idea for the boys to do so.

In fact, over 2 billion people speak English in the world today, only 250 million speak Portuguese, and some 560 million speak Spanish. So with just 200 million people globally speaking French, Lady C makes a good point. 200 million sounds a lot, but when you consider other European languages, it puts everything into perspective regarding the decline of the need to speak French anymore. In its heyday in the 1800s it was a common language across Royal courts that ruled Europe, and those in society from England to Russia all grew up speaking French. It was expected. Times have changed as I told my son's French mistress at his boarding school when she asked if I did not think French important, and that my son should pay more attention in class. I thought he would have been better off studying Spanish or Chinese.

Lady C's boys' French schoolmistress had warned that, *"It's a very socialist country now so beware Lady Campbell."* But until she was living there, she did not realize how horrid it was going to be. The boys' French mistress said to do it now for schooling before the new term starts, which was within two weeks, and Lady C moved and got them into a local school full time, which they were not expecting either, so it was a bit of a shock to the boys they told me.

The kids would lose a year by switching back to England after only one year of learning French properly, so it seemed logical to let them stay in the French system long term until high school graduation, so the teacher's advice was fair. As they only had the most basic conversational French when they arrived, they needed longer than one year in France to become fluent, which was Lady C's goal. It made sense, as it would have handicapped them by changing the language of their lessons again too soon, so in the end she kept them in France for school right through to and including High School.

It was not easy for the boys and a significant sacrifice for Lady C as she was marooned in a not wholly or properly done up house, not speaking the same French language dialect as the locals and pronouncing her words in French far better than any local she felt. Not knowing anyone and no one locally making any effort to welcome her originally did not help. Nevertheless she felt it was the right call for the boys and their education, albeit a very lonely time for her.

She was obliged for her research and work to be back in England almost weekly, and so the boys became weekly boarders. The school felt this was an essential benefit so that they spoke French day and night at school. At weekends when Lady C was home, every weekend, the boys would only speak English. So she now found herself traveling five or six hours from London to the South of France every weekend, door to door, both ways – *"It was horrid,"* she said, and yet she felt this was a key sacrifice she had to make for the sake of the boys.

The boys were allowed to ride small engine motorbikes as they became of an age to be licensed; by now they made some friends locally and as they grew older could commute independently from home to friends on time-off. This gave them a great sense of trust and freedom and in the country they were relatively safe, so Lady C felt this worked well for them.

In England at the time there was an Anthrax disease outbreak, and a threat against public figures and one person the police said was responsible for seventy threats. One letter was addressed to Lady Colin Campbell and family at her

London residence – suggesting that the kids may be kidnapped. The man that was found to have written the letter turned out to be a paedophile, and when he tried to make off with someone's kids in England he was caught and arrested, and we assume imprisoned. France to be fair is very family orientated she said, and there is a strong respect for children, so on balance she felt comfortable that the boys would be safer there, and they were.

Lady C's London homes

Let's talk about her other homes over the years, as many were her true favorites. Bourne Street, Belgravia, London SW1, was one. Lady C said that it was her previous favorite – she loved the surrounds and the buildings and lived in the area for thirty years. She thought it a fabulous house, sweet, charming and the largest of the original old houses left untouched. It was an end of terrace house, so bright and airy. She described charming corners but said that architecturally the house was not quite perfect, with the ground to lower ground floors having unnecessary ledges. Perfect for little ornaments, though, and it had lovely lights and chandeliers. She said that the house was well situated and that she had lots of pals around the area. She sold it when she bought her rural retreat in France. She had decided that she was spending so much time in France, and virtually none in England that it made sense to sell the house, but she moved to Kennington later.

West Eaton Place, Belgravia, and Cundy Street, Belgravia were two other homes Lady C had in London over the years. She loved the flat on West Eaton Place, where she occupied one floor. Next door was Andrew Lloyd Webber and Sarah Brightman. West Eaton Place was a charming flat she said, she just loved it. The Grosvenor Estate (owned by the Duke of Westminster) were redeveloping and moved her to Cundy Street, Belgravia, and she spent several years at each address – the Cundy Street flat looked directly onto Eaton Terrace and Ebury Street and was very nice too, very light as she described it. It was a friendly community and the Duke of Westminster had grace and favor flats there too. Lady C got Janet Milford-Haven into those flats in a roundabout way, and then Janet's mother. Lord Alec Douglas-Home lived there before he was Prime Minister. As a resident once said of Cundy Street: *"It was the highest concentration of Aristos at the time I left in 1995."*

Belgravia, for those that may not know, is in the City of Westminster and the Royal Borough of Kensington and Chelsea. It is noted for its very expensive residential properties and is one of the wealthiest districts in the world. Much of it, known as the Grosvenor Estate, is still owned by the Duke of Westminster's Grosvenor Group. The area takes its name from one of the Duke's subsidiary titles, Viscount Belgrave, and lies mostly to the south-west of Buckingham Palace, and it is close to Knightsbridge, Pimlico and Sloane Street to the west.

I am pleased to include some photographs in the book of Lady C's almost completely restored new home of Castle Goring in West Sussex, England, which I took myself. They are mainly from the thick of the restoration period in late 2014, which continued extensively through to the summer of 2015. If you look at the photo of Castle Goring from the front, the old Gothic windowed Church is to the left center, and the Ballroom to the castellated far right. I have included pictures of both the castellated front of the Castle, and the rear which was built in the Palladian style. It is extraordinary for a house to have such an architectural double aspect, and Castle Goring is a completely unique building which had been in the hands of the same aristocratic family for hundreds of years until they sold it to Lady C.

Castle Goring was built in 1797 for Sir Bysshe Shelley, 1st Baronet. It was intended that his grandson, the famous poet, Percy Shelley would inherit and live there; however, the poet drowned in Italy aged just 29, so he never took possession of Castle Goring. The castle is Grade I listed and is over 15,600 sq. ft. in size. It's been owned by the Somerset family since 1845, whose current scion sold the castle to Lady C and who she invited as a guest to her house-warming Ball this summer, to celebrate the castle becoming her home and its restoration work almost completed.

If you want to see what it looks like now and consider renting it for a special event, wedding or corporate event, please, go to *http://www.castlegoring.com/*

There are photos in the book of the magnificent glass cupola over the castle's grand entry sweeping staircase, and shots off the first floor landing facing into the castle's private family chapel. The grand staircase has been completely restored by Jamaican carpenters under the watchful eye of English Heritage and an elevator is being fitted. Photos of one of the *less grand* rooms on an upper floor, kept for private family use only – which I think you'll agree is never the less very grand in its own right.

The property was expected to be completely restored by the Autumn (Fall) of 2016 and become available as a unique wedding, private event and corporate meeting venue – whilst also being the country seat of Lady Colin Campbell; a huge restoration project, but ending up with a home in cracking condition and a going business concern.

What would soon have been a totally collapsed heritage building, and one which may never have been saved, has been saved for the nation by Lady C buying it and investing huge sums of money into it. The entire roof, the complete outer fabric of the building, and the interiors of priceless architecture - from ceilings to ornate columns - have all been secured for generations to come. The home intended for the famous English poet and one of the nation's most famous writers has been saved for posterity and history by her actions – that's quite ironic. By opening up the castle to weddings and events, Lady C is enabling everyone to enjoy its splendors and be part of the castle's history and upkeep.

A grand private Ball was held in Castle Goring in June 2016 as a house-warming event for all of Lady C's friends and family.

Lady C's London residence today

This is a complete four-story house in Kennington in London. It's close to one of the world's great homes of cricket, The Oval. The Oval is in the London Borough of Lambeth, and has been the home ground of Surrey County Cricket Club since it was opened in 1845.

Kennington is just south of the river Thames, and proximity to central London was key to the development of the area as a residential suburb. As more moved out from places such as Chelsea, Belgravia and Knightsbridge, Kennington has become part of inner central London itself, and these last few years it's rapidly become a *chic* place to live.

Lady C's house has a large double aspect drawing room, with exquisite antiques and paintings, a picture of which is in the book. There is a small private garden, a lower ground floor sumptuous dining room, and three bedrooms on upper floors. There were four bedrooms, but one was converted to a 'serious' dressing room to house Lady C's collection of clothes and her couture ball gowns and outfits, not to mention the shoes I'm sure.

"What do you love about your neighborhood in Kennington Lady C?" I asked. *"It's so easy to get to anywhere in London and get down to the south coast quickly to Goring."* Although she could have done that from Bourne Street too, in reality it's simply a different route, same journey time. Belgravia was wonderful she explained, but not for everyday shopping and the like – *"It was a palaver,"* she said – *"Nothing was on your doorstep."* But there were people and restaurants a-plenty. Kennington on the other hand has everything within walking distance. Her favorite Tesco supermarket, a corner shop, and two high streets full of ordinary everyday shopping five or ten minutes' walk away. It's seven minutes by car away from Sloane Square, from the city of London, from PC World, from everything…. so one can see why she chose to buy there.

Kennington (which sounds so much like Kensington, it's posher more expensive Royal borough across the Thames) is today very much a village, with lovely bistros and restaurants you can walk to – and more and more people are moving out there from Belgravia and Mayfair, just as people did to Battersea some years ago (Batt-ers-ea as it's lovingly referred to, as it sounds so much posher). She said,

"It's a more mixed area in Kennington, more levels of real life, every race and level of society – and I like that."

Many of the grand houses built in the late 1700s and 1800s for the very well-to-do slipped into very poor housing districts in the 20th century, but the whole area is seeing a huge renaissance and you increasingly have to be doing very well indeed to live there! Its location and ease for transport has made it very popular, and prices have skyrocketed.

The famous William Bligh, Captain of HMS Bounty, against whom the Mutiny on the Bounty was brought, occupied a house at Lambeth Road. He died in 1817, and was buried at St. Mary's, Lambeth. The historical Manor of Kennington continues to be owned by the current monarch's elder son (HRH the Prince of Wales, Duke of Cornwall). The Duchy of Cornwall maintains a substantial property portfolio within the area. Scenes from the 2014 film *Kingsman: The Secret Service* were filmed at The Black Prince pub in Kennington. Kenneth Clarke, Member of Parliament, Secretary of State for Justice and Lord Chancellor, lives there. Kevin Spacey, the American film actor appearing on the British stage has lived there. Bob Marley stayed in a home there regularly in the 70s and Charlie Chaplin was born there too.

The adjoining town of Streatham (pronounced Stret-em) and a magically posher way of pronouncing it, which Lady C shared with me, which resulted in us both collapsing in laughter is Saint Reatham (St-Reatham)! I love it. It's like Battersea also a place nobody smart wanted to live in during the 1900s, suddenly as people started to move over the water from Chelsea and Kensington, priced out of the housing market, called it, Batt-ers-ea as it sounded so much smarter. But whether Kennington or St. Reatham, a lot of celebrities like Lady C and *Homeland* star and British Actor David Harewood live in the area. Naomi Campbell has and Simon Callow was born around here. Eddie Izzard used to host the comedy club at the White Lion and the comedian Greg Davies lives in the area.

Chapter 11
Political satire, any regrets, and what's next?

Political satire

LADY C AND I CHATTED TOGETHER about politics on either side of 'the pond', from Blair days right up to Brexit. Her satire on the political characters we all know was so wonderfully frank, humorous and at times cutting that I thought you'd enjoy hearing her views on some of the players.

We'll not dwell on stuff that's old history, but her comments on Tony Blair are worth flagging and because his actions as the Prime Minister who took us to war in the Iraq are the subject of a July 2016 enquiry's results.

Tony Blair is someone whose name one senses, as I ask her views on him, immediately brings up Lady C's hackles. She felt that he certainly had charisma, but that he should be prosecuted for crimes against humanity (along with Bush Junior), as she felt that he flagrantly abused the democratic process, lied to the British people and dragged them into a war that was not in its best interests. She felt too that it was directly contrary to justice and Britain's national interests and not in the best interests of the Middle East as a whole either. She signed a petition when the results of the inquiry came out, demanding that he be prosecuted in the Courts of Justice and said: *"He's simply, a disgrace."*

Lord Butler a former senior civil servant said on the BBC that Blair wanted to help the US because he genuinely thought Saddam Hussein was a dangerous person to the world and to the Middle East. He criticised the way Blair reported the intelligence, as he felt that he had exaggerated the reliability of the intelligence in trying to persuade the UN and the world that there was a proper legal basis for taking military action. Britain's Intelligence Committee had told Blair, Butler claims, that the intelligence was sporadic and patchy but Blair told the British House of Commons that it was extensive, detailed and authoritative. As Butler said, *"He may well have thought it was extensive, detailed and authoritative, but it wasn't."*

The Iraq Inquiry, also dubbed the Chilcot Inquiry, was published at the beginning of July 2016 to a huge furor. It was one of the most highly anticipated political reports in Britain's history. *"It is now clear that policy on Iraq was made on the basis of flawed intelligence and assessments. They were not challenged and they should have been,"* the head of the inquiry John Chilcot said in presenting its findings. Families felt it did not go far enough in proportioning blame, but as a lawyer representing many has said, it was an inquiry and it is for the law courts to decide if Tony Blair is guilty of lying or of crimes against humanity if cases are brought against him. One mother of a British soldier who died in the war accused Tony Blair in July of being, *"the greatest terrorist of all."*

Sir John Chilcot is a British Privy Counsellor and former senior civil servant. His appointment as Chair of an inquiry into the circumstances surrounding the March 2003 invasion of Iraq and its aftermath was announced in June 2009. Thirteen years after the UK invaded Iraq with the US and other allies, the long-awaited Iraq Inquiry has given its verdict on British involvement in the conflict.

The Iraq Inquiry was scathing in its attack on Tony Blair's government. It said that war was *"not a last resort"* and that other peaceful options could have been explored.

The UK's Labour party Government of Tony Blair was claiming to act on behalf of the international community *"to uphold the authority of the Security Council,"* knowing that it did not have a majority in the Security Council in support of its actions. In those circumstances, the UK's actions undermined the authority of the Security Council it has been claimed.

On Tony's wife, Cherie Blair, when asked, Lady C said that she was as ugly a personality as he was repellent. *"Too goodie, goodie."*

Gordon Brown, who was Tony Blair's chancellor and who became Prime Minister after him, she felt had no charisma, but was infinitely a better Prime Minister than he's been given credit for. She felt that he was essentially a decent human being and she had a lot of respect for him as an individual and as PM. As Chancellor of the Exchequer Britain flourished magnificently under him she said, and added, *"No doubt he made mistakes, but he was well worthy of respect."*

As for Ed Miliband who sought to become the next leader of the British Labour party, she was not impressed. She found him flagrantly a committed Marxist, who would in the misguided belief that he knew best for humanity, ruin everything had he ever become Prime Minister. She felt that the Ed Milibands of this world are the greatest scourge to humanity. *"Because Marxists believe their objective is good,"* she said, *"doesn't mean they are."* She gave the example of Hitler, who believed that his objectives were good when he said that Jews, Gays, the mentally ill or even Mormons were all scourges to be eliminated – Marxists believe that all those who don't believe in what they believe have to be removed Lady C said. *"He's proud to be a Marxist,"* she said.

She related how she had seen Leninist - Marxist philosophy first hand in Russia, and in Jamaica witnessed Fidel Castro's attempt to influence Jamaica with his Marxist speeches and support of the Michael Manley government. Many young Jamaicans today I can add, do not realize that in the 70s Castro supplied Jamaica with teachers, doctors, police and army advisors, to try and influence Jamaica's next generation to shift to Marxist communism – those that talk of Michael Manley in almost saint like terms as the last PNP Prime Minister did seem to forget his complete history and the damage he almost irrevocably did to the economy of Jamaica, and only remember the good things; and he did also do plenty of good things. But Lady C sees evil in Marxism trying to pass under the guise of love of fellow man.

Looking at current British politics, she saw David Cameron the British Prime Minister until July 2016, as an extremely capable politician, and in her view he was in some ways the ultimate pragmatist. She simply questions whether he did not sometimes in his prognosis become extremely naive. She felt that there had been no reason in the first place to have a Scottish referendum for example. In the wake of the time and money it seems folly and created the politics of today. She felt that he was in love with his own views and believed that if he managed things enough we'd all follow on behind him, both the Scottish referendum and Brexit – but he got the last one wrong didn't he?

As for Jeremy Corbyn, who at the time of writing was the British Labour Party leader and who recently, post Brexit's vote to leave Europe, saw almost 85% of his Labour MPs pass a vote of no confidence in him; and yet he refused to go until a challenge is raised against him and the whole party votes! Lady C feels that he is a very nice individual, but very immature about the world at large. She sees in him a decent person, but that he would be a car crash waiting to happen as Prime Minister – and he too seems like a confirmed Marxist in ideology to her. Interesting that when aged 19, and I'm not sure if Lady knew this, Corbyn spent two years in Jamaica doing Voluntary Service Overseas. Returning to the UK, he worked as an official for the National Union of Tailors and Garment Workers. Corbyn began a course in Trade Union Studies at North London Polytechnic, but left after a series of arguments with his tutors over the curriculum. He worked as a trade union organiser for the National Union of Public Employees and Amalgamated Engineering and Electrical Union, and unions are backing him heavily against elected Members of Parliament who are overwhelmingly demanding he go. I'm sitting writing, wondering whether he will be gone by the time you read this book or not – politics today are history tomorrow. Lady C feels that Corbyn does not understand the consequences and that Marxists destroyed much of the 20ᵗʰ century and said just look at Russia, Poland and China.

Brexit was the next logical question to ask Lady C's views on and she was clear up front, she voted to leave the EU. She voted, she said, for independence. Living in France for many years she saw how the EU rode rough shod as she describes it over France, or those who didn't follow their directives. She cannot see any long-term damage to Britain over Brexit and ultimately she sees the EU's collapse. By mid-July this last year Theresa May replaced David Cameron as leader of the Conservative Party and British Prime Minister. At the time of writing, Theresa May has been too recently elected for Lady C, who considers such matters carefully, to come to a definite conclusion, but she hopes that Mrs. May will turn out to be an effective Prime Minister. She feels that, *"Mrs. May has started promisingly, in her negotiations with the European Union leaders, some of whom have made it clear they are going to try to be as vicious as possible to discourage other EU member states from leaving, and she seems to be playing a canny hand with those who are less hostile and more realistic about the fact that the European Union should always have remained a trading market and not headed towards becoming a European super-state."*

Lady C feels these are interesting times and if Mrs. May acquits herself well she will go down in history as a successful Prime Minister.

Turning as I did to current US politics, President Obama is someone she's had a lot of respect for and saw him as a liberal conservative. She felt that he displayed sincerity and signs of trying to do things the right way – but that he was often unable to. But responsible government she said needs to be aware of those who are the underbelly of society and provide for those most in need. Looking ahead to the American general election of 2016 Lady C's view is that Hillary Clinton is someone who is no doubt very professional and a brilliant woman but if elected, she does not think she has the stuff of greatness, but that she is bright, willing and capable; and that she will prove an efficient and effective President.

On Donald Trump, she sees him as a great showman, not slow to express his opinion, and that much of what he says resonates with the American people and the world, where nobody tells them what they believe. No doubt if he is elected she felt, he'd ultimately be reined in by the responsible working bureaucracy of government who on a day-to-day basis run the country; much as the civil service does in the UK. Shades of *Yes Minister* and *Yes Prime Minister* come to mind.

Regrets.

I asked Lady C in looking back on her life so far, if she had any regrets? She said that she had no regrets, *"Other than marrying Lord Colin Campbell, and in hindsight I should have held onto my house in Bourne Street."* She regretted too, not working out earlier that one or two people close to her were social climbing off her name and were not real friends at all and abused her friendship. One or two of her friends had commented to me that it was sad that some supposed friends of Lady C over the years had used her, but that she had wised up and let them go. She believes that they were simply insecure people – so she didn't regret having befriended them in the first place.

She had expected that her first book on Princess Diana would make her *persona non grata* in all Royal circles, but it didn't. But then she didn't peddle negativity, just facts, and kept a balance of the true story she believes. She felt that she had written a measured attempt to be fair to both Diana and Charles with events that were truthful. She felt that she didn't write a book seeking to bury Charles as the next author Morton did, which was not fair in her view; so she didn't regret writing it, or indeed any other book.

Her social circle, on the whole, did not change after she wrote the book on The Queen Mother either, just one or two so-called friends slipped away. *"I'd like to think that our Queen knew such things would come out eventually, and at least, I feel they got out safely and sensibly in my hands,"* she said.

She was clear that she never sets out to trash anyone in her books, but has simply shared what those close to events and who knew have told her, or what the persons themselves told her face to face, like Princess Diana. As she says, *"That's history, not gossip."*

What's next?

In April 2016 there had been constant speculation that she may still take part in the reality TV show *Celebrity Big Brother* and that's possible for 2017, let's see. One thing's for sure, her presence if she ever takes part in Big Brother will likely turn it into the most watched series ever I imagine, if *I'm a Celebrity... Get Me Out of Here!* viewer ratings are anything to go by!

She landed an ITV contract for her own reality TV show as well – *Lady C and the Castle*, which aired in September 2016. It follows her life renovating her castle and launching the Castle Goring business. It features herself, her sons, and lots of others as the work progresses. The boys seemed to take it all in their stride that they will be in and out of filming too. It's just following them all going about their daily life, and they will, knowing them, just be themselves. It will also feature her castle-warming Grand Ball, which has now taken place in June this year. *Lady C and the Castle* will have aired on TV by the time you are reading this book.

In August 2016 she had a highly successful run with her one-woman show *A Cup of Tea with Lady C* at the world's largest performing arts festival, the Edinburgh Fringe Festival in Scotland. She was offered her very own one-woman show and as she explained to me, *"It's being scripted by professionals. It's me being myself."* I know from talking to her that she was really looking forward to what she described as more like the audience having afternoon tea and a chat with her, and that she eagerly awaited the script to read and learn – and no doubt knowing she was be ad-libbing and going with the flow of each audience, which is very much what happens at the festival.

While she will continue to write books and remain as she has for decades a well- known socialite, of that I have no doubt, her career continues to evolve into a TV personality and stage performer, a British household name and unique personality. Her new high profile media career is growing stronger, and she is often sought out as a guest celebrity on chat shows, as a commentator on other shows, or for newspaper articles or special magazine feature articles such as at Christmas.

She said to me when I asked her what's next in your life: *"I'll continue my friendships with great pals around the world. Continue my writing and TV work as it evolves, and make Goring as successful a business as I can. I write so that in fifty years from now people can say, "She was right." And what I write stands the test of time."*

Postscript

IF I LOOK AT EVERYTHING that I have learned from all to whom I have spoken, the decades of Press releases which I have read, and all that I have witnessed in her company, I'd summarize Lady C and her life with the following comments.

She's learned from childhood what suffering and mental pain are, and she's experienced what bullying is from a decade or more at an all-boys school - and is not going to let either happen again. This became apparent in *I'm a Celebrity... Get Me Out of Here!* when she held nothing back and went for the throat verbally to pull down her attackers. She was like a lioness defending herself and her cubs, a lioness who held her captives in a suffocating grip of words, and she scratched and bit verbally – if it was TV reality show sport the producers wanted, they got their money's worth, with an additional 5 million viewers per night thanks to her, paying to give their votes.

She enjoyed working with ITV even though she did not appreciate what she saw as that program's over-editing in the Jungle, which she and others saw as unfair as to how she was portrayed to the public.

She learned on the Jamaican social circuit early, from being a model and moving within both the New York and London Society set, just how important family and personal connections are in life. Life is still not so much about what you know, but more who you know. That rule holds fast in social circles today, as it does in corporate careers.

She will never forget the lessons of a violent marriage to a man and his then Machiavellian family as she saw them, who viewed her father's money as more important than herself, as she's said.

I was surprised that after all that she's been through over the years at the hands of some journalists, she retains great respect for journalists and the media as a whole. They are professionals, which she much admires, but she has abhorrence for the small number of conniving journalists who only seek to push their career and sell newspapers with sensational headlines rather than be concerned with reporting the news honestly and with integrity.

Being fearless, she is a threat to those that want to take her on, as there is nothing for her to hide from or stop her speaking out. The world now knows the most intricate and intimate parts of her whole life story. Attackers know that she will strike back – and she more often than not gets the better of those who have a go.

Well-born Jamaican ladies have been brought up to be strong, independent women and raised to cherish good manners and decorum – but they speak plainly – and boy, if you have crossed them or gone a step too far, they are going to let rip at you. All I can say is that the momentary silence after your action is simply the storm gathering, so be sure that the hurricane shutters are down – because as they say in Jamaica, *"You are about to get a good licking!"*

Lady C from all that I have seen in her 'real' world, is no different to most of us, although maybe a tab quicker to let rip and a quicker use of choice expletives; and some in the Jungle certainly experienced being on the wrong side of her when they were all put under such extreme and exceptional pressure. As Kieron Dyer, the English footballer said, *"You wouldn't want to be on the wrong side of Lady C though, would you?"*

I also believe that what we see is what you get with her – a feisty, witty, self-assured, honest, loyal friend and a good listener. She is someone who's straight-forward and who's a highly entertaining host.

Lady C is a very practical person, and if the floor needs sweeping or an interview needs attending she just gets on with it, grabs what she needs – from a bucket and mop to a couture outfit – and she's off. Cars or cab journeys are simply opportunities to be on the phone and lining up the next event or confirming an appointment; a socialite's life with her foot fully on the throttle.

We've learned that she has a memory like an elephant and an enormous capacity to remember names, places, dates, and numbers. I can think of only two other people that I have known with this ability. One a friend from Hong Kong days, now living in the South of France, Clare Wadsworth (a Sassoon by birth and wife of the late and wonderful Freddy, publisher of *The Far East Economic Review* based in Hong Kong), the other a late aunt of my wife's in Jamaica, Wellie Lionhall (a Sharp by birth – citrus people). Both had the ability to meet a dozen strangers who friends may have asked to come to a party they were hosting and had invited amongst scores of friends, and an hour later introduce them to additional newly arriving strangers, remembering every person's name and something about them to share with each guest. True *grandes dames* and *doyennes* of the social scene seem to have such a skill in common.

Lady C is also quite an authority on historical or scientific events, and is very knowledgeable of world politics. She can reel off a Royal's ancestry or discourse on a scholastic matter at the drop of a hat. We have someone in our family like that, my wife's brother, David Harvey. He's a doctor and consultant of anesthetics who we call 'the family oracle'. He always seems to *know everything and anything,* and the annoying thing is, he's usually right!

It will be exciting to see what the future holds for this ever changing, ever evolving, and never tiring woman who like the phoenix has risen out of the ashes of her life's fires, and gone from strength to strength, recreating herself anew.

To those who are not friends of Lady C, I thank them for their very public announcements of what they felt about her, which created a balance to be considered when looking at who Lady C is. As she says herself: *"I am no angel!"*

Writing a book about a multiple *New York Times* best-selling author with an enviable writing style and grasp of the English language and an extensive vocabulary is very humbling, to say the least! I very much hope that I have done her story some justice.

The extraordinary life and amazing times of Lady C continue, and she has become an unexpected British treasure to many. Whether you love her or hate her, Lady C is a force to be reckoned with - and the lioness is here to stay! Or at least for a good while yet I hope!